CALIFORNIA GOVERNMENT

R. L. Cohen

ISBN: 9781988557809 (Hardcover)
ISBN: 9781988557816 (Softcover)

Published in New Zealand

Humanities Academic Publishers

A catalogue record for this book is available from the National Library of New Zealand.

Kei te pātengi raraunga o Te Puna Mātauranga o Aotearoa te whakarārangi o tēnei pukapuka.

Contents

CHAPTER I

Early California

1.1. Expeditions in California

The contacts of Europeans with California started in the mid-1530s when the men of Hernan Cortez entered Baja California. In 1542, the Spaniards sailed north to Alta California, and the expedition of Juan Rodriguez Cabrillo's expedition was the first to made landings as far north as modern Santa Barbara. In this regard, the Spanish navigator Juan Rodriguez Cabrillo was the first European to discover California in 1542. During this period, the territory was inhabited by about 130,000 Native Americans (Madley, 19-20).

The territory did not receive proper attention from Spain for more than two centuries because of the enormous poverty in the region as well as the general slowdown of the Spanish exploration (Crosby, 90-91).

At the request of the Viceroy of New Spain, Juan Rodriguez Cabrillo led an expedition in search of the Anian Strait. The Cabrillo expedition is one of the most important in history because it resulted in the European discovery of Alta California. Cabrillo left the port of Navidad on the west coast of New Spain on June 27, 1542. His two ships, San Salvador and Victoria, were small and of poor quality. Among his crew of 250 sailors and soldiers were some twenty Africans and Native Americans in captivity.

The expedition progressed slowly, mainly because of the prevailing winds from the northwest. They reached the coast of San Diego on September 28, 1542. Cabrillo was very excited about his findings and described the port as closed and very good. The expedition continued its journey north, passing through the San Pedro Bay and the Santa Barbara channel. After reaching the Russian River, Cabrillo decided to change the course and headed back south. The personal life of Cabrillo continues to be a secret, as not much is known about him. According to some historians, Cabrillo was Portuguese, and according to others, he was Spanish. The most important fact is that he left an estate that was one of the richest in the Americas after his death. The work of Juan Cabrillo is one of the most important because it has provided the earliest descriptions of Native people in California. Noticing the ships of Cabrillo in the San Diego Bay provoked an escape of the Native Americans. A few days later, some of them approached the ships of Cabrillo. They described that bearded people with clothes were going about in the inland part of the land by using signs and mimics. According to historians, the Native Americans referred to the Coronado's expedition that traveled through today's New Mexico and Arizona two years earlier (Goetz 47-61).

Passing through the Chumash territory, Cabrillo described that he had seen an Indian town next to the sea with larges canoes to enter into the Santa Barbara channel. Cabrillo named the place Pueblo de las Canoas, the Town of the Canoes.

Except for the expedition of Cabrillo, another explorer that visited the land of California was Cortes. His expedition sailed northward from Acapulco to the peninsula of Baja California in 1535. Cortes is famous because he was one of the first explorers to set a colony in California. He described the land as hot, dry, and sterile; the only exploitable resources were pearls in the coastal waters. For these reasons, they abandoned this post in 1536. The final voyage of exploration was directed northward from Acapulco's port in 1539.

Francisco de Ulloa led the next expedition consisting of three small vessels. They sailed northward along the coast of Mexico to the Gulf of

California. Ulloa believed that Baja California is an island. Thus, he was trying to find an exit to an open sea. The expedition of Ulloa was of great importance because it provided much knowledge about the lower regions of California. The expedition should have proved that Baja California was a peninsula and not an island. However, the European cartographers continued to produce maps presenting Baja California as an island (History of California, 24-27).

Merchant Sebastian Vizcaino sailed from Mexico to the south coast of California in 1602, discovering and naming San Diego, the island of Santa Catalina, Santa Barbara, and Monterrey. Because they were using inaccurate maps, Vizcaino and several later researchers believed that California was an island and lost hope when they could not draw the surrounding seas (Wagner, 33-34).

Pressure for settlement came from missionaries eager to convert the Native Americans to Christianity, from the intrusion of Russian and British traders, primarily in search of sea otter pelts, and from the quest for the Northwest Passage across the North American continent. In 1769 the Spanish viceroy dispatched to land and sea expeditions from Baja California, and the Franciscan friar Junípero Serra established the first mission at San Diego. Gaspar de Portolá set up a military outpost in 1770 at Monterey. Colonization began after 1773 with the opening of an overland supply route across the southwestern deserts intended to link other Spanish settlements in the present-day states of Arizona and New Mexico to the coast (Douglas, 226).

The 21 missions established by Serra and his successors were the strongest factors in developing California. While attempting to Christianize Native Americans, the Fathers taught them farming and crafts (Gonzales, 29). With the forced labor of Mission Native Americans, Fathers irrigated vast ranches and traded hides, tallow, wine, brandy, olive oil, grain, and leatherwork for the manufactured goods brought by Yankee trading vessels around Cape Horn.

The reasons for forming the first missions in Alta California are well known to all of us. Chief in importance was the desire of the Fathers to convert Native Americans to the Christian faith. More than a century and a half after Vizcaino anchored in Monterey bay, missionaries had been asking for permission to start to work in California but unsuccessfully. The chains of missions completing the long Spanish frontier line, which beginning on the Atlantic coast, ran across Florida and extended westward along the Gulf of Mexico, through Texas, New Mexico, Arizona, and upward through California. According to Bolton, this line was twice as long as the famous Rhine Danube frontier held by Rome (Beattie, 250).

In 1769, Spain was leading a chain of 21 missions across the length of Alta California, from San Diego to Sonoma, to gain new territories in the new land. These missions ended in 1834, but the architectural legacy is still present, which can be seen in the state's red tile roofs, whitewashed walls, arched colonnades, and bell towers (Allen, 90-93). The text below covers all of the 21-mission established in California in the period from 1791 to 1834.

1.2. Mission Basilica San Diego de Alcala

As mentioned above, the Spanish have been the founders of 21 Mission along the coast of California in the late 18th century. The Mission of San Diego de Alcalá represents a very significant part of the nation's Spanish heritage because it was the first mission formed by the Spanish. It was founded by Father Serra in 1769, together with the first Spanish colony and the presidio in Alta California. Years after the initial founding, the Mission was moved to its present location. It was initially completed in 1813, and the same church is still used as an active parish church and cultural center (Sandos, 25-26).

The period before the Spanish expeditions touched the land of California, and Native Americans are known as the Kumeyaay people, which populated this area. The first Spanish colony – San Diego, was formed on July 1, 1769. (Barnes, 330). Two weeks later, Father Serra established the San Diego de Alcala Mission, first for the Spanish colonists and later to attract the local Native population. Six years later, the mission moved to its present location because the former place was poor in water, making it difficult to raise different agricultural products. The second location was near the river of San Diego, and the need for water was no longer a problem. The first church of the Mission was built in 1774, and it was made all of the wood, which unfortunately burned to the ground because of the Native uprising in 1775. The second church was built in 1777, but this time instead of wood, it was all of the adobe bricks. The Mission of San Diego was one of the richest. At the beginning of the 19 century, the Mission had at its disposal 50,000 acres on its name. The church went through a lot of modifications and changes between 1808 and 1813.

The process of secularization of the missions started after Mexico gained its independence. Unfortunately, after the Mission was no more under the control of the Franciscans, the mission started to fall apart. In 1862, the United States returned the mission and its buildings to the Catholic Church (Johnson, 168-202).

1.3. Old Mission San Luis Rey de Francia

The Mission of San Luis was established in 1798 by Father Lasuen, the successor of Father Serra. The Mission of San Luis was the only Mission to be named after a king, St. Lous IX, the King of France. The history of this Mission is separated into five different periods of occupation: Luiseño Indian, Spanish Mission, Mexican Secularization, American Military, and Twentieth Century Restoration (Worden and Leffingwell, 27).

Before the Spanish colonization, the Luiseno people Native Americans lived in the area for a long time. Interestingly, the Mission system was not accepted by the Native Americans until the threat of the Russian approach of the area (Street, 97). As an experienced colonizer, Spain learned that the land could be claimed inexpensively by establishing missions and sending dedicated Fathers to spread Christianity. Shortly after Mexico won its independence, the law on secularization passed. From 1847-1857 the Mission was used as an operational base by U.S. soldiers. Notable figures that served at the Mission include General Stephen W.

Kearny, Kit Carson, and the Battalion of Mormon Volunteers, who served at the Mission for six weeks.

1.4. Mission San Juan Capistrano

The mission of San Juan Capistrano was founded on November 1, 1776, and it was the 7th mission formed. This mission is the beginning of what would later be called Orange County. The mission was destroyed just one month after the founding by the Kumeyaay military formation. In 1776 was founded for the second time by Father Serra, but this did not mean the end of its bad fate. It was built of stone and brick in 1806 and represented a jewel, the most beautiful church of all the missions in California (Geiger, 37-45). According to the words of Father Zephlows: "The mission San Juan Capistrano is the most important and pretentious building of the whole mission period which began in 1797." It was built of solid stone masonry, and its special features were the tower, a spacious and imposing altar, and a vaulted roof".

In 1812 was destroyed by an earthquake. The earthquake killed 40 worshipers and several bell-ringers. The mission was named after the Italian warrior saint John of Capistrano, who led the Crusaders against the Ottomans during the siege of Belgrade in 1456. The mission was returned to the Roman Catholic Church in 1865 by Lincoln, and the church still owns the land, but the mission is run by a non-profit organization. The mission is known for the annual migration of swallows from Mexico and Central America on March 19. Urbanization has significantly reduced the number of swallows that used to reach 6,000. In 2012, the mission launched a project to attract swallows back, which includes bird calls and static nests (Smith, 255).

1.5. Mission San Gabriel Archangel

The mission of San Gabriel Archangel was founded on September 8, 1771, and it is the 4th mission by order of creation. Founded on the hills north of modern-day Montebello but moved to its current location in 1775. The

San Gabriel Mission was one of the most prosperous missions since it has owned a quarter of the livestock and grain of all missions. The mission's most prosperous period was in 1829, when the mission's herds consisted of 25,000 cattle and 15,000 sheep. The mission architecture is very reminiscent of the Moorish fortress, similar to the style of the cathedral in Cordoba (Meadows, 339).

Its founders are Fathers Serra, Pedro Benito Cambón, and Angel Fernandez Somera y Balbuena. It was at this mission that Fr. José Zalvidea introduced the first of California's large-scale vineyards. The Viceroy and inspector general had the privilege to choose the name of San Gabriel Archangel, which gave the right of choosing the fathers of the new mission to father Junipero. In this regard, the first fathers of this mission were Father Fr. Angel Somera, from the College of San Fernando, and Fr. Pedro Benito Cambon, of the province of Santiago de Galicia. The most important thing to mention is that the invasion of this country by the Spaniards was met by strong opposition. As the Spaniards entered more deeply on the Indian's land, the chieftain in defiance ordered that measures against the Natives should not be loosened.

Although in July 1771, the Natives of the district began a life different in every aspect from that to which they were accustomed. At the Fathers' request, they went into the woods for timber necessary for the construction of their buildings. Nevertheless, first of all, branches were gathered that there might be a shelter for the celebration of Mass. The Fathers made clear that the community might be successfully maintained only by providing occupations for the Natives (Smith, 252).

1.6. Mission San Fernando Rey de España

The Mission of San Fernando Rey de Espana was founded on September 8, 1797, by the Franciscans (Engelhardt, 12). The exact place of the mission was in the north part of the Valley, which the Native Americans called Achois Comihabit (Robinson, 76). Among the features of the surrounding land were water sources, limestone, and pine for timber.

In the first year, the mission operated in a building in ownership of Francisco Reyes, Alcalde of the Pueblo of Los Angeles, in the period until the first church was being constructed. The church was built in 1798, along with the Priests' dwelling. Also, during this year, the Fathers were involved in litigation with the Pueblo of Los Angeles over water rights. The permanent church was completed in 1806. By this time, there were about 1,000 Native people at the Mission; their village had 70 houses and its plaza (Baer 1958:101). The Mission of San Fernando included people from some rancherias or villages, including Cahuenga, Topanga, Camulos, Piru, Simi, and Tujunga (Robinson, 78; Kroeber, 12) stated that they spoke three distinct languages: Chumash, Gabrielino, and Serrano (like Gabrielino, a Takic language).

Between 1797 and 1820 or 1825, a total of about 2,000 Native Americans were pulled from their villages. In the 1850s, the church was damaged several times by the gold diggers who believed that treasure was buried underneath. (Weinerth, 184-185)

1.7. Old Mission San Buenaventura

The old Mission of San Buenaventura was founded on Easter Sunday on March 30, 1749, and it was the last mission founded by the priest Junipero Serra. (Medina and Genet, 83) Father Junipero Serra was canonized as a Saint on September 23, 2015. Serra left in charge of the new mission padre Cambon. The most important feature of this church is that it was close to the water, a fact that meant a lot at that time. Thus, the living conditions in this mission were much more manageable in terms of garden maintenance, plant irrigation, food mirroring, etcetera. Unfortunately, the entire irrigation system that was built was destroyed in 1862 by floods that swept through the region. Also, the mission's first church was destroyed by fire. In 1792 the foundations of the present church were laid, as well as smaller auxiliary rooms. Although half-finished in 1795, the church was not fully completed until 1809.

The series of earthquakes that took part in 1812 influenced the Fathers and Natives to seek shelter in a different place, a few miles inland. The mission has been the subject of frequent robberies. Even at some point, Father and their followers were forced to flee to the mountains or even to remove valuable items to protect them from theft.

Under the Mexican government in 1833, the fathers received a secularization decree, which gave them administrative control over the missions. In this regard, in 1845, the Mission of Buenaventura was rented to Don Jose De Arnaz and Narciso Botello, which later illegally sold its part to Don Jose De Arnaz.

In 1982, the mission marked its two-century anniversary. In January 2001, a new three-story school building with pre-kindergarten, kindergarten, and grades 1-8 was located at the base of the hill behind the mission. The Mission celebrated its 225th Anniversary with a year-long series of events and activities during 2006-07. Today, the church and its garden are all that remain from the original mission. Also, the church continues to be an active catholic parish for approximately 1200 families. On June 9, 2020, Pope Francis elevated the Mission to a minor basilica, which represents the first basilica in the Archdiocese of Los Angeles. (The Old Mission Basilica, San Buenaventura).

1.8. Old Mission Santa Barbara

The Presidio of Santa Barbara was founded on April 21, 1782, after the establishment of San Buenaventura with the efforts of padre Serra and governor Neve with support of the soldiers and army on a place called Yanonalit, well known to the Native Americans (Worden and Leffingwell, 172). Padre Serra was very disappointed that the mission was not founded right after the presidio. This led to his death which occurred on August 28, 1782.

Two years later, Neve's successor Fages, permitted padre Serra's successor, padre Lasuen, to proceed with the foundation of the mission. At that time, there was a fear that the fathers will not have control over the temporal affairs of the Native Americans, but the guardians of the colleges refused to send missionaries to the new establishments. Fages had no other choice but to allow the fathers to control the temporal affairs of the Native Americans. Finally, the mission of Santa Barbara was founded on December 4 with the rise of the cross on the place called Taynayan by the Native Americans and Pedragoso by the Spaniards. (Gidney, 153). However, the first mass was said on December 16 by Fages. Padre Lasuen was helped by Fathers Antonio Paterna and Cristobal Ormas.

The chapel of Santa Barbara began to build early in 1787. In the years after, other buildings started to rise on rocky heights. By the end of 1807, the Indian village, which extended Southwest of the main building, was composed of 252 separate housings, including many Indian families. The current Mission building was completed by the end of the 18th century. The mission had a large fountain, and the water from the fountain was used for laundry purposes of the Indian village. The chapel at the beginning was small, but a year later, it was enlarged. However, by the year 1792, the people who lived there still considered it as small.

In 1793, the old chapel was torn down, and, in its place, a new one was built with a size of 25 by 125 feet. Unfortunately, the earthquake that happened on Monday, December 1812, damaged the chapel to the extent that it was unrecognizable, so it was removed. In the next period, Padre Antonio builds another chapel. It was open on 10th of September 1820. This was considered the most solid church in whole California (O'Keefe, 10).

The number of people who lived in Santa Barbara was the highest in 1803, consisting of 1792 people. In 1812 another earthquake took place, and the biggest part of the chapel was destroyed. At the end of the year, another unpleasant event happened with the arrival of the Bouchard pirate. To protect themselves, the Fathers send all the valuables to Santa Ines, and the women and children were warned that if an attack happens, they need to go to Santa Ines as well. No attack happened, so the people continued their lives on this mission.

Maybe the most important event in the period of the existence of Santa Barbara was the Indian revolt in 1824. They use the chance that Padre Ripoll was absent and armed themselves. Native Americans claimed that they were put in a dangerous situation by the rebels from Santa Ines if they do not join them. Ripoll and Guerra acted accordingly to the situation. In the battles that happened, several Native Americans and soldiers were hurt and wounded. The army of Guerra, despite the protests of the padre's, attacked the Indian's houses and killed all the people they found regardless of their innocence.

The escaped Native Americans refused to return and proceed further over the mountains. This revolt spread to the missions of Sa Buenaventura, San Gabriel, and some Native Americans from these missions also escaped. After these happenings, the Mission started to decline rapidly. Although the building was in excellent condition, and the manufacturing industry also was kept up, everything else suffered.

In 1833, president Duran in discussion with Governor Figueroa, tackled the question of secularization and suggested some kind of a change need to take place in some of the oldest missions, among which Santa Barbara as well.

The Micheltorena's decree in 1843 returned the control of the Fathers, but in the following year, Padre Duran reported that it had achieved the greatest difficulty in supporting its 287 souls. The Pico's decree in 1845 allowed retaining of the principal building for the Fathers but all of the remaining lands and buildings needed to be reentered. Keeping in mind that the Native Americans were becoming careless and improvident, padre Duran was so willing to give the mission's land to the renters. After the death of Padre Duran in 1846, Padre Rubio Gonzales succeeded in its function for almost 30 years, and it was one of the last missionaries.

In 1853 following a petition sent to Rome, Santa Barbara was erected into a Hospice, marking the beginning of an Apostolic College to educate Franciscan novitiates who are to go forth, wherever sent, as missionaries. (Wharton 22-26)

1.9. Old Mission Santa Inés

The Mission of Santa Ines was founded on September 17, 1804, by Estevan Tapis which later became president of the Missions. At the opening ceremony, Tamis himself conducted the ceremonies (Bellezza, 111).

With Lasuen in charge, the Missions in California reached their maximum. After him, an immediate decline was noticed. This was because of the lack of activities within the missions as well as the establishments of a lot of villages and towns. The decline of the missions was also because widespread mortality has affected Native Americans, so Governor Sola suggested that the infected Native Americans should be transported to a new location, which is more healthful on the north shore of the San Francisco Bay.

On December 14, Padre Saria, along with several other priests, conducted the consecration ceremony of San Rafael Archangel. The original purpose of this mission was to assist the San Francisco mission. However, although there is no record that it was ever officially elevated to the status of an independent mission, it is referred to and listed as such since 1823 in all Fathers' accounts. Today there are no traces of its existence. The only proof of its existence is the few old pears planted at the beginning of its history. Some claim that San Rafael was founded as a direct response to the southern aggression of the Russians, who founded Fort Ross in 1812, only sixty-five miles north of San Francisco. However, there seems to be no solid evidence of this, although the Spanish authorities' concern over the immediate proximity of the Russians was evident. The further cases of anxiety were accelerated by the independence of Mexico, which gave the leaders enough to fill their minds.

The final founding took place in 1823, without the idea of establishing a new mission. The change in San Rafael was of great significance to the ailing Native Americans, which influenced the decision of Canon Fernandez, Perfect Payeraz, and Governor Arguello to transfer the San Francisco Mission from the mainland north of the bay and make San Rafael dependent on it (Worden and Leffingwell, 158-159). An exploring expedition was sent to examine the whole quarter and finally to reported in favor of the Sonoma Valley. The report was accepted, and on July 4, 1823, a cross was placed and blessed at the place, which was named New San Francisco.

Preceded by appeasement of all controversy, the new mission was formally consecrated on Passion Week on April 4, 1824, by Altimira, in San Francisco Solano, "the great apostle of the Native Americans." There were now two San Francisco, de Assis and Solano, and because of the inconvenience of this confusion, the popular names Dolores and Solano, and later Sonoma, came into use (Wharton 27-28).

1.10. Misión La Purísima Concepción De María Santísima

The Mission de la Purisima Concepcion de Maria Santisima was established in 1787 by Father Fermin Francisco de Lasuen. Purisima was the eleventh of the 21 Spanish missions. The mission complex consisted of an enclosed quadrangle with a chapel; military and secular buildings were located outside the mission walls (Lightfoot, 55). An earthquake destroyed the mission in 1812, so the Fathers build another mission under the same name that was constructed at another site. The famous revolt among Native Americans that affected Santa Ines and Santa Barbara did not bypass the Purisima. After the attack at Santa Inés, the rebels fled to Purísima. The Native Americans also seized the buildings of the Mission. After few more attacks, Native Americans settled down, but the Native Americans in Santa Barbara were not calmed yet. Such riots, occasional outbursts, followed by floods, earthquakes, epidemics, have reduced the population living in this area.

Joaquin and Jose Antonio Ezequiel Carillo bought the ruined site of La Purisima following the secularization, and the Franciscans lost control, and many of the Chumash moved into pueblo communities to work at nearby ranchos (Hardwick) Jonathan (Juan) Temple bought The remainder of the mission lands, including the mission buildings which later have been sold to Ramón Malo, who had been granted adjacent Rancho Santa Rita.

In 1874, the Lompoc Temperance colony bought the former mission, and the Lompoc city grew in that area.

1.11. Mission San Luis Obispo de Tolosa, San Luis Obispo

The Mission of San Luis Obispo was founded on September 1, 1772, and in one year, there were only 12 converts. Father Serra founded this mission and left Father Cavalier in charge, with two Native Americans and four soldiers (Bellezza, 75). At this time, they have only a few hundreds of flour on disposal and a barrel of brown sugar. The chapel of the Mission was built by Father Cavalier. In the beginning, Native Americans were not attracted to the Mission, and the only thing that attracted them in the begging was the clothes.

The most important thigh for this mission is that Padre Lasuen and Tapis served here as a missionary and in 1798 father Luis Antonio Martinez began his long-term service at the Mission of San Luis. The highest population was reached in 1794, where the number of people who lived in this Mission was 946. In 1834, San Luis had 264 Native Americans, and this number started to decrease rapidly in the following period. In 1840, there were only 170 Native Americans left. The order of secularization was put into effect in 1835 by Manuel Jimeno Casarin (Helmbrecht, 480.)

1.12. Mission of San Miguel

The Mission of San Miguel was founded by Father Lasuen in 1797, with the purpose to close the gap between Mission San Antonio to the north and Mission San Luis Obispo to the south (Doyce, 230). The church that was built in 1797 was destroyed in the fire that happened in 1806. After this event, the preparations for building a new church started. The church was completed in 1821. The property of San Miguel extended 18 miles to the north and 18 miles to the south, 66 miles to the east, and 35 miles to the Pacific Ocean. The mission was successful thanks to the work of Father Juan Martin, who was in charge of the Mission until 1824.

The secularization of the San Miguel Mission took place in 1834. The exile of the Spanish Franciscans also had an impact on the Salinan people who loved there. This was the main reason for leaving the mission and going back to their ancestral homelands.

In 1859, president Buchanan returned the Mission's buildings to the catholic church, and in 1878, a diocesan priest was assigned, and the parish of San Miguel was established.

1.13. Mission of Nuestro Señora de la Soledad

There is not much evidence in history for the Mission of *"Our lady of Solitude,"* and the present conditions suggest that not much have been restored. In 1791, Padre Lasuen, in pursuit of suitable locations for opening new Missions, spotted a place in the middle way between San Antonio and Santa Clara. The Indian name of Soledad was Chuttusgelis (Mornin and Mornin, 83).

On October 9, the Mission was finally established. The number of Native Americans was not very high in this region, and only a few of them converted to Christianity. Also, the land was not suitable for production and work, so the Fathers were obliged to increase the number of Native Americans. At the end of the 9th year of its founding, 512 Native Americans lived in Soledad, and their property included a thousand cattle, several thousand sheep, and horses. Five years later (in 1805), there were 727 Native Americans, although a severe epidemic a few years ago significantly reduced their numbers and caused many to fear the mission. A new church was started in 1808.

For about forty years, priests and Natives lived a peaceful and comfortable life in this secluded valley, with abundant food and resources. that they lived in prosperity and well-being is evidenced by the fact that they handed over 1150 USD to the presidency in Monterrey. At one time, they owned over six thousand cattle; and in 1821, the number of cattle, sheep, horses, and other animals was estimated at over sixteen thousand. After the changes brought about by political administration, the number of Native Americans rapidly decreased, and the property acquired by their united toil quickly dwindled until little was left but poverty and suffering.

In the time that secularization took place, the estate of Soledad, aside from the church, was evaluated at $36,000. After six years of secularization, the number of Native Americans declined to 70, and the effects were evident to the property as well. On June 4, 1846, the Mission of Soledad was sold to the Feliciano Soveranes for $800 (Farnsworth, 71).

The death of Padre Sarria is considered one of the most important events in the period of decline of the Missions. Padre Sarria was one of the most prominent priests who refused to take the oath of allegiance to the Mexican republic and were arrested for that. His last year, he spent it at the Mission of Soledad. there are not many remnants of the church at that time in the Soledad's Mission. One family from Soledad claimed that the present ruins of the church are from the building erected in 1850 by their grandfather (Wharton 79-81).

1.14. Mission San Carlos Borromeo del Rio Carmelo

The Mission of San Carlos Borromeo was founded in 1769 by the father Junipero Serra in Caramel, California (Smith, and Smith, 25). The purpose of this mission, as in others, was to convert Native Americans to Christianity. Interestingly, the Mission in Caramel was the second established, after the first mission in San Diego.

In the beginning, the Native Americans were not attracted to the Mission, so to make it more approachable to the Natives, Serra moved the Mission from Monterey to Caramel. This site was also very good because of the source of fresh water and better land. The Mission in Caramel served as a Missions' headquarters from 1770 – 1803.

This place is also important because this was the place where Serra Lived and from this place, he inspired to build the other missions. After the Mexican independence, followed by the secularization, the mission's system started to collapse. As California became part of the United States, the government returned the mission to the Roman Catholic Church in 1859. In 1884 restoration of the mission began. The stone church was largely restored in the 1930s (Morgado, 160).

1.15. Old Mission of San Juan Bautista

The Mission of San Juan Bautista was founded on June 24, 1797, in the place called San Juan Bautista by Father Lasuen. This mission was the 15th of the Missions established in California. The Native residents of the valley, the Ohlone people, were brought to live in San Juan and to start to engage in agriculture. Rapidly after its foundation, the population of San Juan started to grow quickly. By 1803, 1036 Native Americans lived there (Mendoza, 5-10).

The mission was founded near the San Andreas Fault, and for this reason, it has suffered a lot of earthquakes. Luckily, the mission was not destroyed at once. The restoration of the Mission started in 1884 and then again in 1949, with funds from the Hearst Foundation. It was subject to secularization in 1835, but it was given back to the roman catholic church in 1859.

1.16. Mission de la Santa Cruz

The foundations of the church were laid on February 27, 1793, and it was completed and officially opened on May 10, 1794, by Padre Penja of Santa Clara, with the help of five other priests (Allen, 8-10), Native Americans, servants, and troops watched the ceremonies with unusual interest, and the next day the church held its first mass. The church was about thirty to one hundred and twelve feet high and twenty-five feet high. The other buildings were slowly erected, and in the autumn of 1796, a mill was built.

With the foundation of the town of Branciforte across the river, a big part of the Native Americans deserted, which was not good for the mission itself in terms of workforce. For a long time, the government intended to fund more villages or towns and missions in California to colonize the country properly. Governor Borica did some personal research and finally chose the right across the Lorenzo River from Santa Cruz from the three proposed sites. Towards the end of the century, all concerned concluded that Bransifort's villa was a bad idea - "the settlers were scandalizing the country with their immorality. "They are disgusting to their persecution and do not do any good" (Allen, 10-12).

For the whole time, the missionaries were against the new settlement. First, because it was on the lands of Native Americans which were used for pasture. On the other side, the Governor stated that the Native Americans were dying off, there were no more pagans to convert, and the Native Americans already had more land and raised more grain than they could attend to. In 1805, captain Goycoechea claimed that because there are no gentiles anymore, the Native Americans need to be divided between the Missions of Santa Clara and San Juan. In the end, nothing happened of this. In the period between 1820 – 1830, the number of people who lived in this mission declined rapidly, but on the contrary, the agriculture of the mission bloomed. In 1823, another attempt was to suppress the Mission, to strengthen the town of Branciforte, but this attempt, like the previous one, was unsuccessful (Jackson, 33).

In 1834 – 1835, Ignacio del Valle effectuated the order for secularization. His property was valued to $47.000, besides $10.000 distributed to the Native Americans. No further distributions were meant for Native Americans. The Native Americans were organized in a village named Figueroa, but this structure was no different from that of the mission, only the name was different.

In January 1840, the tower of the church fell together with several tiles. This was considered as a premonition of the final disaster of 1851 when major damage happened, followed by the attack of the treasure seekers. The Community of the Mission vanished from 1841 to 1842, and everything that was once under the mission auspices now belonged to the town of Branciforte. In 1845 only about 40 Native Americans were known to remain. At present, there are no evident sights of the Mission. (Wharton 26-28).

1.17. The mission of Santa Clara

Years before the arrival of the first Europeans on Californian land, the South Bay was inhabited by a large Native population. They were organized in 40 different tribes. One of the many communities, called Thamien, lived on the place where the now campus stands. Their descendants today call them Ohlone. The Spanish colonization in 1769 was a milestone that provoked major changes in the whole organization and living of the Ohlone people. Few generations were needed for Ohlone society to transform from hunting and gathering to agriculture and to accept the catholic Christian faith (Jackson, Howard and Castillo 4-5).

The whole process of conversion began with different channels rather than conquest, primarily with strategic trade and outright gifts. Once the Native people decided to join the mission, they were not allowed to leave. Another motivator for joining the mission was the increasing scarcity of foods and animals brought by Spanish people.

The Santa Clara Mission was originally established about three miles near Alviso, the San Francisco Bay, near the Guadalupe River, in what the Native Americans called So-co-is-u-ka (laurel tree). The mission was at that location for only a short time, as there were floods on several occasions, forcing the fathers to relocate. In 1780-1782 the new mission was built about 150 yards southwest of the current wide-gauge depot (South Pacific). The mission operated at this location until 1812, when the earthquake did not cause significant problems. The second earthquake in 1818 caused the Mission to move to a new location, where it continued to function for a long time (Skowronek and Wizorek, 55-56).

On November 29, 1777, the village of San Jose was founded near the Mission. for this reason, the fathers rebelled because whites inhabited the village. Hence, their activities and way of life greatly influenced the whole process of conversion of the Native Americans initiated by the priests. in 1820 the number of people living in this mission was 1357, mostly Native Americans. The maximum population was reached in 1827 when the mission numbered 1464. In the following period, the number of inhabitants began to decline.

The process of secularization took place in the Mission of Santa Clara as well. Although it has been proclaimed as an early success, the fall of the Mission was very fast. The population of the Native Americans in 1832 was 1125, in 1834 about 800, and at the end of the decade, about 290, with another 150 scattered in the area.

Several factors, among which the clash of cultures and waves of epidemics, were the main reason for the fall of the Mission. Mexican independence in 1822 only fostered the collapse of the Mission and undermined the planned return of mission land ownership to the Ohlone. The California gold rush was the last chain link that pushed the Ohlone people to the margins of Californian society (Panich, 40-42).

1.18. Mission of San José de Guadalupe

The Mission of San Jose de Guadalupe was founded on April 23, 1809, when the new church was opened with the blessings of President Tapis. Two years later, the fathers from the church went to explore the Sacramento and San Joaquin valleys. They found Native Americans very timid during their journey and concluded that the Sacramento valley is a suitable place for starting a new mission. In 1820, the population in San Jose was 1754. The maximum population was achieved in 1824, consisting of 1806 people. Until the secularization took place, the Mission of San Jose was one of the most prosperous. At this time, Jesus Vallejo was an administrator for secularization, and in 1837 Padre Gonzales funded the mission with $155,000, paying all the church debts (Beilharz and DeMers, 25-28).

Up to the time of secularization, the Mission continued to be one of the most prosperous. Jesus Vallejo was the administrator for secularization, and in 1837 he and Padre Gonzalez Rubio made an inventory that gave a total of over $155,000 when all debts were paid. Even now, it seemed to prosper for a while, and not until 1840 did the decline set in. With Micheltorena's decree from 1843, the mission in San Jose was restored to the temporal control of the Fathers. The Pico's decree from 1845 inventoried the Mission, but there is no trace of it in present times. In 1846, Pico sold the Mission's land to Alvarado for $12,000, but the sale never went to effect (Winther, 170-172.).

1.19. Mission of San Rafael Arcángel

The Mission of San Rafael Archangel was founded on December 14, 1817, in San Francisco to provide health support for sick Native Americans. The original name of the place was Nanaguani. In the beginning, 140 Native Americans lived there and by the end of 1820, their number increased to 590. With the foundation of San Francisco Solano, 92 Native Americans were sent there from San Rafael. Despite this, the population in San Rafael grew reaching 1140 in 1828 (DeBaker, 4-5).

Governor Echeanadia was upset about the positioning of the Russians at Fort Ross and accused them of attracting the Native Americans to a place outside San Rafael. The secularization in 1835 ordered that San Rafael should be placed at a first-class which means that it needed to pay $1500, which is much more expensive than for those of the second class - $1000. In 1837, General Vallejo was permitted to collect everything and care for it, explaining that the Native Americans are not using their liberty well. In 1840 Native Americans expected that the promise of returning what belongs to them should be fulfilled. Despite the governor's opposition, Vallejo succeeded in obtaining an order for the distribution of the livestock.

In 1845, Pico ordered all Native Americans to return to San Rafael within a month. Otherwise, their possessions would be sold. In 1846, the land and buildings were sold to Antonio Sunol for $ 8,000. However, the buyers did not receive proof of ownership, and their titles were declared invalid (Leffingwell, 30).

1.20. Mission of San Antonio de Padua

Mission San Antonio De Padua was founded in 1771 and is the third of 21 missions along the California coast between San Diego and Sonoma (Broom, 10). Father Serra also founded the Mission of San Antonio de Padua. He left Fathers Miguel Pieras and Buenaventura Sitjar behind to continue the building efforts, though the construction of the church proper did not begin until 1810. By that time, 178 Native Americans lived at the Mission (De Padua Mission, 1834).

The number of Native Americans increased to 1300 by 1805, but the secularization itself was the reason for decreasing Native Americans. Thus their number was 150 in 1834. Another important factor for the Mission of San Antonio de Padua is that there was no town forming near the Mission, as was the case in other Missions. In 1845, Mexican Governor Pío Pico declared all mission buildings in Alta California for sale, but no one bid for Mission San Antonio.

After 30 years, the Mission was returned to the Catholic Church. In 1894, roof tiles were salvaged from the property and installed on the Southern Pacific Railroad depot located in Burlingame, California, one of the first permanent structures constructed in the Mission Revival Style. Most of the missions became public churches except for Santa Barbara, San Luis Rey, San Miguel, and San Antonio. Mission San Antonio is one of four still run by the Franciscan religious order, urban social workers concerned with the needs of the poor.

1.21. Mission of San Francisco de Asís

The Mission of San Francisco De Asis was named by the founder of the Franciscan Order, Frances De Assisi, also known as "Mission Dolores" owing to the presence of a nearby creek named Arroyo de Nuestra Señora de Los Dolores, meaning "Our Lady of Sorrows Creek (Mission San Francisco de Asís). The original Mission was dedicated on October 9, 1776. The present Mission church, near what is now the intersection of Dolores and 16th Streets, was dedicated in 1791. The greatest period of activity of the Mission was achieved in the early 19th century.

In the period between 1810 – 1820, the Mission achieved its peak with 1100 people. In 1810 the Mission owned 11,000 sheep, 11,000 cows, and thousands of horses, goats, pigs, and mules. Its ranching and farming operations extended as far south as San Mateo and east to Alameda. The Mission of San Francisco De Asis is one of the two surviving buildings and the Mission in San Capristiano, also known as the Father Serra Church (Newell, 415).

The Mexican War of Independence worsened, thus deteriorated relations between the Mission of California and Mexico. Together with the diseases and the worsened health conditions, these conditions were the reasons for the death of a large number of Native Americans.

In 1834, the Mexican government adopted secularization laws with which most church properties were sold or granted to private owners. In the period that followed, Mission Dolores fell on very hard times. By 1842, only eight Christian Native Americans were living at the Mission (Blind et al., 146).

1.22. Mission San Francisco de Solano

Fifty-four years after founding the first Franciscan Mission in California, the site was chosen for the twenty-first and last, San Francisco Solano. This Mission was established in Sonoma under conditions already narrated. The first ceremonies took place July 4, 1823, and nine months later. The Mission church was dedicated. A year and a half from the time the location was selected, the necessary Mission buildings had been erected, and many fruit trees and vines were already growing. The number of Native Americans was 693, but many of these were sent from San Francisco, San José, and San Rafael. The Native Americans at this Mission represented thirty-five different tribes, according to the record, yet they worked together harmoniously, and in 1830 their possessions included more than 8000 cattle, sheep, and horses. Their crops averaged nearly 2000 bushels of grain per year (Byram et al., 249).

In 1834 the Mission was secularized by M.G. Vallejo, who appointed Ortega as majordomo. Vallejo quarreled with Padre Quijas, who at once left and went to reside at San Rafael. The movable property was distributed to the Native Americans, and they were allowed to live on their old rancherías, though there is no record that they were formally allotted to them. The pueblo of Sonoma was the center of the secularized church of San Francisco and also presented a home for colonists brought to the country by the Fathers. In this same year, the soldiers of the presidio of San Francisco de Asis were transferred to Sonoma to protect the frontier from the Russians and check the incoming of Americans. Vallejo supported the presidial company, mainly at his own expense, and made friends with the Native chief, Solano, who aided him materially in keeping the Native Americans peaceful (Schneider and Kathryn, 227-228).

The general statistics of the Mission for the eleven years of its existence, 1823-34, are as follows: baptisms 1315, marriages 278, deaths 651. The largest population was 996 in 1832. In 1845, when Pico's plan for selling and renting the Missions was formulated, Solano was declared without value, the secularization having been completely carried out. However, there is an imperfect inventory of buildings, utensils, and church property. It was ignored in the final order. In 1880 Bishop Alemany sold the Mission and grounds of San Francisco Solano to a German named Schocken for $3000. With that money, a modern church was erected for the parish, which is still being used. For six months after the sale, divine services were still held in the old Mission, and then Schocken used it to store wine and hay. In September 1903, it was sold to the Hon. W.R. Hearst for $5000. The ground plot was 166 by 150 feet. It is said that General Vallejo built the tower in 1835 or thereabouts. The deeds have been transferred to the State of California and accepted by the Legislature. The intention is to preserve the Mission as a valuable historic landmark (Truman, 7).

1.23. California's Missions and Growth

The foundation of Spanish missions in California had an enormous historical significance for the west part of the country but also for the whole state. The economic success of these missions proves the development of the economically viable community in circumstances of extremely limited recourses (Doti, 2)

The case of Spanish California is unique when trying to portray the Spanish conquest's effects in terms of economic growth and prosperity. In a short period, California managed to transfer from a struggling frontier bastion to economically independent by 1810 and independent from the Spanish empire by 1821. While domestic events did not influence political independence, economic independence resulted from the development of the missions.

The missions of Alta California manage to approximate the ideal of the mission as the main institution (besides the lots of failures but successes as well). Their primary functions they performed remarkably. In this regard, the processes of Hispanicization and Christianization were implemented successfully. The indigenous people have trained in the basic principles of Christianity and were taught how to survive in the new form of living. The Native Americans provided the main necessities for the communities.

During the Mission's period, each mission became an economic community built by the labor of the local Native Californians. The earlies studies of the Spanish California missions present the bad treatment of the local Native people. In this regard, the death rate, especially among women and children, was high. The labor of the Native people was compensated for food, clothes, and beads. By joining the mission, the Natives needed to build churches, housing, warehousing, and manufacturing facilities, which meant to change their entire lifestyle. "So why did Indian people join the missions in large numbers even after their repressive regime became widely known?" because the benefits of joining the mission were larger than the effects of the repression (Dugan, 24).

The California missions have often been accused of evading government orders and of malevolently depriving the military of needed sustenance. To be sure, the situation of the military has to be appreciated. They must have felt abandoned and forgotten by the authorities they were presumably serving. The missions, however, attempted to protect their functions as guardians of Native Americans. Supplying the military was not their obligation, while seeing to the needs of the neophyte community was not only their duty but also the basis upon which they were certain they would be judged in the hereafter.

Consequently, missionaries were reluctant to deprive Native Americans in favor of the military. Nevertheless, there is no evidence that anyone, Indian or Hispanic, ever starved because of refusal by the missions to provide necessities. It was practically incomprehensible to the military that missionaries should attach equal importance to the survival of Native Americans and Gente de Razon. Such conflict was endemic in the Spanish colonial system, and its repetition throughout the empire was widespread.

It was expected that institutions would conflict on the local level to protect their roles and functions. Spheres of authority were deliberately poorly defined to allow for change and adaptation to local situations. Ultimately, resulting conflicts would be settled concerning local circumstances upon appeal to a higher authority that could command the obedience of both parties to the dispute (Archibald, 183-184).

1.24. California during Mexico Independence

At the beginning of the 19th century, the Spanish colonies in America struggled for their independence. California felt the effects of these movements in terms of limited supplies to the missions, the pressure of the navy making them unable to spare ships and to bring supplies and other needed products for the missions and villages north of San Diego. These provoked the local authorities to relax restrictions and to start trading with non-Spanish merchants to provide basic needs for the survival of the colonies. The main trading partners in this period were England, Russia, France, and the USA. The year 1821 is known as the year when Mexico achieved independence, and this news reached Alta California in the following year.

The colonial policies of the new republic were quite different from those of the Spanish monarchy. This meant that Californians were allowed to trade with foreigners, but the novelty was that foreigners now could also hold land once they have been naturalized and converted to Christianity. There were some differences in the way in which the Mexican rule differed from the Spanish monarchy. The Mexican rule allowed more grants for individual ranchos, while the land grants to individuals were only a few in numbers under the Spanish monarchy's rule.

Also, the most important change brought by the Mexican independence was the secularization of the missions and limiting the control of the Franciscan missionaries. This kind of process of secularization started in 1834. In the beginning, the Franciscans administered the lands of missions for the Natives that lived here when the missioners arrived, but only some of them benefited at the end of the mission system. In this period, the biggest part of the mission's churches and buildings began discouraged, but some priests at some missions were doing their best to continue their missions to convert Native people to Christianity. Most of the mission's land was offered to white Californians or the recently arrived from Mexico. In ten years, the number of grants for ranchos increased from 50 to 600 new grants (Clay, 210).

The Mexican independence created conditions for the development of a new culture in California. The symbol of this new culture was the Californian ranchero, and his family was raising cattle. The breeding of beef and hides became the most important factors of economic life. Well-connected families (such as the Vallejos, Alvarados, and Peraltas in the north and the Carillo's, de la Guerras, and Picos in the south) could secure grants for each family member, creating an elite class of rancheros who controlled hundreds of thousands of prime acres. These families mainly raised cattle for an emerging hide-and-tallow trade with American ships that sold the hides to Boston tanneries and the tallow to South American candle and soap factories. These elite Californios — as they became known — held themselves apart from non-land-owning Mexicans and Natives, intermarrying with each other and with the American and European entrepreneurs who began settling in California during the 1830s (Hyde, 205).

However, the end of the missions provoked discontinuity of the manufacture having in mind that the main part of goods needed came from Spain. But the merchants from Britain, Canada, and the USA, which came to California searching for the hides, again revived the manufacturing, but this time using goods from the foreign merchants.

Like the mission system, Native Californians provided the biggest part of the working force for the emerging ranching economy. Some of the Spanish-speaking Natives married working-class Mexicans and further complicated the already complicated racial categories. Spanish became the common language for the Native groups, which struggled to survive in the complexity of the social system followed by diseases and environmental degradation. All of these factors influenced the process of "ethnogenesis," which symbolizes the creation of new ethnicities and identities (Bancroft, 439).

As for the ethnic structure of the people, before 1824, there have been few permanent residents from non –Hispanic descent, but their number increased in the Mexican era. The first citizens of the United States who came to California were trappers led by Jedediah Smith in 1826. Also, the first organized group of people who came to California was a party led by John Bidwell and John Bartelson in 1841.

After its arrival to California, Bidwell started to work for Johann August Sutter, a German-born Swiss businessman (1803 - 1880), one of the most important foreign immigrants in Mexican California. Sutter possessed a grant of 48,000 acres, where he established the so-called "New Helvetia," a settlement with vineyards, wheat fields, and orchards. The Sutter's settlement attracted a lot of American settlers who followed the example of Bidwell.

During the 1830s and 1840s, increasing numbers of Europeans and Americans arrived in California wishing to start a life in the land of California. Like Scottish sailor John Gilroy left their ships, some became Mexican citizens, converted to Christianity, and married Californian families. Others like John Marsh from Massachusetts and John Sutter from Switzerland crossed the ocean to come to California and to set up profitable ranches in the Central Valley.

Although the successful start of its independence, Mexico was faced with difficulties in ruling the Californian province. The last governor who was sent to California from Mexico was Manuel MIcheltorena, who came to California in 1842. The people of California were not satisfied with him, and he withdrew in 1845. The next governor was a local rancher of African descent. Unofficially, this meant that California had achieved home rule.

California, during the Mexican independence, presented a society in dramatic transition. In political terms, the change of power from Spanish to Mexican distributed new laws, new rulers, and the most important thing, a shift of power from missionaries to secular governors and created powerful rancher families. Also, the demographic structure suffered changes. The intensified emigration of Mexicans, colonists from Europe among Russians, Francs and Britons, American trappers, and homesteaders created conditions for new social complexities. California's natural spaces were transformed with Europan cattle and horses' arrival and weeds and crops. Much of California was unrecognizable to Native groups that had witnessed the coming of the Spaniards less than 80 years before, by the time the US-Mexican War broke out in 1846.

The mission system, which functioned for 60 years and converted to Christianity 53600 Natives, now were disappearing because they were a target for Mexican republicans, which after gaining their independence from Spain, started to call for privatization of the church property (Bancroft, 438).

1.25. Mexican – American war

The Mexican-American war (1846-1848) was the first conflict that the USA fought on foreign ground. The American president James K. Polk believed that the USA had a manifest destiny to expand the American influence through the whole continent reaching the Pacific and confronted the politically divided and militarily weak Mexico. In the war that took almost two years, Mexico lost about one-third of its territory, including present-day California, Utah, Nevada, Arizona, and New Mexico (Griswold del Castillo, 28).

Texas gained its independence from Mexico in 1836. The United States did not intend to align Texas into the union because they were against adding a new southern slave state. The government of Mexico was also preparing its troops and knew that any attempt at annexation would lead to war. In his campaign, president Polk considered that Texas should be annexed, and after his election, the annexation procedures quickly started. Polk also had in interest California and New Mexico and the rest of the territories which today belong to the U.S. southwest (Samora, 22).

The Mexican – American war started on April 25, 1846, with the attack of the Mexican cavalry on a group of American soldiers in the disputed zone under the command of General Zachary Taylor. These battles were the reason for Congress to declare war on May 13. It is interesting that no declaration of War ever came from Mexico. The U.S. forces under Col. Stephen W. Kearny and Commodore Robert F. Stockton entered on a Mexican territory north of the Rio Grande river. At that time, only about 75,000 Mexican citizens lived there, so it was easier to conquer those lands with minimal resistance. As defeats lined up, Mexico began to rely on General Antonio Lopez de Santa Ana, a charismatic strongman who lived in exile in Cuba. General Santa Ana convinced Polk that he would end the war on favorable terms for the United States if he were allowed to return to Mexico.

Nevertheless, when he arrived in Mexico, he did not keep his promise to Polk, taking control of the Mexican army and leading it into battle. At the Battle of Buena Vista in February 1847, Santa Ana suffered heavy losses and was forced to retreat. Despite the loss, he took over the Mexican presidency next month. At the same time, U.S. troops led by General Winfield Scott arrived in Veracruz and captured the city. The march to Mexico City was very reminiscent of the route taken by Hernan Cortes when he invaded the Aztec Empire. The Mexicans opposed Cerro Gordo and elsewhere but were defeated each time. In September 1847, Scott successfully laid siege to Chapultepec Castle in Mexico City. During that clash, a group of military school cadets - the so-called niños héroes - allegedly committed suicide rather than surrender (Foos, 103).

Because Mexico refused to pay the U.S. claims, general Polk, on May 9, 1846, started to prepare a war message to Congress. The same day he received a message that a Mexican troop has crossed the Rio Grande river and started with attacks on American land. In this regard, Polk sent the war message to Congress on May 11, 1846, stating that Mexico attacked American territory and shed American blood on American soil. (Glass, 1-2).

Congress approved a declaration of war on May 13, but the United States entered the war divided. Democrats, especially those in the Southwest, strongly favored the conflict. Most Whigs viewed Polk's motives as conscienceless land grabbing. Indeed, from the outset, Whigs in both the Senate and the House challenged the veracity of Polk's assertion that the initial conflict between U.S. and Mexican forces had taken place in U.S. territory.

Further, legislators were at odds over whether Polk had the right to declare that a state of war existed unilaterally. Principally at issue was where the encounter had taken place and the willingness of Americans to acknowledge the Mexican contention that the Nueces River formed the border between the two countries. Active Whig opposition to the legitimacy of Polk's claim and the war itself continued well into the conflict. In December 1846, Polk accused his Whig doubters of treason. In January 1847, the by-then Whig-controlled House voted 85 to 81 to censure Polk for having "unnecessarily and unconstitutionally" initiated war with Mexico (Winders, 4-8).

The United States planned to invade the heart of Mexico by sending its army from the Rio Grande river, under the command of Taylor, and the second force under Col Kearny. Kearny's campaign was, in the biggest part, successful because the people in Mexico and California did not oppose this campaign. They rather accepted it. Among the victories of Kearny is that of Monterey, Buena Vista.

Nevertheless, Taylor did not show much enthusiasm for a major invasion of Mexico and, on several occasions, failed to expel the Mexicans after defeating them vigorously. For this purpose, Polk was forced to revise his military strategy. He ordered General Winfield Scott to take an army by sea to Veracruz, capture a key port, and march ashore to Mexico City. Scott took over Veracruz in March after a three-week siege and began marching on Mexico City. The Mexicans put up some resistance, but it was not enough. Scott defeated and captured Mexico City on September 14, 1847. The fall of the Mexican capital ended the military phase of the conflict (Olguín, 88).

During the conflict between the soldiers, many diseases and illnesses prevailed. Eventually, infection and disease claimed many more lives in the United States than in the war. At least 10,000 soldiers died of disease, while about 1,500 were killed in action or wounded in battle (estimates of war casualties vary). Poor sanitation also contributed to the spread of the disease, within volunteers - who were less disciplined in sanitation practices than regular troops - dying more than regular ones. Another cause of death was yellow fever and measles, mumps, and rubella - taking their toll, especially on rural troops whose immunities were less developed than those of their urban compatriots.

1.26. The Treaty of Guadalupe Hidalgo

Guerrilla attacks on U.S. supply lines continued into the following period, but the war's end was imminent. General Santa Ana resigned, and the United States has been waiting for a new government capable of negotiating. Finally, on February 2, 1848, the Treaty of Guadeloupe Hidalgo was signed, declaring the Rio Grande, not the River Nueces, to be the border between the United States and Mexico (Del Castillo, 11). Under the deal, Mexico also recognized the U.S. annexation of Texas. It agreed to sell California and the rest of its territory north of the Rio Grande for $ 15 million-plus certain damages claims. In this regard, the treaty enriched the U.S. territory with an additional 525,000 square miles, including present territories of Arizona, California, Colorado, Nevada, New Mexico, Utah, and Wyoming.

President Polk assigned Nicholas Trist to negotiate the peace treaty terms as a chief clerk in the State Department. Polk recalled Trist because he thought it was too slow in reaching the peace agreement. Not signing a peace agreement was because problems persisted on the Mexican side, leading to delay information of a new government. Trist did not resign and signed the peace agreement with Mexico on February 2, 1848. Both national congresses ratified the treaty. Mexico made significant concessions in favor of America, giving Mexico, Utah, Nevada, Arizona, California, Texas, and Western Colorado for $ 15 million (Guadalupe, 692).

At the end of the war, Taylor emerged as a national hero and became president in 1849 after the mandate of President Polk. On August 8, 1846, Representative David Wilmot of Pennsylvania attempted to add an amendment to the peace agreement. This amendment, which was never passed, banned, among other things, slavery in any territory acquired by Mexico. Although never passed, it led to serious debate and greatly contributed to the rise of sectarian antagonism. The status of slavery in the newly acquired countries was finally resolved by the Compromise of 1850, but only after the nation was on the brink of civil war.

Works Cited

"1821-1847: Missions, Ranchos, and the Mexican War for Independence" was written by Joshua Paddison and the University of California in 2005 as part of the California Cultures project. https://www.loc.gov/collections/california-first-person-narratives/articles-and-essays/early-california-history/mexican-california/

Archibald, Robert. *The Economic Aspects of the California Missions*. Vol. 12. Washington, DC: Academy of American Franciscan History, 1978.

Bancroft, Hubert Howe. History of California. Vol. 7. History Company, 1890.

Barnes, C. Rankin. "Saint Paul's Church, San Diego, California 1869-1944." *Historical Magazine of the Protestant Episcopal Church* 13.4 (1944): 320-345.

Beattie, George William. "Spanish Plans for an Inland Chain of Missions in California." *Annual Publication of the Historical Society of Southern California*, vol. 14, no. 2, 1929, pp. 243–264. *JSTOR*, www.jstor.org/stable/41168838. Accessed 17 May 2021.

Beilharz, Edwin A., Donald O. DeMers Jr, and Donald o. Demers jr. *San Jose: California's First City*. Vol. 29. Grand Lake Media. LLC, 1980.

Bellezza, Robert A. *Missions of Central California*. Arcadia Publishing, 2013.

Blind, Eric Brandan, et al. "El Presidio de San Francisco: At the edge of empire." *Historical Archaeology* 38.3 (2004): 135-149.

Broom, Michelle. "Mission Life: Can You Dig It?." *Cal Poly Magazine* 2.1 (1998): 7.

Crosby, Harry W. *Antigua California: mission and colony on the peninsular frontier, 1697-1768*. UNM Press, 1994.

de Padua, Mission San Antonio, and Founding Order. "Mission San Antonio de Padua." *Governing* (1834): 2.

DeBaker, Cassidy R. *The Rediscovery of Mission San Rafael Arcangel: An Archaeological Snapshot of the 20th California Mission.* Diss. Cultural Resources Management Program, Sonoma State University, 2012.

Del Castillo, Richard Griswold. *The Treaty of Guadalupe Hidalgo: A legacy of conflict.* University of Oklahoma Press, 1992.

Doti, Lynne. "Spanish California Missions: An Economic Success." (2019).

Farnsworth, Paul. *The Economics of Acculturation in the California Missions: a Historical and Archaeological Study of Mission Nuestra Senora de la Soledad (Spain, Mexico, Native-American).* Diss. University of California, Los Angeles, 1987.

Foos, Paul. *A short, offhand, killing affair: soldiers and social conflict during the Mexican-American War.* Univ of North Carolina Press, 2002.

Geiger, Maynard. "New Data on Mission San Juan Capistrano." *Southern California Quarterly* 49.1 (1967): 37-45.

Glass, Andrew. "Congress votes to declare war against Mexico, May 13, 1846." *Politico,* 13/05/2018, p. Page Number.

Goetz, Rebecca Anne. "Juan Rodríguez Cabrillo and Native Enslavement in California in History and Memory." *Traces and Memories of Slavery in the Atlantic World.* Routledge, 2019. 47-61.

Gonzales, Manuel G., and Cynthia M. Gonzales, eds. *En Aquel Entonces: Readings in Mexican-American History.* Indiana University Press, 2000.

Green, Terisa Marion. *Spanish Missions and Native Religion: Contact, Conflict, and Convergence.* University of California, Los Angeles, 1999.

Griswold del Castillo, Richard. "Manifest Destiny: The Mexican-American War and the Treaty of Guadalupe Hidalgo." *Sw. JL & Trade Am.* 5 (1998): 31.

Hardwick, Michael R. *La Purisíma Concepción: The Enduring History of a California Mission.* Arcadia Publishing, 2015.

Helmbrecht, Brenda. "Revisiting Missions: Decolonizing Public Memories in California." *Rhetoric Society Quarterly* 49.5 (2019): 470-494.

Hyde, Anne Farrar. *Empires, Nations, and Families: A History of the North American West, 1800-1860.* U of Nebraska Press, 2011.

Jackson, Robert H. "Disease and demographic patterns at Santa Cruz mission, Alta California." *Journal of California and Great Basin Anthropology* 5.1/2 (1983): 33-57.

Jackson, Robert Howard, Edward Castillo, and Edward D. Castillo. *Native Americans, Franciscans, and Spanish colonization: the impact of the mission system on California Native Americans.* UNM Press, 1995.

James, George Wharton. *The old Franciscan missions of California.* Little, Brown, 1913.

Johnson, Hildegard Binder. "The location of Christian missions in Africa." *Geographical review* (1967): 168-202.

Lee, Antoinette J. "Spanish missions." *APT Bulletin: The Journal of Preservation Technology* 22.3 (1990): 42-54.

Leffingwell, Randy. "California missions & presidios: the history & beauty of the Spanish missions." (2005).

Lightfoot, Kent. "3 Franciscan Missions in Alta California." *Native Americans, Missionaries, and Merchants.* University of California Press, 2004. 49-81.

Luna, Guadalupe T. "On the Complexities of Race: The Treaty of Guadalupe Hidalgo and Dred Scott v. Sandford." *U. Miami L. Rev.* 53 (1998): 691.

Madley, Benjamin L. "California Native Americans." *Oxford Research Encyclopedia of American History*. 2021.

Meadows, Don. "The Original Site of Mission San Juan Capistrano." *Southern California Quarterly* 49.3 (1967): 337-343.

Medina, Mariana, and Donna Genet. *Father Junipero Serra: Founder of the Missions of California*. Enslow Publishing, LLC, 2015.

Mendoza, Rubén G. "Archaeology and Architectural History Mission San Juan Bautista, CA." *Consultant* 12 (2009): 20.

Mission San Francisco de Asís. Available at: https://www.secret-bases. co.uk/wiki/Mission_San_Francisco_de_As%C3%ADs [Accessed on: 02.06.2021].

Morgado, Martin. "Non-Recedet Memoria Ejus: The Story of Blessed Junipero Serra's Mission Carmel Grave." *California History* 67.3 (1988): 150-167.

Mornin, Edward, and Lorna Mornin. *Saints of California: A Guide to Places and Their Patrons*. Getty Publications, 2009.

Newell, Quincy D. "The varieties of religious experience: baptized Native Americans at Mission San Francisco de Asis, 1776-1821." *American Indian Quarterly* 32.4 (2008): 412-442.

Nunis, Doyce B. "The Franciscan Friars of Mission San Fernando, 1797-1847." *Southern California Quarterly* 79.3 (1997): 217-248.

O'Keefe, Joseph Jeremiah. *The Buildings and Churches of the Mission of Santa Barbara*. Independent job printing house, 1886.

Olguín, Ben V. "Sangre Mexicana/Corazón Americano: Identity, Ambiguity, and Critique in Mexican-American War Narratives." *American Literary History* (2002): 83-114.

Panich, Lee M. "Mission Santa Clara in a Changing Urban Environment." (2015).

Panich, Lee M. "Spanish missions in the indigenous landscape: a view from Mission Santa Catalina, Baja California." *Journal of California and Great Basin Anthropology* (2010): 69-86

Pope Francis declares Mission San Buenaventura a Basilica. Available at: https://www.vaticannews.va/en/church/news/2020-07/pope-francis-declares-mission-san-buenaventura-a-basilica.html [Accessed on: 01.06.2021]

Samora, Julian. *The History of the Mexican-American People. Revised Edition.* University of Notre Dame Press. 2019. Project MUSE.

San Diego Mission Church San Diego, California. Available at: https://www.nps.gov/nr/travel/american_latino_heritage/San_Diego_Mission_Church.html [Accessed on: 27.05.2021]

Sandos, James A. *Converting California.* Yale University Press, 2008.

Schneider, Jeannine Kathryn Elizabeth. *Colliding Cultures: The Changing Landscapes of Mission San Francisco Solano, 1823-1846.* Diss. Washington State University, 2010.

Skowronek, Russell K., and Julie C. Wizorek. "Archaeology at Santa Clara de Asís: the slow rediscovery of a moveable mission." *Pacific Coast Archaeological Society Quarterly* 33.3 (1997): 54-92.

Smith, Frances Norris Rand, and Frances Rand Smith. *The Architectural History of Mission San Carlos Borromeo, California.* California Historical Survey Commission, 1921.

Smith, Frances Rand. "The Spanish Missions of California." *Hispania* 7.4 (1924): 243-258.

The Old Mission Basilica, San Buenaventura). Available at: https://www.sanbuenaventuramission.org/history Accessed on: 19/05/2021.

Truman, Benjamin Cummings, and Benjamin Cummings. *Missions of California*. M. Rieder, 1903.

Wagner, Henry R., and Antonio de la Ascension. "Spanish Voyages to the Northwest Coast in the Sixteenth Century. Chapter XI: Father Antonio de la Ascension's Account of the Voyage of Sebastian Vizcaino (Continued); Chapter XII: The Project to Settle Monterey." *California Historical Society Quarterly* 8.1 (1929): 26-70.

Weinerth, Catherine A. "Art as communication: Indian rock art and mission art of the San Fernando Valley, California." (1985).

Welcome to Mission San Luis Rey de Francia, King of the Missions. Available at: https://www.sanluisrey.org/museum/history [Accessed on: 27.05.2021].

Winders, Richard Bruce. *Mr. Polk's Army: the American military experience in the Mexican war.* No. 51. Texas A&M University Press, 2001.

Winther, Oscar Osburn. "The Story of San Jose, 1777-1869: California's First Pueblo." *California Historical Society Quarterly* 14.2 (1935): 147-174.

CHAPTER 2

The rise of the Southern Pacific

2.1 Introduction

In its most prosperous days, the Southern Pacific was the most influential company in California. Founded in 1865, the railway connected two main cities - San Francisco and San Diego. In 1868 extended its routes to New Orleans. Additionally, in 1885, its routes spread over the Central Pacific Railroad, which was the western half of the nation's first transcontinental railroad. (Southern Pacific, 1996).

Positioning as a giant in the US railroads system, connecting the Pacific Northwest, Texas, and New Orleans, the Southern Pacific system included narrow gauge railroad operations in California and Nevada. The Southern Pacific was also one of the leading players on the Los Angeles Railroad. Fearing competitors and their rapidly expanding market, Southern Pacific fought battles to control intercity railways in the region in the first decade of the 20th century. The merger in 1911 helped the Southern Pacific gain control over Pacific Electric.

With the help of Southern Pacific, Pacific Electric has become one of the largest intercity electric rail networks. Southern Pacific also had a considerable passenger train lane in California, most notably the Daytime

Running Lights between Los Angeles and San Francisco (Winston, Maheshri, and Dennis, 2). One of the most famous locomotives of the Southern Pacific, which is still successfully preserved despite the ravages of time, is the steam locomotive SP 4449. In 1996 the South Pacific merged with the Union Pacific Railway (Kwoka and Lawrence, 28). Additionally, the museum has 25 cars and locomotives from the Southern Pacific, including U-Boat freight locomotive 3100 and San Diego & Arizona Eastern (an SP subsidiary) passenger combine 175. Several Southern Pacific narrow gauge cars are also included in the collection.

The construction of the Southern Pacific Railroad marks a turning point in US history and a moment of national unification. It was a realization of Manifest destiny. The six-month trip to California from other parts of the continent was reduced to two weeks. In just a few years, this line helped to develop the western parts of the continent through European-American settlement, business, and trade development, and the end of indigenous life in these parts of the continent (Carlisle and Golson, 80).

The Southern Pacific Railroad is the last line to complete the Transcontinental Sunset Route from New Orleans to California, emphasizing its impact on overall Pacific rail traffic. By connecting Central Pacific with the eastern-based Union Pacific in Utah, "the big four" started to search for new alternatives to increase their influence over the West Coast shipping and was making efforts to extend the California-based Southern Pacific southward. The Southern Pacific was very successful, and by 1877 this railroad possessed 85% of California's railroad mileage. Responsible for managing the company was Huntington, who immediately saw an excellent opportunity to establish a transcontinental line through the south of the United States.

The first move he needs to do was to confront the competition. As Texas and the Pacific railroad were already heading towards the Pacific, Huntington started to develop its line eastward. He managed to win in 1881, when he connected the Southern Pacific to the Santa Fe Railroad at Deming, New Mexico, creating the second American transcontinental railway. In the next period, the control of Hungtinton's power only increased. He linked several smaller railroads and created the creating the Southern Pacific's "*Sunset Route*" from New Orleans to California. He confirmed his domination over California rails by gaining power over the smaller railroads and transforming them into one more prominent railroad (Orsi, 22).

Of course, these steps were not easy and involved great financial risks. Huntington's position allowed him to be number one in rail traffic, so his competitors began to charge higher shipping rates to shake his position. Often referred to as the "Octopus" because of its position, occupying more than half of California's economy, the Southern Pacific inspired Californians to create some of the first public solid regulations over railroads in American history. However, despite negative comments about Huntington's exploitation, the role of the Southern Pacific Railroad was crucial to the growth of California's economy in the years to come (Wilson, 3).

2.2. The importance of the Southern Pacific railroad

The Southern Pacific railroad brought the West part of the country to the world and the world to the West because it helped California to move from a once-isolated place to a significant economic and political force and helped lead to the state's rapid growth (Ronda, 25). It also enabled trade and commerce. By 1880, the transcontinental railroad was transporting $50 million worth of freight each year. The railroad also facilitated international trade. According to Brands (228), the Constitution provided the legal framework for a single national market for trade goods the transcontinental railroad provided the physical framework. Finally, the Southern Pacific railroads created the opportunity for the rapid expansion of the industry, having in mind that already in 1890, the USA was the most powerful economy on the planet.

It also made travel more affordable. If travel across the USA was accounted for $20,000 in today's dollars), the use of the railroads allowed e cheaper traveling, i.e., the cost of a coast-to-coast trip became 85 % less expensive. On the other hand, it created more places to live. Some of the workers who worked on the railroads lived in tents and wooden shacks. After finishing the work, some disappeared, but the biggest part evolved into towns that provided rail terminals and repair facilities, such as Laramie and Wyoming. Also, another 7000 cities and towns appeared soon as Union Pacific started to transfer passengers. Maybe the most important characteristic of the railroad system was that it helped the immigrants spread across the country (Patrick, 2019).

Thus, it changed the concept of reality among Americans. According to naturalists (Muir, 17), the transcontinental railroad "annihilated" time and space. Moreover, it changed the way that people viewed distances. In the West, where the distances are so great, the railroad brought near and far closer together.

Furthermore, it helped to develop postal traffic. In 1872, the first mail-order catalog was started by Aaron Montgomery Ward. The first transcontinental railroad—and other transcontinental lines later—made it possible to sell products far and wide without a physical storefront and enabled people all over the country to furnish their homes and keep up with the latest fashion trends (Ronda, 32).

However, it took a heavy toll on the environment. The impacts of the construction of the railways were not only positive. Thus, during the construction of the railway, a large part of the forests was destroyed, the wilderness was no longer inaccessible. Furthermore, the railroad establishments made it possible for hunters to travel westward and kill millions of buffalo (Hanner, 239). In addition to, it increased racial conflicts. According to Williams (42), the construction of railways encouraged the development of inter-racial conflicts as white workers from the East Coast, and Europe could more easily travel westward where immigrants were working. Upon completion of the railroad, many Chinese workers returned to California in search of employment. This led Congress to pass the Chinese Exclusion Act of 1882, one of the few laws that blocked Chinese laborers from entering the USA until 1943.

It set the basis for government-financed capitalism as well. The built of the Central Pacific helped to develop a policy of capital investments with funds of the government. Without these assets, implementing such a project would not be possible (White, 88). It comes as no surprise then that the transcontinental railroad had a major effect on how Americans perceived their nation. It became a symbol of America's growing industrial power and a source of confidence that led them to take on even more ambitious quests. According to Ronda, it was one of the most transformative moments in American history.

2.3. The Big Four: Colins Huntington, Mark Hopkins, Leland Stanford, and Charles Crocker

In the East, settlement promoted railroad construction. In the West, railroads promoted settlement. There are plenty of researches that provide information about the colonizing activities of the two western roads, the Northern Pacific and the Santa Fe. However, little attention is given to one of the most influential companies, the Southern Pacific Railroad of California1. One of the main reasons for this enormous project was to stimulate immigration to Southern California from 1875 to 1890 (Parker, 103).

Since the opening of the first line between San Francisco and Los Angeles in 1876, settlement started more energetically. The railroad's large land grant and the scarcity of population made this necessary.

The Southern Pacific conducted an intensive advertising campaign to promote its plans and to attract more immigrants with the final purpose of developing some specific locations (Brunet, 37). Pamphlets became a popular promotional tool in the region sometime in the 1870s when they began to appear in appreciable numbers. Over the fifty years, two things were apparent in railroad promotional literature; first, the most significant number of pamphlets issued was to sell land and promote settlement, and second, the literature had a choice once the area was developed to either change purpose and become more valuable or disappear (Brunet, 35).

The statistic on how many people settled in California as a result of the company's direct propaganda is scarce. However, the success of the feat is not discussed since there has been an increase in the population by 250% in the period between 1880-1890 (McKay, 25).

Before the construction of the transcontinental railway, travel, especially in the southeastern part of the country, was a real challenge, crossing long rivers, deserts, and mountains. The diseases that prevailed in that period were also dangerous to human lives. In that direction, the construction of a railway was inevitable. The construction of the railway that connected the continent began after the invention of the locomotive (Brunet, 36).

In the 1830s, the first trains started to operate in the Eastern part of the continent. By the 1840s, the continent already developed railroads that connected the East, South, and Midwest. In this period, the idea of building a railroad that connects the Pacific with the rest parts of the continent gained momentum. One of the main reasons for this was the annexation of the territory of California, following the Mexican-American War, the gold rush, as dozens of immigrants and miners were in pursuit of their happiness in the West (Orsi, 105).

During the 1850s, Congress put much effort into sponsoring several surveys to explore possible transcontinental routes. Due to the terrain specification, no particular route was a favorite as political groups were divided over whether the route should be north or south. Theodore Judah, a civil engineer who designed California's first railroad, promoted Route 41, passing through Nebraska, Wyoming, Utah, Nevada, and California. Because he was obsessed with the idea of a transcontinental railroad, he became known as "Crazy Judah." Although Judah's plan was one of the most successful, opponents noted the considerable obstacles to his proposal, the most serious of which was the Sierra Nevada mountain range. A railroad built along this route required tunneling through granite mountains and crossing deep gorges, an engineering feat that no one in the United States had yet dared to undertake (Parker, 110).

In 1859, Daniel Strong, a warehouse keeper in Dutch Flat, California, offered to show Judah the best route along the old immigrant's road through the mountains near the Donner Pass. Because a gradual increase characterized the crossing, it required the route to pass only through the top of one mountain rather than two. Judah accepted the offer, and he and Strong prepared a project proposal for the construction of a railway. The beginning was not easy, but Judah managed to find investors convincing them that constructing a railway in the region would help develop trade in that area. The first people to agree to give the needed support to Judah's idea were Collis P. Huntington and his partner, Mark Hopkins; dry goods merchant Charles Crocker; and wholesale grocer, soon to be governor, Leland Stanford. These backers would later become known as the "Big Four" (Williams, 65).

The term "transcontinental railroad" is misused in the United States because they never had a railroad owned by one company that connected the Atlantic coast to the Pacific. The first transcontinental line and its successors stretched across that part of the Missouri River to the Pacific coast. Two companies took the task. The Union Pacific established the railroad west from Omaha and the Central Pacific east from Sacramento. Both of the lines of the railroads had their meeting point in Utah. The leaders of both companies were making efforts to acquire more funds to build the routes, and the acts of 1862 and 1864 provided several forms of assistance. Both companies received government bonds of $16,000 for a mile-built route. For the plateau between the Rocky and the Sierra Nevada Mountains, the amount per mile went up to $32,000 per mile, and for the mountain regions, $48,000 (Williams, 67).

In practice, the provisions were not so generous because the land grants were challenging to sell because they had first to be examined, and the overwhelmed government land once issued patents (titles) to parcels at a glacial pace.

The leadership of both companies differed in the most significant part. The Central Pacific was led by the so-called "Big Four": Collis P. Huntington, Mark Hopkins, Leland Stanford, and Charles Crocker. All of them were tough-minded men who managed to drive the project firmly, despite their differences. Huntington from New York was responsible for raising capital, Crocker was responsible for the actual construction works, while Hopkins took care of the accounts in California. Finally, Stanford did a little bit of everything. As mentioned below, responsible for the management part of the works was Durant. His successors Oliver and Oakes Ames continued their work in the next period. Oakes was a good manager but was busy while performing his role as a congressman (Wilson, 5).

To build the railroad, both groups formed separate construction companies and dominated the management of them and the railroad. At this time, the conflict of interests was still a primitive concept. They made contracts with themselves to achieve profits for their companies at the expense of the railroads.

Huntington and his partners paid Judah to do the necessary research. During the presentation of the idea to Congress in October 1861, Judah used maps from his research. Many members of Congress opposed the idea of building a railroad because of the high cost, especially during the Civil War. However, President Abraham Lincoln, an avid supporter of the railroad project, agreed. On July 1, 1862, Lincoln signed the Pacific Railroad Act, approving $ 32,000 inland and government bonds per mile of the railroad to two companies, the Central Pacific Railway and the Pacific Rail Union.

Immediately after this act, conflicts arose between Judah and his business partners. In October 1863, Judah traveled to New York City in search of investors to cover his Sacramento partners. He did not survive the trip due to yellow fever and died on November 2, a week after arriving in New York. Unfortunately, Judah did not experience seeing the Central Pacific Railway start operating on October 26, 1863. The Big Four replaced Judah with Samuel Montego, and construction teams in the Central Pacific began building the line east of Sacramento (Rogers, 4).

Furthermore, they decided that the eastern terminus of the Transcontinental Railroad would be Council Bluffs, Iowa, across the Missouri River from Omaha, Nebraska. Grenville Dodge and his assistant, Peter Dey, surveyed the Union Pacific's potential route at the eastern end of the project. They presented an idea that recommends a line following the

Platt River and the North Fork, crossing through Continental Divide at South Pass in Wyoming, and continuing along to Green River. President Lincoln authorized this route and decided that the eastern terminus of the Transcontinental Railroad would be Council Bluffs, Iowa, across the Missouri River from Omaha, Nebraska (Rogers, 5).

Thomas C. Durant, a medical doctor who turned into a businessman, bought over $2 million in shares and installed his own man as a president. Durant established the Credit Mobilier of America, which later was the independent constructor to build the railroad. The owners of Credit Mobilier were the Union Pacific investors, which in the course of a few years, managed to pay tens of millions of dollars by charging extortionate fees for the work. Because the payment was per mile track built, Durant unnecessarily prolonged the length of the route to make more gains for himself. After the completion of the railroad, the scandal of Durant's business was disclosed.

The Big Four acted in the same way by awarding the construction agreement to Charles Crocker, who, although resigned from the board, still owned an interest in the railroad building. The rest of the Big Four also owned an interest in Crocker's company, and they profited from the contract (Klein, 2).

To perform the activities of the construction works, Durant hired Grenville Dodge as chief engineer and General Jack Casement as construction boss. The workforce was easy to find. Thousands of war veterans, out of work, have agreed to work on the railroad. The workforce mainly consisted of Irish men, who occasionally went on strike over wage arrears.

Although Strobridge was initially against the idea that the Chinese were too slight in stature for the demanding job, he agreed to hire 50 men on a trial basis. After only one month, Strobridge grudgingly admitted that the Chinese were conscientious, sober, and hardworking.

Finding workers to build the Central Pacific Railroad was much more difficult because Irish immigrants found it more tempting to go to work in the Nevada silver mines. Lacking human resources, Durant tried to find Mexican, African-American workers and even petitioned Congress to provide 5,000 war prisoners, but without success. Wanting to offer an acceptable solution, James Strobridge suggested to Durant that they hire Chinese workers. Although Durant was initially opposed to the idea, he eventually agreed because, in a trial run of 50 Chinese workers, they proved quite valuable and effective (Ong, 119).

Over three years, 80 % of the Central Pacific workforce was made up of Chinese workers, as they proved to be a critical factor in advancing the line across the Sierra Nevadas. The Chinese workers accomplished amazing and dangerous feats no other workers would or could do. They blasted tunnels through the solid granite - sometimes progressing only a foot a day. It often happened that they stayed in the tunnels for several days, save time and resources, and save energy, i.e., not to waste time by going in and out every day.

The construction of the railway in the Central Pacific has faced different types of problems and obstacles in terms of penetration through mountains, gorges, snow cover, etcetera. In contrast, the Union Pacific faced resistance from Indian tribes living in the area. Seeing their homeland change day by day, they could not restrain themselves and attack the railway workers. For that reason, and to protect themselves, the workers began to arm themselves.

Both railway companies successfully fought against all obstacles and challenges. Although the Central Pacific had a two-year advantage due to earlier start-up, the steep terrain of the Sierra Nevadas limited their construction to only 100 miles by the end of 1867. After successfully crossing the Sierra Nevadas, construction on the rest of the track continued at high speed, reaching the border with Utah in 1868. On the east side, the Union Pacific completed its line through Wyoming and moved at an equal pace from the east.

No endpoint had been set for the two rail lines when President Lincoln signed the Pacific Railway Act in 1862, but a decision had to be made soon. By early 1869, the Central Pacific and Union Pacific were closing in on each other across northern Utah, aided by a Mormon workforce under contract to both companies. Nevertheless, neither side was interested in halting construction, as each company wanted to claim the $32,000 per mile subsidy from the government. Indeed, at one point, the graders from both companies, working ahead of track layers, actually passed one another as they were unwilling to concede territory to their competitors (Angevine, 2).

An interesting point in the whole story is that no end was set for the two railways when President Lincoln signed the Pacific Railway Act in 1862, but the decision was to be made soon. By early 1869, the Central Pacific and the Union Pacific were closing in on each other through northern Utah, aided by Mormon labor under an agreement with the two companies. By 1869, the two railroad trails overlapped across northern Utah, aided by the Mormon Work Force. None of the companies wanted to stop because they wanted to continue earning a $ 32,000 per mile subsidy from the government. At one point, both companies overlapped on the tracks because they did not want to make concessions in favor of their competitors (Angevine, 3).

The Congress established the meeting point on April 9, 1869, on the Promontory Summit, north of the Great Salt Lake. one month later, the locomotives of the two companies met face to face to signal the joining of the two lines (Spude and Delyea, 5).

It is essential to mention that the original SP was founded in San Francisco in 1865 by a group of businessmen led by Timothy Phelps to build a rail connection between San Francisco and San Diego, California. The company was purchased in September 1868 by the "Big Four." The "Big Four" had, in 1861, created the Central Pacific Railroad (CPRR). Later, CPRR was merged into SP in 1870.1 The Southern Pacific was acquired by the Union Pacific Corporation in 1996. The merged firm represented the largest railroad company in the United States and controlled most of the rail-based shipping in the western two-thirds of the country.

Works Cited

Brunet, Patrick J. "Can't Hurt, and may do you Good": A Study of the Pamphlets the Southern Pacific Railroad used to Induce Immigration to Texas, 1880-1930." *East Texas Historical Journal* 16.2 (1978): 8.

Carlisle, Rodney P., and J. Geoffrey Golson. *Manifest Destiny and the Expansion of America*. ABC-CLIO, 2007.

Hanner, John. "Government response to the buffalo hide trade, 1871-1883." *The Journal of Law and Economics* 24.2 (1981): 239-271.

Kiger, Patrick. *10 Ways the Transcontinental Railroad Changed America*. Available at: https://www.history.com/news/transcontinental-railroad-changed-america [Accessed on: 09/06/2021].

Klein, Maury. "Financing the Transcontinental Railroad." *Gilder Lehrman Institute of American History, viewed July* 17 (2019).

Kwoka Jr, John E., and Lawrence J. White. "Manifest Destiny? The Union Pacific-Southern Pacific Merger." *New York University, Center for Law and Business, Working Paper* 98-012 (1997).

Lew-Williams, Beth. *The Chinese must go Violence, Exclusion, and the making of the alien in America*. Harvard University Press, 2018.

McKay, Seth Shepard. "Texas and the Southern Pacific Railroad, 1848-1860." *The Southwestern Historical Quarterly* 35.1 (1931): 1-27.

Muir, John. "Rambles of a botanist among the plants and climates of California." (1872).

Ong, Paul M. "The Central Pacific Railroad and Exploitation of Chinese Labor." *The Journal of Ethnic Studies* 13.2 (1985): 119.

Orsi, Richard J. *Sunset limited: the Southern Pacific Railroad and the development of the American West, 1850-1930*. Univ of California Press, 2005.

Parker, Edna Monch. "The Southern Pacific Railroad and Settlement in Southern California." *Pacific Historical Review* 6.2 (1937): 103-119.

Rogers, J. David, and PE ROGERS. "Theodore Judah and the Blazing of the First Transcontinental Railroad Over the Sierra Nevadas." *Rogers/ Pacific, Inc., and Department of Civil and Environmental Engineering, University of California, Berkeley, nd*: 4-10.

Schwantes, Carlos A., and James P. Ronda. *The West the railroads made.* University of Washington Press, 2008.

Southern Pacific Railroad completes New Orleans to California route. Available at: https://www.history.com/this-day-in-history/southern-pacific-railroad-completes-sunset-route [Accessed on: 09/06/2021].

Southern Pacific Railroad. Available at: https://socalrailway.org/collections/southern-pacific-railway/ [Accessed on: 09/06/2021].

Spude, Robert LS, and Todd Delyea. *Promontory Summit, May 10, 1869.* Cultural Resources Management, Intermountain Region, National Park Service, 2005.

The Pacific Railway: A Brief History of Building the Transcontinental Railroad. Available at: https://railroad.lindahall.org/essays/brief-history.html [Accessed on: 08/06/2021].

White, Richard. *Railroaded: The transcontinental and the making of modern America.* WW Norton & Company, 2011.

Williams, John Hoyt. *A Great and Shining Road: The epic story of the transcontinental railroad.* U of Nebraska Press, 1996.

Wilson, Michael G. "The Octopus, resurfaced: California and the Southern Pacific Railroad, 1874-1894." (2019).

Winston, Clifford, Vikram Maheshri, and Scott M. Dennis. "Long-run effects of mergers: The case of US western railroads." *The Journal of Law and Economics* 54.2 (2011): 275-304.

CHAPTER 3

The rise of California's Progressivism

3.1. The progressive movement in California

The construction of the railroad is the main reason for turning California into a cradle of political turmoil. The importance of this railway was excellent in terms of the development of the overall social, economic and political life. This sounded even better when considering the vast state subsidies for the construction of the same from which many people managed to gain profit and power (Williams, 128).

For most Californians, the railroad was a simple technology whose sole purpose was to transport people, but it was still a monopoly corporation that almost enjoyed complete control over all rail traffic. According to some historians, the railroad has increased California's growth and development, while others have been a source of corruption and scandal. No one assumed the railroad was terrible for California, given that the state's agriculture, industry, and trade depended on it. The railroad was also the largest employer in California and, at the same time, the most significant private landowner. It acted as a promoter of local products and allowed many tourists from other parts of America to visit California.

The problem was that the railroad focused on increasing California's growth to take more of the profits (Gendzel, 37). In the late 19th and early

20th centuries, California had the highest and least predictable railroad rates in the world. The railways, not the manufacturers, grabbed most of the profits that were to be made by delivering products from one place to another. As a result, California farmers, traders, and producers were often priced out for transportation costs. Railroad owners also routinely blackmailed California towns and villages into taxpayer subsidies and land grants in exchange for the privilege to be part of a rail link. Charles Crocker, co-owner of the Central Pacific, told the Los Angeles City Council in 1872 that if they did not pay the ransom, he stated: "I will make the grass grow on the streets of your city." (O'Flaherty, 35). Today, large employers and professional sports teams play this tough game of corporate blackmail, but Western railways, such as the Central Pacific, invented the technique in the late 19th century.

The new Constitution of California was adopted in 1879 to regulate railroad taxing, and this was one of the main reasons the company entered politics (Willis, 77). Lobbyists and attorneys were making efforts to influence California's legislators and judges in exchange for favorable legislation that would accommodate their interests. The railroad's owners were deeply engaged in politics. Moreover, they were the main sponsors of party conventions, regulatory decisions, etcetera (Callow, 345).

Corruption in California was widespread. People could not see it, but it persisted in the form of relentlessly pro-railroad public policy, year after year. Periodic upsurges took place from time to time but were not sufficient to defeat the Southern Pacific. The company charges high rates, pays low taxes, blackmails communities, monopolizes land, and pays off politicians while soaking up subsidies and tax breaks (Wilson, 5). California was not the only country that suffered from the evils of corporate domination. Many western countries also felt the consequences of political corruption. Although not unique, it was still an exceptional case in the way how it was dominated by the so-called "The Octopus."

Long before the advent of Frank Norris's novel The Octopus in 1901, many cartoonists had already depicted the octopus, a railroad wrapped around farmers, workers, traders, and producers, sucking the life out of them (Martin, 20). After 1900, Californians envied the progressive movements already taking place in other states. They were particularly impressed by how the state of Wisconsin under Governor Robert La Follett was led. So they asked the question: "*Why not in California*'? Several campaigns ran in California by anti-rail reformers by the populist and Democratic parties but without much success. In 1910, the Progressives took control of the Republican Party in the country (Burchell and Williams, 119). They nominated Hiram Johnson, an avid lawyer, and anti-railroad advocate, to run for Governor. In this regard, Johnson's credit is immense.

Namely, he was in the role of the chief prosecutor of the trials in San Francisco from 1906 to 1909, when he put the corrupt boss of San Francisco in prison. Johnson and his fellows Progressive Republicans won the state elections in 1910, and when the next state legislature convened in 1911, the Reformers finally had control. (Blythe, 7). They did not, however, expect their victory to be permanent. Governor Johnson and his comrades expected the Octopus to recover from the temporary setback and somehow overcome them in the next election.

3.2. Hiram Johnson

Hiram Johnson was born on September 2, 1866, in Sacramento, California. Johnson studied law in his father's office in Sacramento, was admitted to the bar in 1888, and moved to San Francisco in 1902. In 1908 he was appointed Assistant District Attorney, beginning his long career in public service. In his first case as a prosecutor, he obtained a conviction in a prominent graft and bribery case, which gave him the directions as an anti-corruption specialist. He was the leader of the Progressive party in California and reform governor of California in the period between 1911 – 1917. In 1910 Johnson being a member of the Lincoln – Roosevelt league, won the elections for Governor (National Governors Association).

This League was famous because of its characteristics as a Progressive Republican movement opposed to the Southern Pacific Railroad. For his campaign, he traveled the country in an open automobile and visited the country's most inaccessible parts. In his campaign, he made a promise to tear the state's politics and economy out of the grasp of powerful corporations and place it straight back into the hands of its citizens. His progressive reforms were an important step towards a revision of the state's Constitution in 1911. He is also credited for easing the process of voting. Moreover, he established rules to facilitate recalls, and that is one of the measures used in 2003 on Governor Gray Davis.

In his political prominence, he was a populist who worked and developed several democratic reforms such as the elections of U.S. senators by direct popular vote, cross-filing, initiative, referendum, and recall elections. Reforms of Johnson are credited for making California the basis where direct democracy was developing, compared to any other U.S. state at that time (Library of California). Maybe the most critical reform of Governor Johnson was the creation of the state railroad commission, which was established to restrict the power of the Southern Pacific Railroad.

In 1912, Johnson formed the Progressive Party, but his candidacy was unsuccessful compared to Theodore Roosevelt's. As a born progressive, he opposed the Republican Party's conservative policies by supporting agricultural laws as well as by supporting a measure to reduce unemployment in the 1930s. He was known for his unwavering isolationism, opposing U.S. support for the Treaty of Versailles, the League of Nations, and the Permanent Court of International Justice known as the World Court. He was a major sponsor of acts of neutrality in the 1930s, opposed to preparations for World War II and the formation of the United Nations. In 1914, he was reelected Governor, and in November 1916, he was elected to the U.S. Senate. On March 17, 1917, he resigned from his state office and went to Washington. Johnson served as a U.S. Senator from California for five terms, 1917-1945.

Elected to the U.S. Senate in 1916, he was the first senator to led investigations into labor conditions in West Virginia coal mines, confronted with the power of private utilities, and supported public works projects during the New Deal era. Reelected four times, he continued serving

Californians in the Senate until he died in 1945. Johnson's stood behind his vigorous nationalistic spirit in the field of foreign relations, and he was popularly termed an "isolationist." The coming of World War II brought Johnson into a headlong clash with Franklin Roosevelt and the New Deal. The disintegration of American neutrality alarmed Johnson and led him into a bitter losing battle from which he never recovered. Once the war began, he gave it a full support, but his failing health kept him more and more from the active business of the Senate. He died in Bethesda Naval Hospital on August 6, 1945.

Hiram Johnson's work for the political system and overall political life of California is of immense importance. Johnson placed principles of solidarity above politics. His vision of progressivism became the stepping-off point for California's journey through the 20th century (Weatherson and Bochin, 1995).

Reforms introduced such as initiative, referendum, and recall processes forever changed the size and scope of California's political system. These rights have played a major role in California's current legacy as a national leader in direct democracy. Johnson's stood behind his vigorous nationalistic spirit in the field of foreign relations, and he was popularly termed an "isolationist." The coming of World War II brought Johnson into a headlong clash with Franklin Roosevelt and the New Deal. The disintegration of American neutrality alarmed Johnson and led him into a bitter losing battle from which he never recovered. Once the war began, he gave it a full support, but his failing health kept him more and more from the active business of the Senate. He died in Bethesda Naval Hospital on August 6, 1945.

3.3. The rise of nonpartisan candidates during progressivism

Johnson's election as Governor of California in 1910 marked a turning point in California's overall political history. Most of the changes introduced then are still in force today. Progressives believed that both political parties were influenced by the Southern Pacific Monopoly (Kurashige,

280.) From this point of view, their main goal was to weaken these political parties internally. The introduction of a popular primary whose role was to reduce the influence of the nomination of candidates by their party leaders. This mechanism allowed members of political parties who were registered voters to nominate candidates.

The Progressives also allowed one candidate to be nominated by several political parties, but this practice was discontinued in 1959. The Progressives also abolished the party ballot, allowing voters to vote on a straight-party ticket because all of a party's candidates appeared in the same column. Nowadays, in California, the so-called office ballot, in which the voter must read the names of all candidates running for a position before moving on to the next block. This feature allows voters to distribute ballots to candidates from different political parties for different positions. Progressives are also credited with introducing nonpartisan elections in local government, the judiciary, and school boards.

In nonpartisan elections, no label of a political party may appear next to the candidate's name, nor is financial party support permitted for candidates. The "at-large" system has been introduced to enable the selection of all candidates, for all districts, instead of for elections by district (Rodgers, 125). Another significant benefit to progressives for the California political system is the introduction of a merit system for all public employments. This system consisted of high criteria that candidates had to meet to qualify for the job. Previously, political parties have traditionally rewarded their activists, party members with local government jobs, a process known as patronage. Hiring professional managers to run operations is also a credit to progressives (Anirudh and Camões, 33).

The progressive movement also contributed to the direct creation of new laws without consulting the selected candidates. Furthermore, the referendum that can annul a law passed by the elected representatives and the revocation by which the elected representatives can be revoked before the end of their term. The application of these measures requires the submission of a petition through the required number of signatures from registered voters, a provision that is also present in the Electoral

Code. The use of these measures of the so-called direct democracy has grown significantly in the last two decades, primarily through the use of mass media, through which many members can be contacted electronically.

Some of the propositions introduced by the progressives changed in the years that followed. For example, The method and level of support for state and local governments were changed radically in 1978 by Proposition 13, which, among other things, cut local property taxes in half. A formula limiting state budget expenditures was enacted by Proposition 4 in 1979, and Proposition 98, passed in 1988, set aside a guaranteed share of the state budget for local elementary school, high school, and community college districts. Proposition 140, enacted in 1990, established term limits for state legislators and executives. Voters relaxed these limits for state legislators in 2012 with Proposition 28, which allows longer terms in a single house (Balotpedia, 2021).

State ballot propositions also allowed the regulation of specific areas of the city-county and respective district governments. For example, the California Coastal Commission is responsible for the regulation of the use of land along the state's coastline. The Fair Political Practices Commission, created via the Political Reform Act, is responsible for regulating campaign fundraising and spending by candidates for all elected offices and by supporters and opponents of ballot propositions. It is essential to mention that the changes brought by the progressive reformists in the area of local self-government are in use to this day.

3.4. Sunshine laws

Reforms in California during the Progressives provided greater transparency and accountability for both institutions and elected officials. To enable the disclosure of all matters of the public institutions and the fact that the elected representatives will first serve the people and will not put the personal interest before the general one, two state laws have been adopted. Such laws are often referred to as "sunshine laws" because they are based on the principles of transparency and accountability (Edwards and Sherry, 85).

The Brown Act requires government legislative bodies such as the city council, the board of supervisors, the special district board, or any other board or commission to conduct their business in open public meetings with adequate public notice. Any time a majority of a body meets, even in social or recreational situations, and any kind of official matter comes up. The event can be construed as an official meeting. Closed session meetings are for pending legal actions or personnel matters, real estate transactions, and collective bargaining negotiations. Any actions that may result must be announced in public (Grodin, 719).

The Brown Act provides for a discussion of issues that were put on the agenda promptly before the meetings. This allows the adoption of laws and decisions to follow a public debate on specific issues (California Brown Act).

The public has the right to inspect the public records of a city, county, or particular area because of the provisions of the California Public Records Act. Local authorities are required to submit annual reports to independent auditors. Such information is submitted to the office of the State Controller. Also, local agencies are obliged to report financial transactions on an annual basis to the State Auditor, which makes this information publicly available.

The Law on Fair Political Practices creates an obligation for elected representatives, committee members, and other staff to disclose most information about their financial interests. This law also applies to spouses, children, as well as to all those who cooperate with them, the so-called close associates. In the event of a conflict of interest, officials must be excluded from the decision-making process. State law also requires full disclosure of all campaign contributions above $ 99. The Committee on Fair Political Practices makes information about these contributions available to the public (California Legislative Information, 2021).

3.5. Civil Service and patronage system

Political patronage is a process of hiring a person to a government or public job as a thankful act for partisan loyalty. This practice is used on all levels: national, state, and local to reward the people who assisted them to maintain their mandate (Baracskay, 2009). The common saying linked to this practice is *"to the victor go the spoils."* On the other side, when those in power use the patronage system to fire their political opponents, the fired have the right to charge that the practice penalizes them for exercising their First Amendment rights of political association.

The history of civil service employment in government dates back hundreds of years. Choosing to hire government workers based on merit and ability (rather than their association with the winning party in government) is a change that swept the nation after high-profile events at an international and national level.

The early Roman Empire had government officials, such as the following: court officials, governors, and mayors – Military commanders. However, these men were entitled to the office by birthright, not merit. The earliest form of merit examination and application for civil service is found in imperial China (SEIU, 2010). Scholar/bureaucrats could be hired without respect to being born into the office. In the 1850s, the British Government reformed their system of government employment by right of landed entitlement to a merit system based upon the following: – that recruitment is based on merit determined through competitive examination, the candidates have a solid general education to enable interdepartmental transfers, recruits should be graded into a ranking system, promotion should be through achievement, rather than preferment, patronage or purchase, – the work is divided between staff responsible for routine ("mechanical") work, and those engaged in policy formulation and implementation in an "administrative" class.

Political patronage has a long history in the United States. It has existed since the founding of the country. The Constitution delegates the power of appointment of the President. This creates space for the President to appoint a large number of officials, among which judges, ambassadors, cabinet officers, agency heads, and other high-positions (Our American Government, 6). The Senate's confirmation powers check the president's appointment powers. This system is paralleled in many state constitutions and local charters. In the early years, patronage was used more frequently. Also, the proponents of the system argued that political patronage promotes direct accountability from administrators to elected officials. They also characterized it as an asset for lowering elitism at all levels by perceiving key positions for commoners.

The 7th president of the country, Andrew Jackson, wanted to bring the government closer to the people thus increasing its representation. This period was known as Jacksonian democracy, where the spoils system flourished by using political patronage to reward jobs to the party members (Matherne, 2019). Jackson stated that every government whose aim is to serve the people truly would appoint and rotate its members instead of establishing a permanent bureaucracy in which civil servants will see their positions as property. In the period that followed, this practice became a norm for a while.

The patronage system existed at all levels of government, and it was particularly evident at a local level in the late XIX and early XX centuries. On a local level, the patronage system was known as a political machine (Berkman, 28.) Moreover, these machines turned into a vehicle in which the political leader, i.e., the boss, dominated government and politics by creating a community for supporters. Political patronage quickly became a synonym for corruption. Moreover, those appointed with political patronage on the places, in most cases, depended on the will of those who hired them, without the option to criticize their bosses and have a different opinion. The prime example of the political machine was Tammany Hall, the political organization of the democratic party. Prominent mayors Frank Hague of Jersey City, James Michael Curley of Boston, and Richard Daley of Chicago qualified as bosses who dominated politics in their locales.

Since the first days of the Republic, the patronage system was considered an imminent method for filling federal positions. In the beginning, the number of positions filled with patronage was relatively small, around 5000 in 1816, 500 of them in Washington D.C. (US. Department of Commerce 1975, 1101). The powers of the president granted with the Constitution allowed them to fill executive-branch offices. However, these positions were not long-term, excluding the possibility to endanger the democratic goals of the government by creating an entrenched civil service elite. The patronage-filled positions were related to simple jobs such as ones-postmasters, postal clerks, land office clerks, surveyors, and customhouse employees.

According to Leonard White, the success of local organizations seemed to depend much more on securing office, contracts, and favors for their members than on campaigning over disputed issues of statesmanship". Patronage positions were guaranteed to the party members who primarily engaged in campaign works and donated part of their salaries to the political party in the form offunding. These assessments on the salaries of patronage workers were a means of transferring federal tax revenues to political parties. The payments ranged between 2 to 10 percent of an individual patronage worker's salary, depending on the position held. Each worker who got the job via patronage was obliged to make contributions to the party. Those who refused to contribute lost their jobs. (Fowler, 157).

Contributions made by the patronage workers were a significant recourse for political party funding in the XIX century. According to Louise Overacker (103), in 1878, the Republican Congressional Committee alone raised $106,000 for political campaigns, of which $80,000 came from federal employees. Responsible for these funds was the local party apparatus. Also, federal employees were required to contribute simultaneously to the national, county, local, and now state committees, and this created serious potential for conflict.

The most significant part of the XIX century, federal workers were a valuable political weapon. Patronage was the main asset of political exchange with which the right to place the local party faithful into relatively high-paying federal jobs, making them postmasters or customs officers, was coveted by members of the House of Representatives, senators, cabinet members, and local political bosses was achieved (Golway, 2014).

The president often traded these positions to members of Congress, local bosses, and other politicians. In return, he expected their support on legislation and reelection. The support of the local party machines for congress candidates was primarily influenced by the ability to obtain patronage positions from the president. On the other side, the president,, as a sign of gratitude, required support on various bills and policies and reelection.

Those appointed by patronage knew that their positions are not permanent. Usually, they were recalled shortly after elections, no matter their patrons were defeated or not. For example, during the Cleveland administration, 43,087 fourth-class postmasters were either removed, suspended, or asked to resign to make room for Democratic party stalwarts (Fowler, 306).

These were the rules of the game that meant partisan federal democracy. In a small government, the relationship between the nominees and their political leaders was close. In such conditions, patronage was considered a standard and generally accepted practice for promoting equality and social mobility and was a cornerstone for the development of political parties. As long as the interests of the federal politicians and the local party machine coincided, the booty system was mutually beneficial.

Party nominations were often achieved through the permission of the machine to take a role in the distribution of positions won in elections, which also referred to the demands of local party leaders. Also, the local leaders used patronage to motivate voters to go out and vote during elections. Jobs were given to those who worked for the organization and voted for the party's candidates.

The widespread corruption on government associated with the political patronage, the sowing immigration rate, and the rise of the middle class contributed to declining the patronage system. Another reason for that is the fact that numerous government scandals eroded public confidence. The situation worsened with the appointment of the country's 20th president James A. Garfield, who was shot and killed just a few months after the appointment in 1881 by an unsatisfied job seeker (Gilded Age politics: patronage, 2017).

This was the reason for the reforms and led to the enactment of the Pendleton Act of 1883, which turned the appointment of government officials from a patronage system into a merit system preceded by testing to determine candidates' competencies rather than party identification. Initially, this law applied only to 10 percent of the employees in the administration. By 1904, only twenty-one years after the Pendleton Act was passed, over 50 percent of the total federal civilian labor force was under merit provisions (U.S. House of Representatives 1976). No longer were federal employees to direct their attention primarily to the political needs of their patrons and party. Instead, they were to provide government services competently and efficiently(Johnson and Libecap, 12).

Moreover, after the Pendleton Act, federal workers were awarded protection from removal through the actions of the president and Congress. By the mid-twentieth century, they effectively had tenure in their federal positions but were required to be politically neutral. With these changes, most vestiges of patronage that had characterized the organization of the federal labor force since the founding of the Republic were replaced by bureaucratic civil service rule. Later, with the enactment of the Civil Service Reform Act by President Jimmy Carter in 1978, more than 90 percent of federal administration employees were covered by the merit system.

To better observe the principle of impartiality, several acts and laws have been adopted that cover the public service employees. One of the most famous acts is the so-called Hatch Act of 1939, which restricts the participation in public policy of public sector employees. Before this act, the Supreme Court upheld the restrictions on political activity of Ex Parte Curtis 1882. Through a series of decisions, the Supreme Court imposed First Amendment restrictions on patronage. In Elrod v. Burns (1976), the Court prohibited a newly elected Democratic sheriff from firing non – civil service Republican employees. The Court reasoned that patronage dismissals infringe on core First Amendment political expression and association rights. The Court extended this rationale in Branti v. Finkel (1980) and Rutan v. Republican Party of Illinois 1990 (Thompson, 460).

The merit system evolved gradually. Although the merit system prevails today, political patronage still exists at all levels of government today, but with a much lower degree of representation than before. For example, presidents now appoint less than 1% of all federal positions. However, these appointments continue to be an essential means by which presidents reward their supporters and influence their parties.

On June 16, 1913, the California State Legislature approved the State Civil Service Bill (Chapter 590 of Statutes 1913), and Republican Governor Hiram Johnson signed it. This bill established the California State Civil Service Commission to oversee California's newly established civil service system. – This State Commission was structured to consist of three members appointed by the Governor to serve four-year terms. However, any commissioner could be removed by concurrent resolution of the State Senate and Assembly, adopted by a two-thirds majority in each house.

Over the next 20 years, the initial reforms were eroded by politics at the State Capitol. A group of state workers formed the California State Employees Association. Although they first tackled protecting the state retirement system, they took on the failing merit system of hiring soon after. The Depression had taken hold across the country, leading to lines of thousands of citizens applying for state jobs. By the 1930s, the state workers had an organization of about 10,000 members. At the same time, there were 23,000 state workers, with about 12,000 in permanent positions, and the rest exempt and subject to immediate termination at any time. This core group of active state workers circulated the ballot measure to collect signatures across the state. The voters adopted the civil service protections in the State Constitution, primarily as we know them today.

3.6. Political Growth and changes to the taxation of 2/3 majority due to proposition 13

Proposition 13, whose official name is the People's initiative to limit property taxation, represents an amendment of the Constitution of California enacted during 1978 with the purpose of an initiative process. The voters approved this initiative of California on June 6, 1978. The same was confirmed as constitutional by the United States in Nordnger Hahn (1992). Also, proposition 13 is embodied in Article XIII A of the Constitution of the State of California (Lefcoe and Allison, 173).

The most important part of the act is its first paragraph, which determines the tax rate for real estate. According to this paragraph, the maximum amount of any ad valorem tax on real property shall not exceed one percent of the total cash value of such property. According to law, the one percent tax shall be collected by the counties and apportioned according to law to the districts within the counties. Proposition 13 reduces the property taxes by accessing values at their 1976 value and restricted annual increases of assessed value to an inflation factor not to exceed 2% per year. Proposition 13 prohibits reassessment of a new base year value except in change of ownership and completion of new construction. These rules apply equally to all real estate, residential and commercial, whether owned by individuals or corporations (Los Angeles County, office of the Assessor).

The other important part of the initiative is that requires a two-thirds majority in both legislative houses for future increase of any state tax rates or amounts of revenue collected including income tax rates. It also requires a two-thirds vote majority in local elections for local governments which aim to increase special taxes[1].

Proposition 13 is known as the most famous and influential ballot measure of California. Its bringing increased the level of publicity in all of the States. The initiative sparked a "taxpayer riot" across the country and

---

[1] A "special tax" is a tax devoted specifically to a purpose: e.g. homelessness or road repair; money that does not go into a general fund.

is now thought to be the reason for Ronald Reagan's election as president in 1980. An enormous contribution to Proposition 13 was the sentiment that older Californians should not be priced out of their homes through high taxes. Proposition 13 was known as the "third rail" (meaning untouchable subject) of the politics of California, and politicians avoid discussions of changing it (Simmons, 1997)

The state has been given the responsibility of distributing the property tax revenues to local agencies. In addition to decreasing property taxes and changing the state's role, Proposition 13 also contained language requiring a two-thirds (2/3) majority in both legislative houses for future increases of any state tax rates or amounts of revenue collected, including income and sales tax rates. Proposition 13 also requires two-thirds (2/3) voter approval for cities, counties, and special districts to impose special taxes. In Altadena Library District v. Bloodgood (June 1987), the California Court of Appeal for the Second District determined that the two-thirds (2/3) voter approval requirement for special taxes under Proposition 13 applied to citizen's initiatives.

There are several theories of the origin of Proposition 13. The evidence for or against these accounts varies. One of the explanations is that older Californians with fixed incomes face difficulty in paying property taxes, which arose as a result of the population growth, increasing house demand, and inflation. One significant inflation in the 1970s increased property taxes so much that some retired people could no longer afford to live in homes they bought years before. According to one study published in Law and Society Review, older voters, homeowners, and voters expecting a tax increase were more likely to vote for proposition 13 (Law and Society Review, 2006).

Another explanation for the origin of Proposition 13 is that it drew its impetus from the 1971-1976 California Supreme Court rulings in *Serano v. Priest*, which somewhat equalized California school funding by redistributing local property taxes from wealthy regions to poor school districts. According to this, property owners were thinking that the taxes they paid were no longer benefiting their local schools and decided to minimize their taxes (Fischel, 607). This explanation is problematic because the Serrano decision and school funding equalization were popular among California voters. While Californians who voted for Proposition 13 were less likely than other voters to support school finance equalization, Proposition 13 supporters were not more likely to oppose the Serrano decision, and on average, they were typically supportive of both the Serrano decision and of school finance equalization (Isaac, 25).

According to one study from 2020 conducted by Mound, the wealthy property owners were more likely to cap their property taxes, instead of arguing that the tax revolt was rooted in lower and middle-income American's years-long frustration with unfair and highly regressive tax distributions in the period after the II World War. According to this study, the "proGrowth Kennedy – Johnson Liberals" minimized the federal income taxes in the 1960s. At the same time, local officials raised regressive state and local taxes, creating the so-called "pocketbook squeeze" that made voters unwilling to approve local levies and bonds, which was the cause to bring Proposition 13. Mound stated that the tax revolt was not associated only with white voters or with rising conservativism and the election of Ronald Reagan (Mound, 28).

The spending of California's government has increased dramatically during the 1970s, and according to some researchers, this is one possible explanation for the bringing of Proposition 13. However, the evidence supporting this explanation is limited, as there have not been so many studies relating Californian's views on the size and role of government to their views on Proposition 13. However negligible is the fact that California's government had grown. Between 1973 and 1977, California state and local government expenditures per $1,000 of personal income were 8.2% higher than the national norm (Shires and Shires, 1999.) From 1949 to 1979, public sector employment in California outstripped employment growth in the private sector. By 1978, 14.7% of California's civilian workforce were state and local government employees, almost double the proportion of the early 1950s (Sears, 55).

In the 1960s, some scandals in California involved county assessors. These assessors were rewarding friends with low assessments, with tax bills to match. These scandals were the main reason for the passage of Assembly Bill 80 in 1950, with which standards were imposed to hold assessments to market value. As a result of this, a lot of Californians experienced a drastic rise in valuation, similar to raise taxes on the asset value, only to be told that the tax monies will be distributed to distant communities. Dissatisfaction with such reforms was growing because this act favored more prosperous and better-off citizens. The ensuing anger began to turn into a reaction to the property tax that rallied around Howard Aarvis, a former newspaper and appliance maker who turned into a retired taxpayer activist.

The most prominent and visible proponents of Proposition 13 were Howard Jarvis and Paul Gann. Officially known as "the People Initiative to limit property taxation", and popularly known as the Jarvis-Gann Amendment, proposition 13 was listed on the ballot through the California ballot initiative process. It was a provision of the California Constitution, that allows a proposed law or amendment of the Constitution to be offered to voters of they collect a sufficient number of signatures on a petition. Proposition 13 was voted with two-thirds of the voters. After the passage, Proposition 13 became article XIII of the California Constitution (Smith, 188).

Proposition 13 states that the annual real estate tax on a parcel of property is limited to 1% of its assessed value. This value can increase by a maximum of 2% per year unless the property has a change of ownership (Property tax, California State Board of Equalization). If a change of ownership happens, the low accessed value may be reassessed to complete the current market value, which will produce a new base year value for the property, but future assessments are likewise to be restricted to a 2% annual maximum increase of the new base value.

In certain circumstances, the property may be assessed, except in the case of a change of ownership, in the event of the occurrence of additions or new construction. The appraised value will also decrease if the property's market value falls below its appraised value, for example, during a downturn in real estate. Such a reduction was not foreseen in Proposition 13 but was possible with the adoption of Proposition 8 (Senate Amendment No. 67) during 1978, which amended Proposition 13. The fall in real estate prices and the reassessment of the downside occurred in 2009 when the California State Equalization Board announced an estimated reduction in the property tax base year values due to negative inflation. *California property tax* is an ad valorem tax which means that the tax assessed (generally) increases and decreases with the property's value (Carolyn, 2009).

One year after Proposition 13 passed, property tax revenue dropped by 60%. However, until 2003, the inflation-adjusted property tax collected by local governments exceeded pre-1978 levels and continued to increase. According to Howard Jarvis Taxpayers Association, proposition 13 reduced taxes paid by California taxpayers by $528 billion.

Some other estimates show that Proposition 13 may not have reduced the country's overall per-capita tax burden or State spending. According to the think thank Tax Foundation in 1978, Californians had the third-highest tax burden as a proportion of state income (tax-per-capita divided by income-per-capita) of 12.4% ($3,300 tax per capita, inflation-adjusted). By 2012, it had fallen slightly to the sixth-highest rate, 10.9%, ($4,100 tax per capita, inflation-adjusted (State and Local Tax Burdens, 1977 – 2012).

California is a country with the highest marginal income and capital gains tax rate, and it is among the top ten highest corporate tax and sales tax rates nationally. In 2016, this country had the country's highest per capita property tax revenue at $1559, up from 31st in 1996.

The public schools in California were among the best in the 1960s but started to show wrong results regarding student achievements. According to some researchers, this was mainly a result of the decline of Proposition 13's role in the change to state financing of public schools because schools financed mainly through property taxes were declared unconstitutional.

Until 1985, California's per capita spending was the same as the state average when it began to decline, resulting in another referendum, Bill 98, which required a percentage of the state budget to be spent on public education.

Before implementing Proposition 13, there was an increase in property tax collection in California, with the share of state and local property tax revenues increasing from 34% at the end of the decade to 44% in 1978 (Schwartz 1998). One measure for spending K-12 public schools is the percentage of personal income the state spends on education. From a maximum of about 4.5% for the nation, and 4.0% for California, peaking in the early 1970s, California spending declined in public education from 1975-1985. California has always spent less than the rest of the nation on education.

According to economics professor Julian Betts, in the period between 1978-1979, a sharp reduction in spending on schools was evident. Compared to other states, Calfornia fell significantly, and according to Betts, they have not fully recovered yet. The lack of funds needed per student decreased the funding in the years that come. Since 1981-1982, California consistently has spent less per student than the rest of the U.S., as showed by data collected by the U.S. Bureau of Economic Analysis and the Public Policy Institute of California.

The most significant development in this period was that California's voters approved higher income and capital gains on the state's wealthiest residents to increase K-12 school funding. This was achieved with Proposition 30, passed in 2012, and extended in 2016 with Proposition 55, which raised tax rates on income and capital gains over $250,000 for single filers and $500,000 for joint filers, with most of the resultant revenue going to schools. These measures have significantly closed the K-12 spending gap between California and the national average. Pupil-teacher ratios have decreased since the passage of Proposition 30. In 2019, California K-12 public school teachers earned the second-highest average salaries amongst teachers of all states.

The *Serrano v Priest* decision in 2013 was the reason for creating the Local Control funding formula with whom more significant recourses for schools are provided. LCFF has provided an additional 20% or more in "supplemental funding" to disadvantaged school districts and can make them better funded than school districts receiving the state-required minimum "basic aid" funding (Local Control Funding Formula).

Proposition 13 is quite popular among California citizens, 64 percent of whom are property owners. According to the results of a survey from 2018, 57% of citizens said that their proposal is a good thing, and 23% said it is terrible. 65% of likely voters say it has been mostly a good thing, as do: 71% of Republicans, 55% of Democrats, and 61% of independents; 54% of people age 18 to 34, 52% of people age 35 to 54, and 66% of people 55 and older; 65% of homeowners and 50% of renters. The only demographic group for which less than 50% said that Proposition 13 was mostly a good thing was African Americans, at 39%.

The survey also found that 40% of Californians and 50% of likely voters said that Proposition 13's supermajority requirement for new special taxes had had a good effect on local government services provided to residents, while 20% of both Californians and likely voters said it had a harmful effect, and the remainder felt it did not affect. At the same time, a majority of both Californians (55%) and likely voters (56%) opposed lowering the supermajority threshold for local special taxes (Public Policy Institute of California).

In 2003, when Arnold Schwarzenegger was elected for Governor of California, his advisor, Warren Buffett, tried to change or repeal proposition 13. However, Schwarzenegger knew that this could mean the end of his political career. According to Gavin Newsom, the political realities are such that Democrats, not just Republicans and Independents, are overwhelmingly opposed to making adjustments in terms of the residential side of Prop. 13. There seems to be a lot more openness to debate (California property tax information).

According to Governor Jerry Brown: *"it was not Proposition 13 that was the problem, but it was what the Legislature did after 13. It was what happened after 13 was passed because the legislature reduced local authorities' power"* (Los Angeles Times, 2011). In his later interview in 2014, he claimed that he would not dare to change proposition 13 as a campaign asset. Driven by the experience and failure of the 1970s, Governor Brown has argued he will not seek a change in the law, the third railroad in California politics. "Prop. "13 is a sacred doctrine that should never be questioned."

Works Cited

Baracskay, D., (2009) Political Patronage. *The First Amendment Encyclopedia*. Available at: https://www.mtsu.edu/first-amendment/article/1140/political-patronage [Accessed on: 06/07/2021].

Berkman, Michael B. *Ten thousand democracies: Politics and public opinion in America's school districts*. Georgetown University Press, 2005.

Blythe, Samuel G. "Putting the Rollers under the SP." *Saturday Evening Post* 183: 6-7.

Burchell, R. A. "R. Hal Williams, The Democratic Party and California Politics 1880–1896 (Stanford: Stanford University Press, 1973, $10.00). Pp. x, 290." *Journal of American Studies* 9.1 (1975): 119-119.

California Brown Act Primer. *First Amendment Coalition*. Available at: https://firstamendmentcoalition.org/facs-brown-act-primer/ [Accessed on: 06/07/2021].

California Legislative Information. Available at:https://leginfo.legislature. ca.gov/faces/codes_displayText.xhtml?division=7.&chapter=3.5.&lawCode=GOV&title=1.&article=1 [Accessed on: 06/07/2021].

California Term Limits, Proposition 140 (1990). Balotpedia. Available at: https://ballotpedia.org/California_Term_Limits,_Proposition_140_(1990) [Acessed on 7/1/2021].

Callow, Alexander. "The Legislature of a Thousand Scandals." *The Historical Society of Southern California Quarterly* 39.4 (1957): 340-350.

Edwards Jr, David N., and Daniel I. Sherry. "Operating with State Sunshine Laws." *JC & UL* 6 (1979): 85.

Fischel, William A. "How Serrano caused proposition 13." *JL & Pol*. 12 (1996): 607

Gendzel, Glen. "The People versus the Octopus: California Progressives and the Origins of Direct Democracy." *Siècles. Cahiers du Centre d'histoire «Espaces et Cultures»* 37 (2013).

Gilded Age politics: patronage. Available at: https://www.khanacademy.org/humanities/us-history/the-gilded-age/gilded-age/a/gilded-age-politics-patronage [Accessed on: 06/07/2021].

Golway, Terry. *Machine-made: Tammany Hall and the creation of modern American politics.* WW Norton & Company, 2014.

Gov. Hiram Warren Johnson. National Governors Association. Available at: https://www.nga.org/governor/hiram-warren-johnson/ [Accessed on: 05/07/2021].

Gov. Jerry Brown talks Prop. 13 Available at: https://latimesblogs.latimes.com/california-politics/2011/01/gov-jerry-brown-talks-prop-13.html [Acessed on 7/1/2021]

Grodin, Joseph R. "Public Employee Bargaining in California: The Meyers-Milias-Brown Act in the Courts." *Hastings LJ* 23 (1971): 719.

History of the California Civil Service. Statewide Bargaining Advisory Committee. SEIU Local. Available at: https://www.seiu1000.org/sites/main/files/file-attachments/history_of_civil_service.pdf [Accessed on: 06/07/2021].

Johnson, Ronald N., and Gary D. Libecap. "2. Replacing Political Patronage with Merit: The Roles of the President and the Congress in the Origins of the Federal Civil Service System." *The Federal civil service system and the problem of bureaucracy.* University of Chicago Press, 2007. 12-47

Kurashige, Lon. "Immigration, Race, and the Progressives." *A Companion to California History* (2013): 278-291.

Lefcoe, George, and Barney Allison. "The Legal Aspects of Proposition 13: The Amador Valley Case."*S. Cal. L. Rev.* 53 (1979): 173.

Library of California. Hiram Johnson. Available at: https://governors. library.ca.gov/ [Accessed on: 05/07/2021].

Local Control Funding Formula. Available at: https://ed100.org/lessons/ lcff [Accessed on: 05/07/2021].

Martin, Isaac. "Does school finance litigation cause taxpayer revolt? Serrano and Proposition 13." *Law & Society Review* 40.3 (2006): 525-558.

Martin, Willard E. "The Establishment of the Order of Printings in Books Printed from Plates: Illustrated in Frank Norris's" The Octopus", with Full Collations." *American Literature* 5.1 (1933): 17-28.

Matherne, Max. "The Jacksonian Reformation: Political Patronage and Republican Identity." (2019).

Mound, Josh. "Stirrings of Revolt: Regressive Levies, the Pocketbook Squeeze, and the 1960s Roots of the 1970s Tax Revolt." *journal of policy history* 32.2 (2020): 105-150.

Newsom on proposition 13. Available at: *https://www.latimes.com/california/story/2020-09-11/newsom-endorses-proposition-15-ballot-measure-prop-13-property-tax-rules-split-roll* [Acessed on 7/1/2021]

O'Flaherty, Joseph S. "An End and a Beginning: The South Coast and Los Angeles, 1850-1887." Exposition Press, 1972.

Orsi, Richard J. *Sunset limited: the Southern Pacific Railroad and the development of the American West, 1850-1930.* Univ of California Press, 2005.

Our American Government. 108th Congress 1st Session. Available at: https://www.govinfo.gov/content/pkg/CDOC-108hdoc94/pdf/CDOC-108hdoc94.pdf [Accessed on: 06/07/2021].

Property tax, California State Board of Equalization. Available at: https:// www.boe.ca.gov/proptaxes/proptax.htm [Accessed: 05/07/2021].

Proposition 13: 40 Years Later". Public Policy Institute of California. Archived from the original on 2018-07-14. Retrieved 2018-10-24.

Rodgers, Daniel T. "In search of progressivism." *Reviews in American history* 10.4 (1982): 113-132.

Ruhil, Anirudh VS, and Pedro J. Camões. "What lies beneath: the political roots of state merit systems."*Journal of Public Administration Research and Theory* 13.1 (2003): 27-42.

Said, Carolyn, 2009. "Lower home values mean lower tax revenue". San Francisco Chronicle. Available at: https://www.sfgate.com/realestate/article/Lower-home-values-mean-lower-tax-revenue-3294709.php [Accessed: 05/07/2021].

Sears, David O., and Jack Citrin. Tax revolt: Something for nothing in California. Harvard University Press, 1982.

Shires, Michael A., and M. Shires. *Patterns in California government revenues since Proposition 13.* San Francisco: Public Policy Institute of California, 1999.

Simmons, Charlene Wear. *California's statewide initiative process.* California Research Bureau, California State Library, 1997.

Smith, Daniel A. "Howard Jarvis, Populist Entrepreneur: Reevaluating the Causes of Proposition 13." *Social Science History*, vol. 23, no. 2, 1999, pp. 173–210. JSTOR, www.jstor.org/stable/1171520. Accessed 5 July 2021.

State and Local Tax Burdens, 1977 – 2012. *Tax Foundation.* 2016-01-20.

Thompson, Joanne J. "Social workers and politics: Beyond the Hatch Act." *Social Work* 39.4 (1994): 457-465.

Understanding Proposition 13. *Los Angeles County. Office of the Assessor Jeffrey Prang.* Available at: https://assessor.lacounty.gov/

real-estate-professionals-toolkit/04-what-is-prop-13/ [Accessed on: 06.07.2021].

Weatherson, Michael A., and Hal Bochin. *Hiram Johnson: Political Revivalist*. University Press of America, 1995.

What is Proposition 13? Available at: https://www.californiataxdata.com/ pdf/Prop13.pdf [Acessed on 7/1/2021]

Williams, John Hoyt. *A Great and Shining Road: The epic story of the transcontinental railroad*. U of Nebraska Press, 1996.

Willis, E. B., and P. K. Stockton. *Debates and Proceedings of the Constitutional Convention of the State of California, Convened at the City of Sacramento, Saturday, September 28, 1978*. Vol. 2. State office, JD Young, Superintendent State printing, 1881.

Wilson, Michael G. "The Octopus, resurfaced: California and the Southern Pacific Railroad, 1874-1894." (2019).

CHAPTER 4

Hyper Diversity of the Population: The influx of Southeast Immigration from the 1960s to 1970

4.1 Introduction

From 1960 to 1970, the working-age population grew by a little more than 6 million—a slow expansion driven by the relatively small birth cohorts in the late 1930s and early 1940s. The figure of 6 million additional working-age people reflects the balance of a net increase of almost 9 million in the third-plus generation population and a net decrease of almost 2.5 million in first and second-generation populations. These figures reflect the mortality experience and aging out of the workforce (attaining age 65) of immigrants and children from early in the 20th century, before the long immigration pause. In short, the foreign-born population in 1960 was composed mainly of the elderly survivors of the early 20th-century immigration. The figure of 6 million persons added to the working-age population during the 1960s is dwarfed by the population changes over the next few decades.

Illegal immigrants from Mexico became relevant in the late 1960s, at the end of the so-called Bracero Program in 1964. This program was designed to enable Mexican migrants to work legally in the United States. Over the next 30 years, illegal migration increased significantly, especially along the southwestern border. Illegal border crossings increased from 200,000 in the 1970s to 1.5 million in 1999. The cumulative product of this illegal immigration is an increase in the number of illegal migrants. In 1997, the number of illegal migrants in the United States was estimated at 3.1 million. Mexicans also represent the largest population of illegal immigrants in the country, at 60 percent. Immigrants from El Salvador, Guatemala, Honduras, and Nicaragua make up another 13 percent of illegal immigration to the United States. (U.S. INS 1999). Some of these immigrants crossed the border legally but exceeded their tourist visas' validity, while others crossed the border illegally without documents. According to a study by (Calavita, 2010), the net inflow of illegal migrants from Mexico between 1987-1996 was about 202,000 immigrants per year.

According to experts, migration is described as a two-way process under the influence of push factors from Mexico and pulls factors from the United States. What primarily facilitates immigration are the family ties and the people who enable it, the so-called smugglers, and low wages and cheap labor are encouraging. Although early border control did not significantly affect migration control, again, the efforts made are practical.

Efforts to prevent immigration encouraged the search for smugglers. However, with the strengthening of control, the risks of crossing the border have increased, which can be seen in many deaths of immigrants who tried to cross the border but unsuccessfully. For these reasons, the need for joint bilateral cooperation is needed to resolve these issues.

Western Mexico, and especially the states of Michoacán, Jalisco, and Guanajuato, is a source of immigrants to the United States. Since the MMP survey, migration rates have increased from 3.7 to 7.5 percent during the analyzed period. The continuous increase in migration is related to the 1970s and 1980s, increasing almost 10% in 1988.

4.2. The Bracero Program

Mass immigration from Mexico is due to the Bracero program, which has been implemented since 1942 (Massey and Liang 1989). This program allowed temporary legal migration from Mexico to the United States to make up for labor shortages in the United States due to the war. The leading proponents of this program were farmers and ranchers in need of workers. Thus, they were the biggest lobbyists, which led the government to continue the program in the 1950s. However, in 1964 this program ended due to the efforts of workers' associations in the United States. (Calavita 1992).

At the time this program was active, more than 200,000 immigrants entered the United States each year. Most of them were concentrated in California, Arkansas, Texas, Arizona, and New Mexico. The unexpected end of the program increased the rate of illegal immigration. However, the influx of migrants was not very significant in the beginning due to the tremendous economic growth of Mexico in the 1960s. Mexico also developed a cross-border industrialization program, known as the Maquiladora program, specifically designed to create jobs for migrant migrants. In the early 1970s, the rate of immigration from Mexico to the United States resumed (Carrillo and Zárate, 340).

4.3. Factors of Illegal Immigration

The increase in the rate of illegal migration is due to several economic and social factors. There was a whole network of people in different positions who in some way enabled and reduced the risks of migrating to the United States to maintain this illegal migration trend. (Massey et al. 1987). An essential link in this whole process was smugglers known as "coyotes," which further encouraged illegal immigration. However, one of the main drivers of illegal migration is higher wages and more jobs in the United States. Another factor is the failure to implement laws that would prevent illegal immigration, such as IRCA employer sanctions, signal tolerance for illegal immigration.

Channels: Despite the vital role of economic factors, they are still not the only ones in directing illegal immigration. For example, an immigrant who crosses the border for the first time must know what awaits him, i.e., he faces a specific type of fixed costs, and for those costs not to increase, he must provide a safe passage. According to immigration experts, family contacts and networks are the ones that provide direct information to immigrants. The Bracero Program is undoubtedly responsible for this, through which the foundations for such communication were laid. Since then, such networks have only expanded.

Nineteen percent of MMP households had access to at least one sibling network in 1965, whereas 41 percent had access in 1991. These same households averaged 1.7 sibling networks in 1965 and 2.3 in 1991. Moreover, an increasing proportion of sibling networks settled permanently in the United States over this period. In other words, both the quantity and quality of migrant networks are changing (Orrenius, 5.)

Smugglers: In parallel with the migrant network, the network of smugglers, also known as coyotes, who transported undocumented migrants, started to spread. Interestingly, the smugglers could be found in the migrants' birthplaces or along the border and usually accompanied the migrant to his final destination. Surprisingly, despite high demand, smugglers' prices have been on a downward trend most of the time (Andreas, 107).

By 1994, prices for migrant smuggling were around $300. One of the main reasons for the falling prices of smugglers is infrastructure development and the absence of barriers to entry into this industry. The construction of infrastructures, such as roads, airports, highways, and the emergence of major cities such as Tijuana / San Diego and Ciudad Juárez / El Paso, made the border more accessible to travelers from Mexico's interior. Before the 1930s, only two railways connected Mexico to the U.S. border. Most of the roads that connected the interior of Mexico to the border were built between 1940-1960.

The airline industry developed similarly, and because of this, the price of smugglers was falling. Another reason for the low prices is the lack of barriers to entry in this industry. For example, every single migrant who enters the United States can use their experience and become a smuggler, i.e., work as a coyote. All of this points to the fact that illegal migration has become a common practice, with more and more migrants entering the business, lowering prices for this service (Gathmann, 1935).

Wages: Networks and coyotes have reduced the cost of illegal immigration, allowing immigrants to adapt to various factors, such as low wages in Mexico. According to Massey and Espinosa (1997) and Orrenius (1999), Economic downturns cause unemployment in cities, depress agricultural prices in the countryside, and make loans challenging to repay. The apparent surge in Mexican emigration in the mid-1980s is consistent with declines in real income at that time. Mexican manufacturing wages tell a similar story and, in 1999, were still below the peak levels reached in 1981. Although less volatile than national output, agricultural sector output fell throughout the latter half of the sample period (Bosch, Manacorda, 128).

4.4. Examine Mexico, Latin, and Central American migration

A study by Manson, Espenshade, and Muller (22) provides an excellent overview of the impact of immigration from Mexico to Southern California. As a labor force, Mexicans were transformed into the California economy, working predominantly in the manufacturing sector. As a result, the workload in the manufacturing sector has increased. Many of the positions were related to the low-wage non-durable goods manufacturing industry, and many may have been created solely by the availability of these low-skill workers.

From the point of view of unemployment, there were no adverse effects, i.e., an increase in unemployment due to the increase in immigrants in California during this period was not detected (Pissarides and McMaster, 820). What is characteristic of immigration in this period is the fact that black workers were considered to be most affected by the influx of lower-income immigrants. However, over time, black workers began to see an available upgrade in their professional status.

Further research is needed to determine whether increased immigration leads to upgrading domestic workers in terms of occupation and income. Increased immigration to California, and especially to Los Angeles, is thought to be the cause of changes in the U.S. model of internal immigration. Although general migration to the West continued during the 1970s, it declined in California as a result of declining migration rates and increasing outmigration rates.[2]

In the years that followed, immigration from Mexico increased, creating the conditions for the introduction of immigration reform. However, significant changes in legislation must be led by competent persons to understand the labor market dynamics, especially in areas where there are more immigrants (Rosenblum and Brick, 2011).

Research data show that in and out immigration differed in several essential respects. While in-immigration applied to young people in their prime and well-qualified and family-free, out-immigrants were less trained and moved with their families. However, Mexican immigrants who came to California during this period were much less qualified. In this way, they were a supplement to the labor market and a replacement for less-skilled workers. This leads to the conclusion that the demand for low-paid and low-skilled labor has now been met by immigrants from Mexico (Dixon and T. Rimmer, 2010).

Some aspects of the issue of immigration from Mexico to California have not yet been clarified. For example, if immigrants contribute to strengthening the economy by employing industries, attention must be paid to immigration reforms, which reduce the number of undocumented workers, their deportation, etcetera.

In the 1980s, the United States experienced one of the largest waves of immigration. With this, the concern among the citizens started to grow and the need for the protection of the workers. Despite growing concern, it must not be forgotten that the United States is a country of immigrants

---

[2] To leave one region or community to settle in another, especially as part of a large-scale and continuing population movement.

and that much of the progress and development would not have happened without the great waves of immigration that lasted for many years. Today, and in the past, outflows have increased fears among workers, especially blue-collar workers, that immigrants could take their jobs.

The fear was that employers would choose workers who would work below the minimum wage and for meager wages, which native workers would not accept and would be acceptable to immigrants. Thus, the prevailing view was that American workers would not be competitive in these conditions, would remain unemployed or unemployed. In a survey conducted by The Urban Institute in June 1983 by the Field Research Corporation, California residents were asked about their perceptions of the impact of immigration on the region. Nearly half (48.2 percent) of the respondents believed that illegal immigrants take jobs away from citizens and contribute to unemployment. Among blacks in the survey, 58 percent believed that jobs were threatened.

Although plausible, this argument would only make sense if immigrants competed with native workers for the same jobs, i.e., if immigrants did not create a demand for new goods and services, the production would increase the need for native workers. According to Piore, 1979, Excess labor demand can increase if labor markets are divided into primary and secondary. In this way, if the secondary labor market offers more undesirable jobs for domestic workers, then the demand for immigrant labor will increase and will be met by workers who want to do that work.

The extent to which substitution prevails among different types of workers is an empirical question to which many researchers have sought to answer. Despite the numerous results, a plausible conclusion could not be drawn from them. (Hamermesh and Grant, 1979; Johnson, 1980). As a result, a draft law on immigration reform was introduced, the so-called Simson Masoli. The law addresses the concerns of American workers by introducing provisions that make it illegal for U.S. employers to employ undocumented immigrants. This law was expected to reduce immigration, as employers would be penalized and would not dare to hire immigrant workers. This law was also called the "jobs bill."

Most of the United States has been hit by large waves of immigration, including California. In the 1980s, a quarter of all legal immigrants to the United States lived in California (Immigration and Naturalization Service, 1981). During the 1970s, both legal and illegal immigration prevailed in California.

Concerns about Mexican immigration stem not only from a large number of immigrants but also from a large number of illegal immigrants with low levels of education and qualifications, as well as poor knowledge of English, which places them at the lowest level for both salary and skills and qualifications. As mentioned above, the influx of large numbers of Mexican immigrants has not increased the unemployment rate in the country, but another feature has emerged, and that is altered the pattern of internal migration to the region.

The evidence suggests that there has been a decline in the rate of low-wage workers migrating to California from other parts of the country during a time when the flow of immigrants from Mexico increased. Most California immigrants in the '60s and 70s settled in the southern part of the country, mainly in Los Angeles. However, contrary to the belief that most immigrants in California are Mexican, they are neither the majority in Los Angeles nor the majority in California, even though they represent the largest single nationality among immigrants.

More than 15 percent of Californians born outside of California, only one-third, were Mexican and more than half were non-Hispanic. Of Mexican immigrants, two-thirds of those living in Los Angeles have settled since 1970, and more than half arrived in the second half of the decade. Of the non-Hispanic group, most arrived before the 1970s, mostly from Europe and after 1970 from Asia. As mentioned above, the most significant cause for concern is illegal immigration. In terms of the impact on the labor market, their number can not be controlled and is largely unknown. Also, to prepare a good analysis that would precede immigration reform, the number of illegal immigrants must be known to see how many eligible immigrants may seek amnesty under proposed immigration reform legislation.

Despite numerous attempts, it is still challenging to determine the number of illegal immigrants due to the lack of direct information. In this regard, Immigration and Naturalization Service data have only partial coverage. In 1984, Passel and Woodrow (1984) attempted to estimate immigration by country, by country, and nationwide. According to their estimates, Mexicans have historically had a higher rate of illegal immigration than immigrants from other countries.

Specifically for California, these estimates show that more than three-quarters, or 73%, of those who entered California in the 1970s are undocumented, while that number is lower in the period before the 1970s. Compared to other countries that have much lower rates of illegal entry into U.S. territory, as a result of not having a common border with the U.S. Of these, 24% entered U.S. territory before 1970 without proper documentation.

In addition to being in large numbers, immigrants from Mexico pose a threat to domestic low-skilled workers due to their low education. According to the 1980 census, 3/3 of Mexican immigrants in California had no primary education, and only 2% had secondary education or more (Chiquiar and Hanson, 245). In Los Angeles, Mexican immigrants showed better levels of education than those in the country as a whole.

Compared to other Spanish immigrants in the country, one in three had not completed primary school, while one in eight had completed four or more years of secondary education. Immigrants of non-Hispanic descent - primarily Europeans and Asians - had much higher levels of education, with only about one-fifth of this group having no secondary education. The 1980 census shows that immigrants from Mexico spoke very little English. Among those who arrived between 1960 and 1980, 32% did not speak English well, and 29% did not speak English at all. Those over 18 and older, mainly in the physician workforce, hardly spoke English at all.

Unsurprisingly, despite their low level of education and poor English language skills, Mexican immigrants mainly worked at the lowest levels of the job ladder. Between 1960 and 1980, Mexican immigrants worked in positions classified as semi-skilled or unskilled, while only about one in eight had jobs classified as white-collar workers.

Black people born in the United States are somewhere between people of Hispanic descent and non-Hispanic whites and Asians. One-third of all black people in Los Angeles have worked in low-skilled jobs, which puts them at potential risk of being taken over by low-skilled Mexican immigrants. Of U.S.-born whites, only one-fifth worked in positions classified as unskilled. To summarize: Immigrants from Mexico arrived in California with deficient levels of education, and most worked in positions that required low qualifications. According to the two eligibility criteria, Mexican immigrants had the lowest status of all immigrant ethnic groups and even lower than those born in California (Cornelius, 139).

The 1970s were marked by lightning-fast job expansion in Southern California. 2/3 of these jobs were the so-called white-collar jobs, which grew by 1/3 above the national average. Although only a few blue-collar jobs were added, their growth rate doubled above the national average, all resulting from employment growth in the manufacturing sector. In Los Angeles, the growth was even higher, with jobs in the manufacturing sector up 14 %, compared with a 5 percent increase at the U.S. Bureau of Labor Statistics. Of all the new positions in California in the 1970s, nearly one-third were held by Mexican immigrants (Raijman, 50).

The group of skilled blue-collar jobs made up ½ of the number of jobs for this period. Most of these immigrants to Mexico worked in the manufacturing sector. Of the 20,000 jobs in the sector, half of the jobs went to Mexican immigrants. A significant percentage of jobs in the manufacturing sector belong to Mexican immigrants. Thus they make up 23% of all production workers and 29 percent of the total in non-durable manufacturing.

After the manufacturing sector, the following areas where Mexican immigrants work are the service sector, sales, and commerce, where one in 6 and one in 7 employees are Mexican immigrants. Overall, net manufacturing employment in California increased by 113,000 jobs during the 1970s. However, in the period after the 1970s, the influx of immigrants was higher, and immigrants occupied thus more of the jobs in the manu-facturing sector. In consequence, there was a decline of 55 thousand jobs among other workers during the decade (Kalleberg, 2011).

However, this does not mean that immigrants caused the drop of 55 thousand jobs. If we take into account the high turnover rate in this sector, such a change may affect domestic workers to leave their jobs voluntarily, with low wages, low skills, for other types of employment. The number of jobs filled by Mexican immigrants in all other sectors was equal to the total number of manufacturing jobs. The number of Mexican immigrants employed in all non-manufacturing sectors was only equal to the total number of manufacturing jobs. Within this group, one of the most dra-matic changes in personal services occurred when all immigrants took 24.4 thousand jobs. Mexicans were looking for 10.3 thousand when the sector lost 7.4 thousand jobs (Holzer et al., 2011).

4.5. Understanding gentrification

Gentrification is a process of changes in the neighborhood that impli-cates economic changes in what used to be a historically not so developed area, in terms of real estate investment and new higher-income residents moving in, as well as demographic change in income but also changes in education or racial make-up residents (Fraser, 437).

The process of gentrification is complex, and for its understanding, it is crucial to focus on three primary factors:

- Historical conditions and policies that made communities suscep-tible to gentrification
- How central city disinvestment and investment patterns are taking place today as a result of gentrification
- The impact of gentrification on communities.

In the period from 1930 to the late 1960s, rules and procedures set by the government, in the most considerable part labeled neighborhoods home to "colored" people, were defined as risky and not suitable for investment. This meant that people of color were denied access to loans that will enable them to buy or repair homes in their neighborhood.

Other housing and transportation policies of the mid-20th century increased the number of suburbs, mostly with white people and the exodus of capital from urban centers in a phenomenon often referred to as "white flight" (Wilson, 677). If we take the GI Bill as an example, we can see that after WWII, this bill guaranteed low-cost mortgage loans for returning soldiers. However, this bill set limitations to which black veterans were able to purchase homes in the growing suburbs (Frydl, 4147.) Moreover, the FHA was strict in its requirements, and that is, suburban developers not to sell houses to black people.

The low-income households and communities were most affected by the built of the highway system and urban renewal programs, resulting in massive clearance of homes and setting the stage for the massive public and private disinvestment in the years that followed (Institute for quality communities). Another factor that led to gentrification was the foreclosure crisis. In low-income communities of color, disproportionate levels of subprime lending resulted in mass foreclosures, leaving those neighborhoods vulnerable to investors seeking to buy and rent homes. Between 2007-2009, there were evident 790 foreclosures for African-Americans, 769 foreclosures for Latinos, and 452 for non-Hispanic whites per 10,000 loans (The Center for Responsible Lending).

The past 40 years have been marked by dramatic changes in the way the United States migrates. If rural-urban migration has been current so far, there has been migration in the opposite direction in recent years, from urban to rural areas. A similar process occurs in other post-industrial economies such as the United Kingdom, Australia, New Zealand, and Spain (Nelson and Nelson, 445).

Residents of the urban parts of the country and the upper classes, driven by the desire to avoid the dynamic city and create their paradise in rural areas, are one of the main reasons for the growth of the population in rural areas. Most scholars who analyze these topics believe that globalization is a crucial factor in the gentrification process. Wealthy urban professionals are the primary beneficiaries of globalized capital accumulation, whether indirect compensation, dividend income, or the increased value of their urban real estate, enabling them to move to high-convenience destinations (Nelson, 2005). According to (McCarthy 129), these processes result from a post-productive, consumer-oriented rural landscape "produced through increasingly globalized forms and relationships."

In the case of the United States, urban-rural migration began in the 1970s, when, for the first time in more than 100 years, population growth occurred in non-urban areas. According to some, this growth is random and represents only a link in the whole chain of rural-urban migration. According to them, the 1980s are again characterized by a return to the big cities. However, the 1990s revitalized urban-rural migration, especially in the high-amenity regions of the Western USA (Frey and Speare Jr. 144.)

Such movements were of particular interest to scientists. They attracted much attention, seeking reasons for such increased instability in the ever-stable process and even the natural population concentration in urban areas. Scientists have described this phenomenon as the "Rural Renaissance," which dates back to the 1970s, to the Arab oil embargo and the search for new energy sources. Scientists focusing on the "Rural Renaissance" of the 1970s in the United States have identified many forces that contributed to rural growth, from the completion of the interstate highway system to the Arab oil embargo and the search for new energy sources. (Frey, 1989; Johansen and Fuguitt, 1984).

According to others, rural growth in the 1970s resulted from counter-culturalist movements seeking to return to the land and rural life (Dillman, 1979). The explanations for the rural return of the 1990s were based on the rise of information technology, information, and the demand for natural habitats. According to Brown et al. (2005), the reason for the growth in the 90s of the last century lies in two types of factors: technological innovations that have reduced the isolation of certain groups and economic restructuring that has increased employment opportunities. Both urban and rural populations have been affected by global pressures and the effects of globalization. As mentioned above, the oil embargo has almost doubled the price of oil in the United States, forcing the state to develop the potential of rural areas to find domestic energy sources (Gipe, 1995).

Until the 1990s, the reasons for the return to rural areas were not related to a single geopolitical event but various economic and industrial factors. Such factors have influenced the wealthy inhabitants of the urban areas to become even richer and easier to transfer to rural areas. Proponents of both currents of the population emphasize the power of a romanticized rural idyll in the movement for population change, as wealthier migrants seek ideal rural space to "escape" the city.

Bunce (2003) argues that the advertised *"village portrait"* sold to the rich of the city aims to paint a picture of a simple understanding of home and "pure" nature. One of the reasons for the relocation of more prosperous residents is the so-called casual atmosphere provided by the rural, quality of life, slower pace of life.

This imagined reality is the number one factor for the process of gentrification, i.e., the arrival of the middle and upper class in rural areas. Social and environmental ideals for the rural environment have been a driving factor throughout all these years. Bunce also argues that fundamental shifts like the global economy have created the conditions under which these migration flows have been produced and maintained over time.

There are indications that such migration movements will continue in the future, as the primary age structure creates new areas for accumulation. The oldest baby boomers turned 65 in 2011, and about 80 million would follow in the next ten years. Never before in the history of the United States has such a retirement rate been recorded, and with retirement naturally comes the need to move from urban to rural areas (Wilson, 130). Conservatives estimate that migration in these categories will add over 5 million immigrants to rural areas by 2020 (Nelson and Cromartie, 2009).

The basis in the migration literature consists of the analysis of the reasons for migration from urban to rural areas and the economic, social, and political impact of migration on rural communities. New migrants often differ from current residents in many ways, thus enabling a transformational process to impose different economic, social, cultural, and political influences. In this regard, the class represents perhaps the most palpable fault-line along which ruptures in the rural idyll emerge as newcomers gentrify their rural destinations (Cloke et al., 1995; Murdoch and Day, 1998; Phillips, 1993).

Newcomers often have different views on many issues from the natives, such as environment, community understanding, economic development. The influx of new residents into rural areas will intensify rural differences in the future, leading to further rifts in these areas (Phillips, 20). According to Ghose (535), in many gentrification communities across the United States, domestic migration accompanied by all the economic, political, cultural, and social influences increases the sense of class differentiation.

According to a study conducted in Missoula, Montana, migrants there are mostly college-educated and work as professionals in the service industries, earning a solid income from the middle to an upper middle class instead of the average long-term resident (Ghose, 2004). Similarly, in the Teton Valley, there is a sense of social and class difference in anticipation of the arrival of wealthier residents. A resident of the Teton Valley said that almost all of the children he went to school with were at the same or similar level from an economic point of view. According to him, there were one or two in each class who were better than the others, and he considered that as Nelson's (2001) golden rule.

Such developments are similar to those in the United Kingdom, Australia, Spain, and New Zealand. Urban gentrification processes allow wealthier residents of certain urban settlements to settle in rural areas. For rural residents, the modern migration dynamics from urban to rural areas amplifies class differences in rural areas and transforms the actual living experience for rural residents.

Although gentrification processes are increasingly considered in the West, many scientists are still beginning to analyze it as a phenomenon in other regions, i.e., countries. Such processes show how wealthy domestic migrants can influence the transformation of traditional values and identities. Such differences can be seen in the environment, i.e., in housing. The processes of gentrification undoubtedly influenced the change of real estate markets. According to Ghose (2004), home prices in Missoula more than tripled during the 1990s. If in 1989 a good house and a good location could be found for $ 50,000 ten years later, the same house cost $ 300,000, almost six times more expensive.

Characteristics of the new way of life were the so-called ranches, closed communities, and private properties, which primarily reflected the new look of housing in rural areas. According to Theobald et al. (1996), this trend is evidenced by the increasing share of land in rural Colorado, in plots of 30-45 acres, too small for agriculture but ideal for 'ranchettes.' The construction of these ranchettes is kind and attractive for newcomers, who strive to equalize to meet the criteria for rural living. From the point of view of cost-effectiveness, these backpacks are not economically efficient at all but only serve aesthetic purposes and fit the image that suits white newcomers.

These ranchettes often set new values and tastes for the rural image. According to Walker and Fortmann, newcomers influence by transforming local environmental policy and discourse, while Jones et al. analyze a similar effect in the Appalachia area. The rural planning discourse is complemented by phrases such as "historical" or natural preservation, thus challenging traditional land uses and environmental ideas.

According to Hamnett (180), gentrification is a complex process that involves physical, social, and economic changes in the environment and an increase in the propensity for rural living. Attracted by rural idyll, wealthy migrants transform local housing markets, introduce new forms of class differentiation, and demonstrate new cultural attitudes and preferences for rural living and rural areas. More importantly, gentrification in rural areas often shatters rural idyll along socio-economic and ethnic lines, creating more rurality for different constituent groups.

The influence of gentrification can be both negative and positive. Moreover, communities react differently to gentrification so to craft effective policies. Policymakers need to understand how different kinds of communities experience the process.

Gentrification's effect on a community spans a spectrum of reactions ranging from appreciated to despised. It is a complex process incompletely defined by scholarly literature and warranting more thorough investigations into how it impacts indigenous residents of varying communities (Nyborg, 2008).

4.6. Latino immigrants in rural America

What is characteristic of Latino immigrants in the United States is that they are concentrated mainly in larger cities, while some of them have begun to settle in rural areas of the United States, a process that is also called secondary migration.

According to Kandel and Cromartie (2004), the increase in the number of Latino immigrants in U.S. metropolises refers not only to new destinations but also to places that are historically dependent on Latino migrants, which have witnessed the transition to permanent and permanent immigration of Mexican immigrants. in the 1990s and later. The literature on immigrants from Mexico abounds with data on the political and economic drivers of this phenomenon and their social, political, and cultural influences on communities.

In analyzing the rural dimensions of Latino settlements, geographers and other scholars take into account the following interrelated issues: the changing nature of labor markets in rural areas and the withdrawal of immigrants to non-traditional destinations, directly from abroad or from other primary origins. Geographers also pay considerable attention to the challenges of social integration and the factors that affect the formation of the community under the influence of low wages of immigrants, lack of documents, and the like.

Articles by Lionel Cantu' 's *The peripheralization of rural America: A case study of Latino migrants in America's heartland (1995) and geographer*

*Altha Cravey's 'Latino labor and poultry production in rural North Caro-
lina' (1997)* represent the first works that provide an overview of the key
dynamics of transformation in rural areas, which was difficult to accept
by the professional public in the years that followed. These authors further examine the impacts on local communities of agricultural expansion
in Iowa and North Carolina and the active recruitment of immigrants
from these industries in the late 1980s and beyond. Cantu's research follows "controversial ideas about community membership, citizenship" in
a small Iowa town.

Cantu analyzes the relationship between marginalization and racial
affiliation among Latinos in the community by asking qualitative questions - whether they are legal, illegal migrants, or born in the United
States. In contrast, Cravey considers the racial division of labor as a result
of the increasing need for a workforce in the North Carolina poultry
industry during the 1980s. In addition to these issues, the analysis also
addresses issues related to immigrant communities' socio-economic, linguistic, and cultural marginalization. Although these developments were
current in the 1990s, interest in them began to grow after 2000, after the
implementation of the census, which dramatically showed these changes
in the population structure.

Gentrification itself is full of challenges and opportunities. Until now,
it was thought that gentrification has only negative consequences. Recent
research shows that gentrification has some positive effects (Atkinson,
126). According to research by a San Francisco neighborhood, some
unexpected results were presented regarding the impact of gentrification
on ethnicities and the working class. Residents also highlighted issues
such as crime, job opportunities, culture, and family. Although many
were concerned about problems arising from gentrification, such as displacement, they were more concerned about issues such as crime and lack
of job opportunities (Byrne, 405).

Interaction between different social categories can affect gentrification differently. For example, higher-rent homes disqualify low-income
residents, thus increasing crime rates and withdrawing most of their

suburban homes. According to this research, just 5 minutes spent on Mission Street, is enough to conclude that violence, prostitution, and drug use prevail.

Mission Street itself shows some aspects of gentrification. On the other hand, just one block to the west, another street gives a greater sense of security, beautified with restaurants and boutiques of expensive brands. For this reason, the competent institutions must understand that the goal is to encourage the positive aspects of gentrification, i.e., to invest in the neighborhoods without forcing the residents to move out and thus destroy the permanent social capital in the community. Moreover, one should invest in healthy neighborhoods by creating opportunities for job creation, education, organization, and crime prevention.

The authorities need additional information on how different communities respond to gentrification to create effective policies. Residents of Harlem and Mission County shared their experiences regarding gentrification. Although, for the most part, negative comments prevailed, perceptions were mixed mainly and varied from district to district. According to Freeman (2011), the people of Harlem are committed to tackling cynicism, while the people of Mission Street believe that it is necessary to preserve social capital. Such a complete picture of the perceptions of the effects of gentrification is quite essential to see how gentrification affects different areas and, more importantly, to determine the right policies for managing the whole process. Finally, more information is needed to identify and warn of early signs of gentrification.

Early measures are crucial to facilitate the process and reduce any potentially harmful consequences. By preserving social capital, cities make communities healthier and set better rules for managing and directing gentrification. In addressing gentrification, cities must also recognize early indicators and help communities organize to allow residents to participate in neighborhood development plans. Gentrification processes are pretty complex, and there is a lack of professional literature for their understanding. Therefore, there is a need to sweat its effects on the native population of different communities.

4.7 Impact of gentrification on communities

While increased investment in an area can be positive, gentrification is often associated with displacement, which means that in some of these communities, long-term residents cannot stay to benefit from new investments in housing, healthy food access, or transit infrastructure.

Another impact of displacement to consider is cultural displacement. Even for long-time residents who can stay in newly gentrifying areas, changes in the make-up and character of a neighborhood can lead to a reduced sense of belonging or feeling out of place in one's own home.

4.8. Further steps

Finally, we can conclude that the adverse effects of gentrification are only a consequence of the model of urban restructuring that has been imposed over the years and has negatively affected specific communities such as blacks and people of Hispanic descent.

The competent institutions are the ones that have the resources to make a change, i.e., to implement strategies for greater utilization of investments in the communities by their inhabitants. One of the measures that need to be taken by the authorities to prevent displacement is the sale of apartments at reasonable prices, protection of residents.

Works Cited

60 years of Urban Change. *Institute for Quality Communities. The University of Oklahoma.* Available at:http://iqc.ou.edu/urbanchange/ [Accessed on 19.07.2021].

Andreas, Peter. "The transformation of migrant smuggling across the US-Mexican Border." *Global human smuggling: Comparative perspectives* (2001): 107-25.

Atkinson, Rowland. "The evidence on the impact of gentrification: new lessons for the urban renaissance?." *European Journal of Housing Policy* 4.1 (2004): 107-131.

Bosch, Mariano, and Marco Manacorda. "Minimum wages and earnings inequality in urban Mexico." *American Economic Journal: Applied Economics* 2.4 (2010): 128-49.

Brown, Ralph B., Shawn F. Dorins, and Richard S. Krannich. "The boom-bust-recovery cycle: Dynamics of change in community satisfaction and social integration in Delta, Utah." *Rural Sociology* 70.1 (2005): 28-49.

Byrne, J. Peter. "Two cheers for gentrification." *Howard LJ* 46 (2002): 405.

Calavita, Kitty. *Inside the state: The Bracero Program, immigration, and the INS.* Quid Pro Books, 2010.

Carrillo, Jorge, and Robert Zárate. "The evolution of maquiladora best practices: 1965–2008." *Journal of Business Ethics* 88.2 (2009): 335-348.

Center for responsible lending. Foreclosures by Race and Ethnicity: The Demographics of a Crisis. Available at: https://www.responsiblelending. org/mortgage-lending/research-analysis/foreclosures-by-race-and-ethnicity.pdf [Accessed on 19.07.2021].

Chiquiar, Daniel, and Gordon H. Hanson. "International migration, self-selection, and the distribution of wages: Evidence from Mexico and the United States." *Journal of Political Economy* 113.2 (2005): 239-281.

Cloke, P. J., Martin Phillips, and N. J. Thrift. "The new middle classes and the social constructs of rural living." *Social change and the middle classes.* UCL Press, 1995. 220-240.

Cornelius, Wayne A. "Immigrant Labor: New Evidence from California." *Theoretical Perspectives: Interdisciplinary Perspectives on the New Immigration* (2014): 139.

Dixon, Peter B., and Maureen T. Rimmer. "US imports of low-skilled labor: restrict or liberalize?." *New Developments in Computable General Equilibrium Analysis for Trade Policy.* Emerald Group Publishing Limited, 2010.

Fraser, James C. "Beyond gentrification: Mobilizing communities and claiming space." *Urban Geography* 25.5 (2004): 437-457.

Freeman, Lance. *There goes the hood: Views of gentrification from the ground up.* Temple University Press, 2011.

Frey, William H. *United States: counter urbanization and metropolis depopulation.* 1989.

Frey, William H., and Alden Speare Jr. "The revival of metropolitan population growth in the United States: An assessment of findings from the 1990 census." *Population and Development Review* (1992): 129-146.

Frydl, Kathleen J. "The GI Bill." (2001): 4147-4147.

Fuguitt, Glenn V. "The nonmetropolitan population turnaround." *Annual Review of Sociology* 11.1 (1985): 259-280.

Ghose, Rina. "Big sky or big sprawl? Rural gentrification and the changing cultural landscape of Missoula, Montana." *Urban Geography* 25.6 (2004): 528-549.

Gipe, Paul. *Wind energy comes of age.* Vol. 4. John Wiley & Sons, 1995.

Hamnett, Chris. "The blind men and the elephant: the explanation of gentrification." *Transactions of the Institute of British Geographers* (1991): 173-189.

Holzer, Harry J., et al. *Where are all the good jobs going?: what national and local job quality and dynamics mean for US workers.* Russell Sage Foundation, 2011.

Kalleberg, Arne L. *Good jobs, bad jobs: The rise of polarized and precarious employment systems in the United States, 1970s-2000s.* Russell Sage Foundation, 2011.

Manson, Donald M., Thomas J. Espenshade, and Thomas Muller. "Mexican immigration to southern California: issues of job competition and worker mobility." *Review of Regional Studies* 15.2 (1985): 21-33.

Massey, Douglas S., and Kristin E. Espinosa. "What's driving Mexico-US migration? A theoretical, empirical, and policy analysis." *American journal of sociology* 102.4 (1997): 939-999.

Massey, Douglas S., and Zai Liang. "The long-term consequences of a temporary worker program: The US Bracero experience." *Population Research and Policy Review* 8.3 (1989): 199-226.

Murdoch, Jonathan, and Graham Day. "Middle-class mobility, rural communities and the politics of exclusion." *Migration into rural areas: Theories and issues* (1998): 186-199.

Nelson PB and Cromartie JB (2009) Baby boom migration and its impact on Rural America, USDA: Economic Research Service, Report 79. Available at: http:// www.ers.usda.gov/publications/err79/err79.pdf [Accessed on: 13.07.2021].

Nelson, Lise, and Peter B. Nelson. "The global rural: Gentrification and linked migration in the rural USA." *Progress in Human Geography* 35.4 (2011): 441-459.

Nyborg, Anne Meredith. *Gentrified barrio: Gentrification and the Latino community in San Francisco's Mission District.* University of California, San Diego, 2008.

Orrenius, Pia M. "Does increase border enforcement trap illegal immigrants inside the United States?." *Federal Reserve Bank of Dallas* (2000).

Orrenius, Pia M. "Illegal immigration and enforcement along the US-Mexico border: An overview." *Economic and Financial Review-Federal Reserve Bank of Dallas* 1 (2001): 2-11.

Phillips M (1993) Rural gentrification and the processes of class colonization. Journal of Rural Studies 9(2): 123– 140.

Phillips, Martin. "Other geographies of gentrification." *Progress in human geography* 28.1 (2004): 5-30.

Pissarides, Christopher A., and Ian McMaster. "Regional migration, wages and unemployment: empirical evidence and policy implications." *Oxford economic papers* 42.4 (1990): 812-831.

Raijman, Rebeca. "Mexican immigrants and informal self-employment in Chicago." *Human organization* 60.1 (2001): 47-55.

Rosenblum, Marc R., and Kate Brick. "US immigration policy and Mexican/Central American migration flows." *Washington, DC: Migration Policy Institute* (2011).

Rothstein, Richard, (2017). *The history of residential segregation in America: "The Color of Law: A Forgotten History of How Our Government Segregated America.* Available at: https://www.nytimes.com/2017/06/20/books/review/richard-rothstein-color-of-law-forgotten-history.html?_r=0 [Accessed on 16.07.2021].

Spectrum News New York City: How *Gentrification Is Affecting the Hispanic Community.* Available at: https://www.ny1.com/nyc/all-boroughs/

in-focus-shows/2019/10/13/how-gentrification-is-affecting-the-his-panic-community [Accesed on: 15.07.2021].

University of Richmond Digital Scholarship Lab. Available at: https://dsl.richmond.edu/panorama/redlining/#loc=4/41.218/-105.499   [Accessed on 16.07.2021].

Wilson, Erika K. "Gentrification and urban public school reforms: The interest divergence dilemma." *W. Va. L. Rev.* 118 (2015): 677.

Wilson, Franklin D. "Components of change in migration and destination-propensity rates for metropolitan and nonmetropolitan areas: 1935–1980." *Demography* 25.1 (1988): 129-139.

Recalls in California

5.1 Introduction: The role of recalls in California

According to article 2 from the Californian Constitution, the citizens of this country have the right to initiate a recall election. This rule applies both to state and local officials but does not apply to federal officials. Also, citizens can recall judges of courts of appeal and trial courts.

5.2 State officials

The procedure to recall a state official is the following: first, the proponent fills a notice of intent to recall petition that needs to be signed by 65 voters to start the petition drive process. In the actual petition, signatures must be equal to the percentage of the total number of votes most recently cast for the targeted office, i.e., 12% for executive officials and 20% for state legislators and judges. Also, the petition must consist of signatures of each of at least five counties equal in number to 1% of the last vote for the office in that county (California's Constitution, Article 2).

5.3. Local officials

The number of valid signatures needed to raise the recall question on a local basis is determined by the following rules:

For the officials of a city, county, school district, county board of education, or any resident voting district, signatures from the following percentage of registered voters is required:

- 30% in jurisdictions with 0 - 1,000 registered voters;
- 25% in jurisdictions with 1,000 - 10,000 registered voters;
- 20% in jurisdictions with 10,000 - 50,000 registered voters;
- 15% in jurisdictions with 50,000 - 100,000 registered voters;
- 10% in jurisdictions with 100,000 or more registered voters.

In Los Angeles, the threshold for a recall is 15% of signatures. This signature requirement is set by the city's charter (Initiative, Referendum & Recall Petition Handbook).

5.4. County judges

According to section 14 of Article 2 of the California Constitution, the required petition for a recall is 20% of the votes cast for the judge in the last election, rather than a percentage registered (California State Consitution).

In the case of a county superior court judge position that did not appear on the ballot at the last relevant election, signatures equaling 20% of votes cast for whichever countywide office received the least total number of votes in the most recent general election in the judge's county must be collected to qualify a recall of the judge for the ballot.

5.5. Can one recall a federal official?

The constitution of the USA does not allow a recall of any federally elected official. However, some state constitutions stated that the citizens have the full right to recall members of congress. The Supreme Court has not ruled on whether this is constitutional at a federal level.

Petition process: The process of submitting a petition begins with the issuance of petitions for a recall, and it is first submitted a notice with the intention of revocation, written in the appropriate legal language, provided that 65 voters sign it. Once this condition is met, the petition can be formally submitted. Voters must sign petitions for the dismissal of state officials, i.e., 12% of the voters for that district. Petitions to recall state legislators must account for 20% of the total votes for that district.

The recall ballot is composed of two components: a yes or no to vote for a recall as well as the names of candidates that are proposed for a substitute, selected by the nomination process used in regular elections. The recall is considered successful if it passes by a majority. In that case, the replacement candidate with a simple plurality of votes wins the office. If the recall measure fails, the replacement candidate votes are ignored.

The language in the recall provision is strictly procedural. Substantive grounds for recalls are not specified. Recalls can be launched to remove corrupt officials and to remove officials whose policies and performance are found wanting. The recall is but one of several mechanisms for removing public officers. Others include the normal criminal process, impeachment, term limits, and, of course, the next election.

Notice of intent: A minimum number for a state recall is 65, and many signatures are required on the nomination paper of the officer against whom recall is sought for local recall. For a recall of an official, Petitioners must submit a notice of intention to the city or district clerk for a local recall and to the California Secretary of State for a state recall. The notice must contain the following elements:

Delivery to the officer to be recalled: This notice of intention must be delivered by the clerk or Secretary of State that received the notice of intent to the officer in question.

Publication of the notice of intent: Proponents must, if possible, publish the notice of intent in a general circulation newspaper. If no such newspaper operates in the officer's jurisdiction to be recalled, proponents must post the notice of intent in at least three public places.

Official's answer: Within seven days of being served with the notice of intent, the official against whom a recall is being attempted can officially file an answer to the recall proponents and a statement of defense against the recall attempt. The official answer can be no more than 200 words in length.

Sample ballot: The reason given on the notice of intent and the officials answering statement must be included on the sample ballot for the election on which the recall will be featured and mailed to each registered voter in the relevant jurisdiction.

Petition form: The Secretary of State must provide a petition format to proponents on request from the county elections department. Proponents must use the provided format to collect signatures.

Each signer must personally write in the following:

- His or her signatures
- His or her printed name
- His or her residence address
- Name of city or unincorporated community of residence

Replacement candidates: The official against whom the recall is sought cannot submit himself or herself as a possible replacement candidate.

State recall: For a state recall, every candidate who wants to be considered to replace the official against whom the recall is sought must submit the standard nomination papers and a declaration of candidacy at least 59 days before the recall election date.

Local recall: For a local recall, every candidate that wants to be considered to replace the official against whom the recall is sought must submit the standard nomination papers and the declaration of candidacy at least 75 days before the date of the recall election (*California elections code Section 11381*).

5.6. Ballot language

On the election ballot, voters are asked the following:

Shall [name of officer sought to be recalled] be recalled (removed) from the office of [title of office]? Additionally, under the recall question, the ballot will include a list of candidates to take the place of official submitted for recall in the event of a successful recall vote. The list of candidates must include a space for voters to write in a candidate of their own (Laws governing recall in California, Ballotpedia).

Election results: If most electors vote "yes" on the recall question, the official in question will be recalled from office. If a majority of electors vote "no," the official will remain in office. In the event of a successful recall, the replacement candidate who receives the most votes will serve the remainder of the recalled official's term. If no replacement candidate is nominated or qualifies for the position, the office will be vacant and filled according to the relevant laws governing vacancies (Laws governing recall in California).

5.7 Notable California recalls

Maybe the most famous recall election in history happened in California in 2003, when Governor Gray Davis was recalled and the actor Arnold Schwarzenegger took his place. This event was a subject of debate among the public. It was given a lot of attention and media space due to both California's size and importance and the fact that many celebrities, such as Arnold Schwarzenegger himself, were running to replace Gray Davis.

Although the primary purpose of the recalls is meant for local officials like mayors and state governors, they also might apply to presidents, MPs, or the entire legislature (Jovanovska, 2). The arguments for the right of a recall are due to the public responsibility of the elected officials. It is a way to prevent inappropriate behavior while doing their job, to which the citizens appoint them, and provide the citizens with a mechanism of protection from bad policies.

On the other hand, the recalls are criticized because they are considered to contribute to a higher level of polarization between political parties. This is because they give an implicit invitation to sabotage a rival's performance. The effects of recall can cause damage in terms of undermining the entire decision-making process, which would prevent politicians from making bold and necessary political decisions (Konrad-Adenauer-Stiftung, 2011).

5.8. Re-conceptualizing representation

This raises a fundamental question: can the recall procedure affect the destruction of the free parliamentary democracy? If dismissals force elected officials to do just what they promised during the election campaign, they may be demotivated to think freely and evaluate things independently. Such constraints are not compatible with the dynamic policy process. Different problems are identified all the time, and solutions are negotiated and discussed. Finally, removing elected officials from critical and constructive thinking can severely limit their ability to do their job correctly (Reynolds et al., 1999).

Nevertheless, will the recalls inevitably contribute to the overthrow of the democratic government? It is important to note that there is evidence to the contrary. Given that the secret ballot does not reveal who voted for the elected and what exactly are their expectations (Goodin, 2008). Hence, it is evident that they can not be bound by the will of the persons who elect them. Furthermore, it is a generally accepted fact that elected officials do not represent only those who voted for them but the entire constituency. Even if their political mandate is a continuous link of ideological sympathy and communication with the plurality of their constituents, they are characterized by sovereign power on behalf of the entire abstract commonwealth (people, state, nation).

As a result, elected officials think in terms of the general will - not in favor of the individual will of those who vote for them. The recalls do not challenge this multidirectional form of representation, and their premise is to represent and defend the community's goals as a whole. Quite the contrary, the recalls contribute to strengthening the legitimacy and representativeness of the legislature (Vandamme, 6).

5.9. Do recalls foster populist politics?

Another feature of recalls is that with the politicization of corruption, they come directly into the hands of populist parties. The impeachments in principle form a bipolar image of corrupt politicians and a united, morally superior citizenship. Instead of political pluralism, the bottom line is that it recalls promoting material and socially exceptional definitions of the people. The recalls are essential because they provide space for debate and debate on allegations of political corruption, protect against conspiracy theories and any baseless allegations that may be perceived as political action (Malkopoulou, 2015).

The recalls may act as pull-outs of the rug from under the populists' feet. This situation results from their political identity, which feeds on a lot of publicity, more popularized scandals but often unsustainable. In search of support, populists are deprived of the opportunity to manage the anti-corruption movement. However, the risk of withdrawing from a political position as a mechanism for getting rid of their rivals remains. Also, the tactics of mobilizing the majority of the population against specific individuals may have discriminatory tendencies. It is particularly risky in countries where political divisions reflect ethnic, linguistic, or other characteristics. However, institutions have mechanisms to avoid both problems, such as denying recalls when elections occur. The challenge for minorities can be overcome by imposing high thresholds for confirmation of recall and requesting a legislative review of recall (Cain, 2015).

5.10. A form of democratic self-defense?

The type of political explanation for the recall deserves special attention. Apart from transparency and accountability, although unrecognized, recall is a tool for democratic self-defense. When the extreme- right is on the rise in Western democracies, counter-policies quickly turn into controversies. Before this, the recall may serve as a possibility for legitimate withdrawal of the mandates of non-democratic politicians. Without impeachments, democracies can embrace one of the two enduring paradigms of pro-democracy action. The first is the form of militant democracy. This model provides constitutional protection for democracy and prohibits the existence of political parties (Birch and Muchlinski, 400).

The first is the model of militant democracy. This constitutionally protects democracy and thus allows for the prohibition of political parties and the restriction of individual freedoms on its behalf. According to this model, representative institutions must be protected from decisions that may undermine democracy, even if this involves circumventing the democratic process. The model is often criticized where democratic goals justify undemocratic means. An alternative option, and at the same time the second model opposite to this one, is procedural democracy, which does not set a framework that restricts political expression.

In a broader picture, the model of procedural democracy favors democratic procedures over the quality of the decisions they produce, even if they are essentially undemocratic. This situation contributes to procedural democracies being often accused of passive resignation and escalating undemocratic movements in democratic societies. However, it may lead to increased security measures and policing, which may reduce individual freedoms. To summarize: what we need are democratic procedures that will oppose extremism without compromising the substance of the decisions produced as a result of their use.

Such a neo-procedural approach to democratic self-defense would mean strengthening democratic procedures explicitly designed to protect the system from internal erosion. Revocations are the best option for this. They take place separately from regular elections, applying the procedural standards of democratic elections, using a particular type (usually negative) political assessment.

The general distrust of the masses is in itself an anti-democratic perspective influenced by post-war elitism. This is partly due to the distorted contribution of the rise of Nazism to mass participation. This ignored the importance of Weimar's "misfortune" with constitutional manipulation and the collapse of intra-party negotiations. Unless this unsubstantiated suspicion of democratic participation is overcome and voters are not recognized as defenders of (and not a threat to) a democratic state, the potential for withdrawals to function as democratic tools against extremism cannot be exploited. (Malkopoulou, 2015).

One of the events that caused turmoil on the political scene in California was the recall of Governor Gray Davis, whom Arnold Schwarzenegger replaced. It is essential to ask the question: what have we learned from this recall? At the outset, it should be noted that recall is a tool of direct democracy. Although the collection of signatures preceded the recall, the success of the withdrawal ultimately depended on the political movement surpassing party politics in the ways that the creators of direct democracy envisioned.

Indeed, the recall of Governor Davis was a pure reflection of the activities of a particular interest group that was able to reach beyond partisan and ideological lines and tap into public discontent with an elected official and change of the public policy.

One of the main factors is the adverse political climate as well as the positive attitude towards the recall process. Surprising, however, is the recall of a newly re-elected governor in a state such as California, which is considered a "safe" democracy during elections.

According to data from PPIC Statewide Surveys, voters are unusually attracted to the knowledge that they have the power to remove an elected official. The fact that the Democratic Party is unable to mobilize the entire electorate to defeat the impeachment is evident in almost all research on this topic. Interestingly, many candidates supported the recall and disapproved of the governor's result. They saw the recall as an appropriate way to oust Davis.

The same trends were observed in all voters. It is important to note that Democratic Party voters did not oppose the recall until next month, but it is evident that this number was not enough to prevent a repeat of the special election. In this election, Republican Arnold Schwarzenegger defeated the governor of the Democratic candidate, Cruz Bustamante, by a large margin (49% vs. 32%). Despite appeals from many Democratic leaders to vote for Democrat Bustamante, the governor's office to continue to be run by a Democrat, according to the Los Angeles Times, Democrats show a fascinating pattern of behavior, with one in three Democrats voting for the opposite party on the ballot for replacement.

The role of partisanship played a significant role in the recall process. Republicans have given strong support in terms of voting to oust Governor Davis. According to some analysts, the impeachment could have taken place with more votes if the Democrats, who disapproved of Davis' performance and considered the impeachment appropriate, voted for the impeachment. Nevertheless, many of them voted for Davis to remain in office. According to a study by Elizabeth Garrett, in California, 6 in 10 Californians said that the recall process itself required changes due to what they observed in the course of the election. A similar proportion said they wanted the law changed so that elected officials can only be recalled for unethical or illegal behavior.

The same number of people preferred to increase the required number of signatures to put a candidate on the recall list, given the ease with which lobbyists mobilized signature collection, and 7 out of 10 Californians wanted to raise the threshold for signatures to nominate a candidate to replace the recalled. Six out of 10 voters thought that the recall process should include a runoff election if no replacement candidate gets more than 50 percent of the vote (Baldasare et al., 2003).

According to the survey, three out of four voters think the recall is good in the last days of the election. Only one in four voters said they were less likely to support a future recall based on their experience. Consequently, some people believe that the recall of Governor Davis could impose a practice for a recall in the following years, mirroring the 25-year history of the citizen's initiative after the passage of the Proposition 13 tax limits.

However, the future use and ultimate success of this tool for direct democracy depend on the likelihood of a recurrence of the adverse political climate and the basis of public support for recall in theory and practice that transcends partisanship and ideology in the memory of the 2003 California governor (Populism, Partisanship, 180).

The recalls are a product of the dramatic fusion between representative institutions and direct democracy. The recalls shed new light on issues important to the electoral process at the national, regional, and local levels. The very act of recall represents an increase in lawsuits as a political weapon. It gives perspective to the issues studied by those working in areas such as political parties, independent candidates, and ballots. A recall is not a radical act but provides a new form of analysis of the important issues for the design of democratic institutions (Garrett, 239).

5.11. Recall history in California from 1913 – onward

Since 1913, there have been 179 recall attempts of state elected officials in California. Eleven recall collected enough signatures to qualify for the ballot, and of those, the elected official was recalled in six instances. One recall effort is currently qualified for the ballot to be held in September 2021 (California Secretary of State, 2021).

The table below presents a chronological listing of every attempted recall of an elected state official in California. For this history, a recall attempt is defined as a Notice of Intention to recall an official that is filed with the Secretary of State's Office.

Year	Elected officials
1913	Senator Marshall Black, 28th Senate District (Santa Clara County) Qualified for the ballot, recall succeeded Vote percentages not available Herbert C. Jones elected successor; Senator Edwin E. Grant, 19th Senate District (San Francisco County) Failed to qualify for the ballot.
1914	Senator Edwin E. Grant, 19th Senate District (San Francisco County) Qualified for the ballot, recall succeeded Vote percentages not available Edwin I. Wolfe elected successor Senator James C. Owens, 9th Senate District (Marin and Contra Costa counties) Qualified for the ballot, officer retained.
1916	Assemblyman Frank Finley Merriam Failed to qualify for the ballot
1939	Governor Culbert L. Olson Failed to qualify for the ballot Governor Culbert L. Olson Filed by Olson Recall Committee Failed to qualify for the ballot Governor Culbert L. Olson Filed by Citizens Olson Recall Committee Failed to qualify for the ballot
1940	Governor Culbert L. Olson Filed by Olson Recall Committee Failed to qualify for the ballot Governor Culbert L. Olson Filed by Olson Recall Committee Failed to qualify for the ballot
1960	Governor Edmund G. Brown Filed by Roderick J. Wilson Failed to qualify for the ballot
1965	Assemblyman William F. Stanton, 25th Assembly District (Santa Clara County) Filed by Jerome J. Ducote Failed to qualify for the ballot Assemblyman John Burton, 20th Assembly District (San Francisco County) Filed by John Carney Failed to qualify for the ballot Assemblyman Willie L. Brown, 18th Assembly District (San Francisco County) Filed by Terry R. Macken Failed to qualify for the ballot Assemblyman William

F. Stanton, 25th Assembly District (Santa Clara County) Filed by Frederick S. Reinheimer Failed to qualify for the ballot Governor Edmund G. Brown Filed by C. Fain Kyle Failed to qualify for the ballot Governor Edmund G. Brown Filed by L.J. Beauchamp Failed to qualify for the ballot

1966   CA State Chief Justice of the Supreme Court Roger Traynor CA State Associate Justices of the Supreme Court: Marshall McComb, Raymond Peters, Mathew Tobriner, Stanley Mosk, Louis Burke, and Raymond Sullivan. Filed by C. Fain Kyle Failed to qualify for the ballot

1967   Senator Joseph Kennick, 33rd Senate District (Fresno and Madera counties) Filed by Charles D. Linza Failed to qualify for the ballot Assemblyman David Negri, 41st Assembly District (Los Angeles County) Filed by Sam Cordova Failed to qualify for the ballot

Governor Ronald Reagan Filed by Nancy L. Parr Failed to qualify for the ballot Assemblyman Charles W. Meyers, 19th Assembly District (San Francisco County) Filed by John Robert Visnick Failed to qualify for the ballot

1968   Governor Ronald Reagan Filed by Joyce A. Koupal and James E. Berg Failed to qualify for the ballot

1972   Governor Ronald Reagan Filed by Margaret Bullard Failed to qualify for the ballot

1977   Governor Edmund G. Brown, Jr. Filed by Patricia Dolbeare Failed to qualify for the ballot

1979   Assemblyman Carmen Perino, 26th Assembly District (San Joaquin and Stanislaus counties) Filed by Doug Carter Failed to qualify for the ballot Assemblyman Carmen Perino, 26th Assembly District (San Joaquin and Stanislaus counties) Filed by A. Guy and B. Wikoff Failed to qualify for the ballot Assemblyman John Thurman, 27th Assembly District

(Merced and Stanislaus Counties) Filed by Roland Lapham Failed to qualify for the ballot Governor Edmund G. Brown, Jr. Filed by Frank James Compton Failed to qualify for the ballot Governor Edmund G. Brown, Jr. Filed by Cecil Gibson Failed to qualify for the ballot.

1980   Governor Edmund G. Brown, Jr. Filed by Cecil Gibson (4/16/80) Failed to qualify for the ballot Governor Edmund G. Brown, Jr. Filed by Cecil Gibson (10/18/80) Failed to qualify for the ballot Senator Alan Robbins, 20th Senate District (Los Angeles County) Filed by Jan Tucker Failed to qualify for the ballot Senator Alan Robbins, 20th Senate District (Los Angeles County) Filed by Andrew Sigel Failed to qualify for the ballot Senator Alan Robbins, 20th Senate District (Los Angeles County) Filed by S. Stevens Failed to qualify for the ballot.

1981   CA State Chief Justice of the Supreme Court Rose Elizabeth Bird Filed by Marvin Feldman, Tony Rackaukas, Ingrid Azevedo Failed to qualify for the ballot Senator Alan Robbins, 20th Senate District (Los Angeles) Filed by Jan Tucker Failed to qualify for the ballot

1982   CA State Chief Justice of the Supreme Court Rose Elizabeth Bird Filed by Marvin Feldman Failed to qualify for the ballot CA State Chief Justice of the Supreme Court Rose Elizabeth Bird Filed by H.L. Richardson and Carol Hallett Failed to qualify for the ballot CA State Chief Justice of the Supreme Court Rose Elizabeth Bird Filed by George Nicholson, Patrick Nolan, and Tony Racauckas Failed to qualify for the ballot CA State Chief Justice of the Supreme Court Rose Elizabeth Bird Filed by Tony Racauckas (4/29/82) Failed to qualify for the ballot

CA State Chief Justice of the Supreme Court Rose Elizabeth Bird Filed by Tony Racauckas (6/21/82) Failed to qualify for the ballot CA State Chief Justice of the Supreme Court Rose

Elizabeth Bird Filed by Tony Racauckas (8/3/82) Failed to qualify for the ballot.

1983 CA State Chief Justice of the Supreme Court Rose Elizabeth Bird Filed by D. Carnessale Failed to qualify for the ballot Governor George Deukmejian Filed by Michael Greenspan and Charles Brookey Failed to qualify for the ballot Governor George Deukmejian Filed by M.P. Baltzer, George Baltzer, Johnny Van Pelt, and Cynthia Van Pelt Failed to qualify for the ballot Governor George Deukmejian Filed by R. Ahl Failed to qualify for the ballot.

1984 Senator John Doolittle, 1st Senate District (El Dorado, Lassen, Modoc, Nevada, Placer, Plumas, Sacramento, Sierra, Siskiyou, Sutter, Trinity, Yolo, and Yuba counties.) Filed by Ranold Kennedy Failed to qualify for the ballot.

1985 Governor George Deukmejian Filed by Michael Bogatirev Failed to qualify for the ballot Senator Henry Mello, 17th Senate District (Monterey, San Benito, Santa Clara, and Santa Cruz counties) Filed by Michael Bogatirev Failed to qualify for the ballot Assemblyman Sam Farr, 28th Assembly District (Monterey and Santa Cruz counties) Filed by Michael Bogatirev and Harry Snell Failed to qualify for the ballot

Senator John Doolittle, 1st Senate District (El Dorado, Lassen, Modoc, Nevada, Placer, Plumas, Sacramento, Sierra, Siskiyou, Sutter, Trinity, Yolo, and Yuba counties) Filed by Ranold Kennedy Failed to qualify for the ballot.

1986 Governor George Deukmejian Filed by Michael Bogatirev, Timothy Grady, and Harry Snell Failed to qualify for the ballot Senator Henry Mello, 17th Senate District (Monterey, San Benito, Santa Clara, and Santa Cruz counties) Filed by Michael Bogatirev, Timothy Grady, and Harry Snell Failed to qualify for the ballot Assemblyman Sam Farr, 28th Assembly District (Monterey and

Santa Cruz counties) Filed by Michael Bogatirev and Timothy Grady Failed to qualify for the ballot Assemblyman Sam Farr, 28th Assembly District (Monterey and Santa Cruz counties) Filed by Peter Austin Failed to qualify for the ballot CA State Associate Justice of the Supreme Court Cruz Reynoso Filed by Michael Bogatirev (8/8/86) Failed to qualify for the ballot CA State Associate Justice of the Supreme Court Cruz Reynoso Filed by Michael Bogatirev (9/4/86) Failed to qualify for the ballot CA State Associate Justice of the Supreme Court Stanley Mosk Filed by Michael Bogatirev (7/21/86) Failed to qualify for the ballot CA State Associate Justice of the Supreme Court Stanley Mosk Filed by Michael Bogatirev (8/1/86) Failed to qualify for the ballot CA State Associate Justice of the Supreme Court Stanley Mosk Filed by Michael Bogatirev (9/2/86) Failed to qualify for the ballot

CA State Associate Justice of the Supreme Court Joseph Grodin Filed by Michael Bogatirev and Timothy Grady (8/15/86) Failed to qualify for the ballot CA State Associate Justice of the Supreme Court Justice Allen Broussard Filed by Michael Bogatirev and Timothy Grady (9/4/86) Failed to qualify for the ballot Governor George Deukmejian Filed by Michael Bogatirev and Timothy Grady (2/3/86) Failed to qualify for the ballot Governor George Deukmejian Filed by Michael Bogatirev and Timothy Grady (2/21/86) Failed to qualify for the ballot CA State Chief Justice of the Supreme Court Rose Elizabeth Bird Filed by Michael Bogatirev, Timothy Grady, and John Hammond Failed to qualify for the ballot CA State Associate Justices of the Supreme Court Malcolm Lucas and Edward Panelli Filed by Michael Bogatirev and Timothy Grady Failed to qualify for the ballot Lieutenant Governor Leo McCarthy Filed by Michael Bogatirev and Timothy Grady Failed to qualify for the ballot.

1987   Senator Henry Mello, 17th Senate District (Monterey, San Benito, Santa Clara, and Santa Cruz counties) Filed by Michael Bogatirev Failed to qualify for the ballot Assemblyman Sam Farr, 28th Assembly District (Monterey and Santa Cruz counties) Filed by Michael Bogatirev Failed to qualify for the ballot Assemblyman Paul Zeltner, 54th Assembly District (Los Angeles County) Filed by Donald Plunkett Failed to qualify for the ballot CA State Associate Justice of the Supreme Court Stanley Mosk Filed by Michael Bogatirev and James Olson Failed to qualify for the ballot

CA State Associate Justice of the Supreme Court John Arguelles Filed by Michael Bogatirev and Gravinski (10/27/87) Failed to qualify for the ballot CA State Associate Justice of the Supreme Court Marcus Kaufman Filed by Michael Bogatirev and Gravinski (10/27/87) Failed to qualify for the ballot CA State Associate Justice of the Supreme Court Allen Broussard Filed by Michael Bogatirev and James Olson Failed to qualify for the ballot CA State Associate Justice of the Supreme Court Edward Panelli Filed by Michael Bogatirev and James Olson Failed to qualify for the ballot Governor George Deukmejian Filed by Michael Bogatirev and Douglas Cupp Sr. Failed to qualify for the ballot Attorney General John Van de Kamp Filed by Michael Bogatirev (5/20/87) Failed to qualify for the ballot Attorney General John Van de Kamp Filed by Michael Bogatirev (6/10/87) Failed to qualify for the ballot CA State Chief Justice of the Supreme Court Malcolm Lucas Filed by Michael Bogatirev and Douglas Cupp, Sr. Failed to qualify for the ballot

1988   Assemblyman Tom Hannigan, 4th Assembly District (Solano and Yolo counties) Filed by Ralph Morrell (5/9/88) Failed to qualify for the ballot Assemblyman Tom Hannigan, 4th

Assembly District (Solano and Yolo counties) Filed by Ralph Morrell, Barbara MacArthur, Maxine Young, Tonie Scott, and David Scott (5/24/88) Failed to qualify for the ballot

Assemblyman Sam Farr, 28th Assembly District (Monterey and Santa Cruz counties) Filed by Michael Bogatirev Failed to qualify for the ballot Assemblyman Steve Clute, 68th Assembly District (Riverside County) Filed by Harold Payne Failed to qualify for the ballot CA State Associate Justice of the Supreme Court Edward Panelli Filed by Michael Bogatirev and Russ Farrer Failed to qualify for the ballot CA State Associate Justice of the Supreme Court Allen Broussard Filed by Michael Bogatirev and Russ Farrer Failed to qualify for the ballot CA State Chief Justice of the Supreme Court Malcolm Lucas Filed by Michael Bogatirev and Russ Farrer Failed to qualify for the ballot Governor George Deukmejian Filed by Michael Bogatirev and Russ Farrer Failed to qualify for the ballot.

1989   Assemblyman Jack O'Connell, 35th Assembly District (Santa Barbara and Ventura counties) Filed by Charles L. Townsend, William E. Cullen, Fayne S. McElroy, and Joseph B. Conyers Failed to qualify for the ballot Assemblyman Rusty Areias, 25th Assembly District (Merced, Monterey, San Benito, and Santa Clara counties) Filed by Robert Keith Alber, Robert A. Adams, and Charles Mark Atkins (5/23/89) Failed to qualify for the ballot Assemblyman Jerry Eaves, 66th Assembly District (San Bernardino County) Filed by Robert A. Estes, Gilbert R. Berry, Arthur E. Throop, Jeff Bell, and Jerry Lee Wilson (4/6/89) Failed to qualify for the ballot

Assemblyman Rusty Areias, 25th Assembly District (Merced, Monterey, San Benito, and Santa Clara counties) Filed by Robert Keith Alber, Robert A. Adams, Edward R. Powers, and Cal J. Eustpaquio (7/31/89) Failed to qualify for the ballot Senator Bill Greene, 27th Senate District (Los Angeles County) Filed by Esther M. Lofton (9/6/89) Failed to qualify for the ballot Senator Bill Greene, 27th Senate District (Los Angeles County) Filed by Esther M. Lofton (9/13/89) Failed to qualify for the ballot Senator Bill Greene, 27th Senate District (Los Angeles County) Filed by Esther M. Lofton (10/6/89) Failed to qualify for the ballot Assemblyman Steve Clute, 68th Assembly District (Riverside County) Filed by Harold Paul Payne, Dennis E. Bransford, Brenton D.Glisson, Stephen T.Goodrich, and Harold Lee Dame (4/5/89) Failed to qualify for the ballot Assemblyman Rusty Areias, 25th Assembly District (Merced, Monterey, San Benito, and Santa Clara counties) Filed by Robert Keith Alber, Robert A. Adams, and Charles Mark Atkins (7/6/89) Failed to qualify for the ballot Assemblyman Steve Clute, 68th Assembly District (Riverside County) Filed by Lee A. Rutledge, David W. Duncan, Clarence C. Martin, Robert Martin, and John Reinken (6/6/89) Failed to qualify for the ballot Assemblyman Steve Clute, 68th Assembly District (Riverside County) Filed by Harold P. Payne, John H. Bray, Ralph P. Mueller, Cecil L.Cook, and James R. Sandidge (6/7/89) Failed to qualify for the ballot Assemblyman Steve Clute, 68th Assembly District (Riverside County) Filed by Lee A. Rutledge, Clarence C. Martin, Darrel W. Martin, Velma Berg, and Harold A. Berg (6/29/89) Failed to qualify for the ballot

Assemblyman Steve Clute, 68th Assembly District (Riverside County) Filed by Lee A. Rutledge, Clarence C. Martin, Raynelle O. Martin, George Kallman, and Leonard V. Martin (7/11/89) Failed to qualify for the ballot Assemblyman Bruce Bronzan, 31st Assembly District (Fresno County) Filed by Mathew B.Gerawan of Sanger and Eric A. Benjamin (9/25/89) Failed to qualify for the ballot Assemblyman Bruce Bronzan, 31st Assembly District (Fresno County) Filed by Mathew B.Gerawan of Sanger and Eric A. Benjamin (10/5/89) Failed to qualify for the ballot Governor George Deukmejian Filed by Michael Bogatirev (9/29/89) Failed to qualify for the ballot Governor George Deukmejian Filed by Michael Bogatirev (11/13/89) Failed to qualify for the ballot.

1990   Assemblyman Sam Farr, 28th Assembly District (Monterey and Santa Cruz counties) Filed By Michael Bogatirev and Daniel E. Donnelly (5/17/90) Failed to qualify for the ballot Assemblyman Sam Farr, 28th Assembly District (Monterey and Santa Cruz counties) Filed By Michael Bogatirev and Daniel E. Donnelly (6/4/90) Failed to qualify for the ballot Assemblyman Sam Farr, 28th Assembly District (Monterey and Santa Cruz counties) Filed By Michael Bogatirev and Daniel E. Donnelly (8/1/90) Failed to qualify for the ballot

1991   Senator Lucy Killea, 39th Senate District (San Diego County) Filed by Joe Naiman (5/14/91) Failed to qualify for the ballot Senator Lucy Killea, 39th Senate District (San Diego County) Filed by Joe Naiman (6/10/91) Failed to qualify for the ballot

Governor Pete Wilson Filed by Deborah Murray, Teresa S. Squier, Herbert C. Redlack, Sharon Moad, and Corinne Lavorico Failed to qualify for the ballot Governor Pete Wilson Filed by Lorna G. Fowler, Emily L. Powell, Patricia L. Williams, and Elmer E. Powell Failed to qualify for the ballot Assemblywoman Deirdre Alpert, 75th Assembly District (San Diego County) Filed by Bernabe Barr Urbano Ambrosio, Henry J. Brantingham, Sally Sue Booth, Elaine A. Brantingham, and Littleton W. T. Waller Failed to qualify for the ballot Assemblywoman Tricia Hunter, 76th Assembly District (San Diego and Riverside Counties) Filed by Alicia L.M.Cross, Randolph A. Cross, George R. Moody, and Lexie B. Boswell Failed to qualify for the ballot

1992   Governor Pete Wilson Filed by Peter James Failed to qualify for the ballot Governor Pete Wilson Filed by Gordon Reynolds,

Joseph DeSiata, Deborah Murray, A. Lee Sanders, and Janice L. Tracey Failed to qualify for the ballot Governor Pete Wilson Filed by Gary Karnes and Ralph White Failed to qualify for the ballot Governor Pete Wilson Filed by Barbara Brammer, Mary Reyna, Patrick Hill, and Robert Cunha Failed to qualify for the ballot.

1993   Senator David Roberti, 20th Senate District (Los Angeles County) Filed by William A. Dominguez, John R. Vernon, Hans Rusche, Dolores White, and Glenn C. Bailey Qualified for the ballot: Recall election April 12, 1994, Recall failed- 40.75% in favor; 59.25% opposed

1994   Assemblyman Michael Machado, 17th Assembly District (San Joaquin County) Filed by Dean F. Andal of Stockton and 62 others Qualified for the ballot: Recall election August 22, 1995 Recall failed -37.02% in favor; 62.98% opposed Assemblyman Sal Cannella, 26th Assembly District (Merced, San Joaquin, and Stanislaus counties) Filed by Jared C. Burris, Cindy L. Burris, and 58 others Failed to qualify for the ballot Assemblywoman Deirdre Alpert, 78th Assembly District (San Diego County) Filed by Marian Uzzalino, Joseph M. Giardiello, and 52 others Failed to qualify for the ballot Assemblyman Paul Horcher, 60th Assembly District (Los Angeles County) Filed by Timothy J. Vrieling, and 59 others Qualified for the ballot: Recall election May 16, 1995, Recall succeeded- 61.63% in favor; 38.37% opposed Gary G. Miller elected successor

1995   Dean Andal, Board of Equalization, 2nd District Filed by Jennet Stebbins and 55 others (1/12/95) Failed to qualify for the ballot Dean Andal, Board of Equalization, 2nd District Filed by Jennet Stebbins and 57 others (1/25/95) Failed to qualify for the ballot Assemblyman Ross Johnson, 72nd Assembly District (Orange County) Filed by Jacob Spaargaren and 46 others Failed to qualify for the ballot Assemblywoman Doris Allen,

67th Assembly District (Orange County) Filed by Edward R. Fafara and 59 others Qualified for the ballot: Recall election November 28, 1995, Recall succeeded - 65.19% in favor; 34.81% opposed Scott R. Baugh elected successor Governor Pete Wilson Filed by Jayne Liera, and 101 others Failed to qualify for the ballot.

1997 CA State Chief Justice of the Supreme Court Ronald M. George Filed by Fred G. Labankoff and 10 others Failed to qualify for the ballot.

1999 Governor Gray Davis Filed by Glenn J. Spencer, and 73 others Failed to qualify for the ballot Senator Kevin Murray, 26th Senate District (Los Angeles County) Filed by Doris Hill and 99 others Failed to qualify for the ballot Assemblyman Roderick D. Wright, 48th Assembly District (Los Angeles County) Filed by Doris Hill and 99 others Failed to qualify for the ballot.

2000 Insurance Commissioner Chuck Quackenbush Filed by Sandra J. Webb and 108 others Failed to qualify for the ballot

2003 Governor Gray Davis Filed by Edward L. Nicholson and 9 others Failed to qualify for the ballot Governor Gray Davis Filed by Edward J. Costa and 98 others Qualified for the ballot: Recall election October 7, 2003, Recall succeeded- 55.4% in favor; 44.6% opposed Arnold Schwarzenegger elected successor

2004 Governor Arnold Schwarzenegger Filed by Henry F. Ramey Jr. and 64 others Failed to qualify for the ballot

2005 Governor Arnold Schwarzenegger Filed by Kenneth Matsumura and 121 others (10/7/05) Failed to qualify for the ballot Governor Arnold Schwarzenegger Filed by Kenneth Matsumura and 105 others (11/16/05) Failed to qualify for the ballot

2007 Senator Jeffrey Denham, 12th Senate District (Madera, Merced, Monterey, San Benito, and Stanislaus counties) Filed by

Gary D. Robbins and 49 others Recall election June 3, 2008, Recall failed- 24.64% in favor; 75.36% opposed

2008   Governor Arnold Schwarzenegger Filed by Mike Jimenez and 84 others Failed to qualify for the ballot

2009   Senator Roy Ashburn, 18th Senate District (Inyo, Kern, San Bernardino, and Tulare counties) Filed by Michael Moore and 50 others (3/10/09) Failed to qualify for the ballot Senator Roy Ashburn, 18th Senate District (Inyo, Kern, San Bernardino, and Tulare counties) Filed by Michael Moore and 79 others (3/20/09) Failed to qualify for the ballot Governor Arnold Schwarzenegger Filed by John D. Fusek and 110 others (3/20/09) Failed to qualify for the ballot Governor Arnold Schwarzenegger Filed by ET Snell and 112 others (3/23/09) Failed to qualify for the ballot Assemblyman Anthony Adams, 59th Assembly District (Los Angeles and San Bernardino counties) Filed by ET Snell and 112 others (3/23/09) Failed to qualify for the ballot Assemblyman Anthony Adams, 59th Assembly District (Los Angeles and San Bernardino counties) Filed by David Bartels and 54 others (4/13/09) Failed to qualify for the ballot Governor Arnold Schwarzenegger Filed by John D. Fusek and 119 others (4/17/09) Failed to qualify for the ballot Assemblyman Jim Silva, 67th Assembly District (Orange County) Filed by Bradford Bach and 49 others (4/20/09) Failed to qualify for the ballot

Senator Bob Huff, 29th Senate District (Los Angeles, Orange, and San Bernardino counties) Filed by Paul Griffin and 49 others (5/06/09) Failed to qualify for the ballot Assemblyman Jeff Miller, 71st Assembly District (Orange and Riverside counties) Filed by Jeffrey Sawyer and 48 others (5/19/09) Failed to qualify for the ballot Assemblywoman Alyson Huber, 10th Assembly District (Amador, El Dorado, Sacramento, and San Joaquin counties) Filed by Anthony F. Andrade, Jr. and 49 others

(7/29/09) Failed to qualify for the ballot Assemblywoman Alyson Huber, 10th Assembly District (Amador, El Dorado, Sacramento, and San Joaquin counties) Filed by Anthony F. Andrade, Jr. and 57 others (8/10/09) Failed to qualify for the ballot Attorney General Edmund G. Brown Filed by Issac Park Yonker and 9 others (9/23/09) Failed to qualify for the ballot Attorney General Edmund G. Brown Filed by Issac Park Yonker and 87 others (10/09/09) Failed to qualify for the ballot.

2012   Governor Jerry Brown Filed by Edgar Origel and 9 others (5/17/12) Failed to qualify for the ballot Governor Jerry Brown Filed by James D. Smith and 9 others (11/01/12) Failed to qualify for the ballot Attorney General Kamala D. Harris Filed by James D. Smith and 9 others (11/01/12) Failed to qualify for the ballot

2013   Governor Jerry Brown Filed by James D. Smith and 90 others (10/23/13) Failed to qualify for the ballot

2015   Senator Richard Pan, 6th Senate District (Sacramento and Yolo counties) Filed by Katherine Duran and 49 others (6/5/15) Failed to qualify for the ballot Senator Bill Monning, 17th Senate District (Monterey, San Luis Obispo, Santa Clara, and Santa Cruz counties) Filed by Michael D. Lelieur and 59 others (6/9/15) Failed to qualify for the ballot

Governor Jerry Brown Filed by Lauren Stephens and 74 others (10/29/15) Failed to qualify for the ballot

2017   Senator Josh Newman, 29th Senate District (Los Angeles, Orange, and San Bernardino counties) Filed by Elvira Moreno and 59 others (4/19/17) Qualified for the ballot: Recall election June 8, 2018, Recall succeeded - 58.1% in favor, 41.9% opposed Ling Ling Chang (R) elected successor Assemblyman Anthony Rendon, 63rd Assembly District (Los Angeles County) Filed by Veronica Osuna and 59 others (7/31/2017) Failed to qualify for the ballot Governor Jerry Brown Filed by Rachel Gunther and 197 others (11/16/17) Failed to qualify for the ballot

2019   Governor Gavin Newsom Filed by Erin Cruz and 69 others (March 15, 2019) Failed to qualify for the ballot Lieutenant Governor Eleni Kounalakis Filed by Erin Cruz and 70 others (March 15, 2019) Failed to qualify for the ballot Attorney General Xavier Becerra Filed by Erin Cruz and 69 others (March 15, 2019) Failed to qualify for the ballot. Secretary of State Alex Padilla Filed by Erin Cruz and 69 others (March 15, 2019) Failed to qualify for the ballot

State Treasurer Fiona Ma Filed by Erin Cruz and 70 others (March 15, 2019) Failed to qualify for the ballot Insurance Commissioner Ricardo Lara Filed by Erin Cruz and 69 others (March 15, 2019) Failed to qualify for the ballot State Controller Betty Yee Filed by Erin Cruz and 69 others (March 15, 2019) Failed to qualify for the ballot Senator Richard Pan, 6th Senate District (Sacramento and Yolo Counties) Filed by Austin Bennett and 53 others (May 8, 2019) Failed to qualify for the ballot Senator Richard Pan, 6th Senate District (Sacramento and Yolo Counties) Filed by Austin Bennett and 76 others (May 29, 2019) Failed to qualify for the ballot Governor Gavin Newsom Filed by Erin Cruz and 137 others (August 2, 2019) Failed to qualify for the ballot Governor Gavin Newsom Filed by James Veltmeyer and 99 others (August 26, 2019) Failed to qualify for the ballot

2020   Attorney General Xavier Becerra Filed by Erin Cruz and 93 others (January 28, 2020) Failed to qualify for the ballot Governor Gavin Newsom Filed by Orrin E. Heatlie and 124 others (February 13, 2020) Failed to qualify for the ballot Governor Gavin Newsom Filed by Orrin E. Heatlie and 124 others (February 21, 2020) Qualified for the ballot: Recall election September 14, 2021, Governor Gavin Newsom Filed by Carla Canada and 9 others (June 3, 2020) Failed to qualify for the ballot.

5.12. Open primary elections

The most significant developments in the laws regulating elections can be found in the legislation in the various states from 1913. These provisions mainly focus on strengthening the direct primary for party nominations, the growth of the non-partisan primary and election for judges and municipal officers, the gradual adoption of the short ballot principle, and the extension of" 'corrupt practices prevention" measures. The most important among these are registration by affidavit, voting by mail, a double election in recall proceedings, and provision for new parties in the primaries (West, 437).

Changes in the electoral legislation of many countries have included constitutional changes to women's suffrage. In California, this constitutional right was guaranteed back in 1911, making California the first state to guarantee equal suffrage for women and men, nine years before the amendment was passed nationally. At the same time, similar amendments were passed in 1913 in South Dakota and Montana.

In California, Kansas, Michigan, New Hampshire, and Wisconsin, in 1913, new provisions were made regarding the participation of new parties in the primaries. Moreover, California, Nevada, and Pennsylvania require the voter to register to state his party affiliation as a condition of participating in the primary. Michigan, on the other hand, adopts the "open" primary. Non-Partisan Primaries have been adopted in varying forms and degrees for city elections in these states: Minnesota, Missouri, Pennsylvania, Tennessee, and Texas.

In anticipation of the adoption of the seventeenth amendment to the federal constitution, the following States make provision for the direct election of United States senators: California, Colorado, Connecticut, Florida, Georgia, Idaho, Illinois, Iowa, Minnesota, New Hampshire, North Carolina, Pennsylvania, Tennessee, and Wisconsin. In these States, nomination and election are in the same manner and at the same time as for state officers or for representatives in congress. In several cases, provision is made for filling vacancies by temporary appointment to be followed by special election (West, 440).

Under new California laws, voters receive by mail sample primary ballots (if they are registered for the primaries) and sample election ballots. A new check against fraudulent ballots is the use in Nevada of specially watermarked paper, arranged to show the watermark when the ballot is folded, the design to be changed from year to year.

A complex history characterizes the election laws in California. Direct primary elections were introduced in 1909 as a reform of the progressive era. The legislation created a closed primary system in which registered voters of a particular party received only that party's ballot. Registered voters who refused to run for office received a ballot containing only nonpartisan candidates. In 1913, in a further progressive reform, cross-filling was introduced. The cross-filling allowed the candidate to appear on multiple party ballots for the same position and to be nominated for more than one party. Cross-filling was eliminated in 1959.

The following significant change in the primary election law followed in 1996 with the adoption of the 1983 Proposal in the March primary elections. Named the "Open Primary Initiative," Proposition 198 created a Louisiana-style blanket primary for California. The blanket primary permitted all voters, both registered partisans and "declined to state" independents, to choose among all the candidates on the primary ballot, irrespective of party affiliation. The intent was to encourage political participation and promote selecting "centrist" candidates who would need to appeal to a broad spectrum of voters to win. The blanket primary system was in effect for the primary elections of June 1998 and March 2000. In June 2000, the United States Supreme Court declared Proposition 198 unconstitutional.

In California, the Supreme court used the First Amendment right of association and ruled that political parties in California have a constitutional right to exclude nonparty members in primary elections.

Later, in September 2000, following the Supreme court's decision, California enacted SB 28, with whom modified closed primary elections were established. This act took effect on January 1, 2001. This Act prescribes that registered voters of a particular party receive only the party's ballot, as it was earlier with California's closed primary law. Also, if the party has permitted the unaffiliated voters to participate in its primary, they may choose a party ballot. This was the case in 2002 and 2004 when the Democratic and Republican parties allowed this kind of participation. Critics say such laws are confusing and vague, citing the fact that many unrelated voters in the 2002 and 2004 primaries were unaware that they had a choice of party ballots.

5.13. The Two Ballot Measures

The November 2004 ballot consisted of two competing primary election measures. In this regard, proposition 62 was placed on the ballot following by an intensive campaign led by a coalition of corporations, business executives, and politicians. This would mean a return to the version of the preliminary blanket in which the first two voters always appeared on the ballot for the general election. Proposal 60 (SCA18) was placed on the ballot of the legislature in June 2004 to oppose Proposal 62. It would essentially preserve the existing modified closed primary system. If both proposals pass, the one with the most votes prevails.

Proposition 62: Proposition 62 refers to a single primary ballot in which all state and congressional candidates are presented together, no matter their party affiliation. The top two candidates with the most votes for each office should appear on the general election ballot, even if one of the two received a majority of the vote (80-90% of the votes), even if both were of the same party. Also, Proposition 62 does not refer to the presidential nominating process. National party rules require that only voters registered with a particular party cast ballots for that party's presidential candidates.

The other name of Proposition 62 is the Voter Choice Open Primary Act, often understood as a version of the blanket primary. The legal and political understanding of this term refers to a system in which each party has a separate ballot, and the voter chooses among the ballots on election day. In this way, Proposition 62 version of the blanket primary differs from its Proposition 198 predecessor in that it would create a "top two" system in which candidates in the general election are the top vote-getters, not the official party nominees (Institute of governmental studies, 2004).

The proponents of Proposal 62 had the same primary purpose as the proponents of Proposition 198: to promote moderate, centrist candidates, even in constituencies that rely heavily on both streams, i.e., which favor Democrats or Republicans; by encouraging primary candidates to turn to a wide range of voters to win enough votes to be the "first two" candidates in the primary elections.

The proponents of proposal 62 also aimed to reduce the phenomenon of third parties in general elections. In this regard, a third party or so-called spoiler is a candidate who is considered to attract the support of the candidate of the largest party and announces the general election to favor the opposite candidate of the largest party. The most egregious instance of the spoiler phenomenon occurs when a third-party candidate receives behind-the-scenes help or is otherwise manipulated to remove the support of a major party candidate. Supporters of proposition 62 also consider that it will contribute to strengthening voter participation.

Legislative districts are so well organized to favor the major party's general election results, usually know before. According to Proposal 62, supporters say that the two best candidates in the general election would be severe, sustainable candidates and thus arouse interest in the general election.

Proposition 62 lies on three basic arguments: first, its opponents consider that proposition 62 will further weaken political parties by reducing the incentive of voters to register with a political party. On the other side, opponents think that weak political parties are dangerous for the state legislature because they already suffer from a lousy organization and lack of discipline. Second, opponents argue that Proposal 62 would turn the primaries into free elections for all candidates, encouraging intra-party competition and creating opportunities for incumbent candidates to gain more votes. As a result, opponents believe that the primary elections with one ballot will create conditions for participation in the so-called spoilers that proponents consider obscene for general elections.

Finally, opponents argue that Proposition 62 would decrease choices in the general election. In this regard, third-party candidates, they maintain, would rarely get enough votes to be "top two" candidates. Voters would find only the top Democrat and the top Republican (or perhaps two Democrats or two Republicans) on the general election ballot, and general elections would be mere runoff elections.

Proposition 60: Proposition 60 is crucial because it inserts a provision into the state constitution that gives the participating political parties the right to advance their top vote-getting candidate to the general election. In the context of primary elections, Proposition 60 states that shall be "primary elections for partisan offices, including an open presidential primary. Authored by Senators Ross Johnson (R-Irvine) and Deirdre Albert (D-San Diego), SCA18), which became Proposition 60, was placed on the ballot as the state legislature's alternative to Proposition 62. SCA18 has rushed through the legislature just ahead of the deadline for placing measures on the November general election ballot and met the two-thirds vote requirement for such measures with broad bipartisan support.

In the beginning, Proposition 60 referred to the requirement that proceeds from the sale of surplus state property to be used to pay down the $15 billion in deficit bonds included in the 2003-2004 budget package. Challenged in court, Proposition 60 was accused that it violates the state constitution's ban on multi-subject ballot measures.

For an Open Primary v. Shelley (2004 Cal. App. Lexis 1259), Petitioners in Californians sought its removal from the ballot altogether. In a July 30, 2004 decision, the California Third District Court of Appeal allowed Proposition 60 to stay on the ballot but ordered that it be split into two separate propositions.

On August 3, 2004, Secretary of State Kevin Shelley announced that the "surplus state property" provision would become Proposition 60A on the November ballot. On August 9, 2004, with the deadline for printing the Official Voter Information Guide looming, the California Supreme Court let stand the appellate court decision bifurcating Proposition 60, but agreed to review the legal issues at a later time, after "adequate briefing, oral argument, and deliberation." The final result of the litigation is that Proposition 60 remains on the general election ballot as a single-subject measure concerned with elections only.

Proponents argue that Proposition 60 would preserve voter choice and that voters need an alternative to the radical changes proffered in Proposition 62. Opponents contend that Proposition 60 is a crude "poison pill" measure intended to sidetrack Proposition 62 and confuse voters.

Works Cited

The *city of Los Angeles,* "Initiative, Referendum & Recall Petition Handbook. Available at: https://clerk.lacity.org/stellent/groups/departments/@clerk_elections_contributor/documents/contributor_web_content/lacityp_023253.pdf [Accessed on: 21.07.2021].

California State Constitution, Article 2, Section 14. Available at:http://www.leginfo.ca.gov/const.html [Accessed on: 21.07.2021].

California Code, Elections Code - ELEC 11381 Available at:https://codes.findlaw.com/ca/elections-code/elec-sect-11381.html   [Accessed   on: 21.07.2021].

Laws governing recall in California, Ballotpedia. Available at: https://ballotpedia.org/Laws_governing_recall_in_California#cite_note-quotedisclaimer-3 [Accessed on: 21.07.2021].

Malkopoulou, Anthoula. "Flipped Elections: Do Recalls Improve Democratic Representation?." *The Conversation (Australia edition)* (2015).

Populism, Partisanship. "The Role of Public Opinion on the California Governor's Recall in 2003." *American Politics Research* 33.2 (2005): 163-186.

Garrett, Elizabeth. "Democracy in the Wake of the California Recall." *U. Pa. L. Rev.* 153 (2004): 239.

West, Victor J. "Legislation of 1913 Affecting Nominations and Elections." *American Political Science Review* 8.3 (1914): 437-442.

Proposition 60. Primary Elections. (2004). Institute of Governmental Studies. Available at: https://igs.berkeley.edu/library/elections/proposition-60 [Accessed on: 26.7.2021].

California Secretary of State. (2021). *Complete list of recall attempts.* Available   at: https://www.sos.ca.gov/elections/recalls/complete-list-recall-attempts [Accessed on: 27.7.2021].

Jovanovska, Tanja Karakamisheva. "Why Fear of Recall for Elected Officials." *Iustinianus Primus L. Rev.* 10 (2019): 1.

Klein, Angelika, Yusuf Kiranda, and Regina Bafaki. "Concepts and principles of democratic governance and accountability." *Uganda: Konrad-Adenauer-Stiftung* (2011).

Reynolds, Andrew, Ben Reilly, and National Research Council. *Electoral systems and conflict in divided societies.* National Academies Press, 1999.

Goodin, Robert E. *Innovating democracy: Democratic theory and practice after the deliberative turn.* OUP Oxford, 2008.

Vandamme, Pierre-Etienne. "Can the recall improve electoral representation?." *Frontiers in Political Science* 2 (2020): 6.

Cain, Bruce E. *Democracy more or less.* Cambridge University Press, 2015.

Birch, Sarah, and David Muchlinski. "Electoral violence prevention: what works?." *Democratization* 25.3 (2018): 385-403.

Direct Democracy: California Initiative's Process

6.1 Introduction to Direct Democracy in California

Democracy is a political regime based on the "rule by the people." In Athens, the first historical model of a society based on a democratic government, collective participation was necessary to respect two principles structuring this republic: *isegoria* and *isonomia*. *Isegoria* meant that all citizens had to be given equal freedom to speak in the public assembly. *Isonnomia* required that all citizens participate equally in the city's government, which was achieved thanks to the rotation in power, which made sure that rulers were ruled in turn (Held 2006; 11-27). Since Athens, societies have changed both in size and in the conception of political representation preferable, so current democracies mostly rely on representative systems where political decisions are in the hands of the politicians. At the same time, citizens' participation is limited to cast their votes at the ballot to elect the representatives they think will better represent them in the following years (Manin 1997).

At the same time, this does not imply that direct forms of democracy have disappeared since most democracies still encompass procedures by which citizens vote directly on laws rather than to elect candidates for office. Direct democracy is thus an umbrella term that covers different procedures, of which the most widespread process is the ballot or proposition. These measures differ according to how they come to the ballot, but overall there are three main types (Matsusaka 2005; 185-186):

1. *Initiatives:* a law proposed by citizens that qualifies for the ballot if a sufficient amount of signatures is collected.

2. *Referendums:* vote on a law already approved by the legislature, also qualified for the ballot by collecting a predetermined number of signatures.

3. *Legislative measures:* placed on the ballot directly by the legislature, either to collect a sense of public opinion or to get the approval of a specific law.

These procedures are widespread in all democratic systems, even though the way they are implemented differs from case to case according to the number of signatures required for an initiative to qualify for the ballot, whether a majority or supermajority is required to pass the law, and other details. In the United States, direct democracy is present since the beginning of the Republic. Nowadays, more than half of all American States feature initiatives and referendums in their policy agenda. In California, the State focus of this chapter, initiatives, and propositions are the part of the constitution since the beginning of the 20th century.

Governor Hiram Johnson proposed these measures in 1911 to counterbalance the immense economic power owned by 'Southern Pacific Railroad' owners, who used their economic power to buy legislature to have them pass the laws preferred by railroad owners. The ballot was thus seen as a way to deal with government corruption, and it was meant to give back political power in the hands of California citizens (Grodin 1993; 1-42). In the following sections of this chapter, we will explain and discuss how direct democracy is enacted in California.

Section 1 describes the initiative process. Currently, only direct initiatives – those where the initiative goes directly to the ballot after the signatures have been collected - are used (section 1.1). However, up until 1966, the California constitution also encompassed indirect initiative (section 1.2), namely the proposition that must first go through the legislative process. To offer an overview of what an actual initiative entails, we will describe three significant propositions of the past (section 1.3), namely proposition 13, proposition 1a, and position 9. In section 2, the chapter analyses another direct power at the disposal of California's citizens, namely the 'Recall process.' This is citizens' power to remove elected state and local officials before their terms expire.

In section 3, the chapter describes one of the main criticisms stressed regarding the initiative process: its outcomes are too affected by money's influence. Even though it is true that money is essential and plays a part in shaping the outcomes, the chapter underlines that initiatives' outcomes are not a direct result of money invested in the process, so there is still room to defend the democratic character of this process. Nevertheless, the influence of money on the initiative process is only one of the problems underlined by critics of the proposition tools.

In section 4, some of the most crucial reform proposals will be described, focusing in detail on how deliberation could improve both initiatives' democratic character and their outcomes. The debate regarding the initiative process results from how divided are the opinions regarding the efficiency of direct democracy procedures.

In section 5, we thus analyze some of the pros and cons of this procedure, concluding that, despite some criticalities, the literature supports the thesis that direct democracy produces good outcomes both from the instrumental and educative points of view (Lupia and Matsusaka 2004). In this way, we will conclude that California State is a "Hybrid" political system where the legislative side and ballot propositions are not separated, but they interact one with another, thus offering political actors various means to pursue their political agenda.

6.2 The Initiative Process

As specified by Article II of the California Constitution, citizens can initiate legislation in several ways, either as a constitutional amendment or a state statute. Ballots are usually held to resolve the most controversial issues – tax measures have been the most recurrent ones - and they thus generate passionate debates across the State. The initiative is of two kinds.

Direct initiatives are those where voters place a proposed statute or an amendment to the constitution directly on the ballot. Instead, indirect initiatives are those where proponents collect signatures and then present the measure to the legislature for enactment. This latter is no longer in use in California since it was repealed in 1966. Let us analyze both in more detail.

6.3. Direct Initiatives

The procedure to qualify a proposal for the ballot must follow a specific procedure. The first step is writing the proposed law by the proponents of the initiative (California Secretary of State 2021; 1). Proponents may either write the text by themselves or ask a private counsel or assistance from the 'Office of the Legislative Counsel'.[3] The procedure to qualify a proposal for the ballot must follow a specific procedure. The first step is writing the proposed law by the proponents of the initiative (California Secretary of State 2021; 1). Proponents may either write the text by themselves or ask a private counsel or assistance from the 'Office of the Legislative Counsel.

Having written the proposal, proponents submit the text - together with their contact information and a signed statement to certify that they are qualified electors - to the 'California Attorney General's Initiative Coordinator,' with a request to prepare a title and one hundred words

---

[3] In this case, proponents must submit 25 signatures from qualified electors.

summary for the circulation (California Secretary of State 2021: 2-3). On top of that, proponents must also disclose in a separate document who are the top official funders of the initiative and deposit 2000$, a sum that will be refunded in case the initiative goes to the ballot within the following two years.[4] All committees formed to support or to counteract the initiative must file semi-annual reports, pre-election statements concerning their activities, quarterly ballot measure statements and 10-business day and 24-hours reports. These two latter are reports concerning contributions and any paid spokespersons.

The day the attorney receives the proposal becomes the 'Official Summary Day', which will be the focal point to set all future deadlines. The attorney should also ask the 'Department of Finance and the Legislative Analyst' to write a fiscal estimate of how revenues to the State will be affected by such a proposal. Once received the fiscal estimate, the Attorney has 15 days to write the title and summary and post the text on the governmental website to facilitate a 30-day public review process. After this process, the Attorney prepares a calendar of filing deadlines and sends comments to the proponents for reviews and amendments (Liebert 1998; 30-31).

Petitions then circulate via mail in the ballot pamphlet, a document that includes copies of each proposition, the specific constitutional provision that each measure would revise, the arguments of those for and against each measure, and finally, the impartial analysis of each measure by the legislative office (Liebert 1998; 32-33). Ballot pamphlet is an essential means at the disposal of proponents in the signature collection phase, which lasts 180 days. There is no distribution requirement in California, so any proportion of the signatures can be collected from any county or congressional district. Those collecting signatures must be older than 18, provide their personal information, and sign a specific declaration

---

[4] In 2015, the filing fee for submitting an initiative to the ballot was increased from $200 to $2,000. The original fee was set in 1943, but the State Legislature decided that it was better to increase it in order to discourage people from proposing worthless measures for the ballot.

whereby they promise to respect the instructions on circulating petitions (California Secretary of State 2021; 7-11).

Collectors can be paid according to the number of signatures collected, but those breaching the elections code with abuses - such as false statements about the content or effect of the petition or giving money in exchange for the signature - can incur criminal penalties. The number of signatures required to place a measure on the ballot varies according to the initiative (California State initiative 2021; 12):

a. *Initiative State Statute (ISS):* signatures must be at least 5% of the total votes cast for the office of governor at the last gubernatorial election (for 2021 the total number is 623,212);

b. *Initiative Constitutional Amendment (ICA):* signatures must be at least 8% of the total votes cast for the office of governor at the last gubernatorial election (for 2021 the total number is 997,139);

c. *Referendum:* signatures must be at least 5% of the total votes cast for the office of governor at the last gubernatorial election (same as ISS).

When proponents collect 25% of the signatures required, they have to notify the Secretary of State. In this way, each chamber in the State legislature has sufficient time to assign the proposed initiative to its appropriate committees and schedule public hearings on it. Once all signatures are collected, they must be filed with the county election officials,[5] and when this happens, petitions can no longer be amended, except by order of a court. County election officials have then eight days to verify signatures (California Secretary of State 2021; 13-14).

Verification of the signatures occurs via a random sample of 500 signatures or at least 3% of the total amount collected (whichever is great) within

---

[5] I.e. all the signatures from those in Alameda County need to be submitted to the Alameda County elections official, Los Angeles County signatures need to be turned in to the LA County elections official, and so on.

30 days,[6] reporting the results to the Secretary of State. The cut-off time to go through this entire process, have all the signatures verified, and get on a particular ballot is 131 days before that election. The procedure varies according to the number of signatures found to be valid with the random sample.

If valid signatures are less than 95%, the initiative is failed. If valid signatures are between 95-110% of the amount required, then each signature must be "fully checked." Finally, if valid signatures are greater than 110%, the proposition qualifies for the ballot without further certification. Due to the problems that may occur in this phase, proponents usually seek at least 50 percent more than the legal minimum number of signatures to compensate for possible duplicate or otherwise invalid signatures (California Secretary of State 2021; 14).

An initiative that has been certified by county officials to have been signed by the requisite number of voters is classified by the Secretary of State as 'eligible' for the following state-wide ballot. At the ballot, initiatives that receive the simple majority of "yes" of those voting on that proposition pass. If they do, they take effect the fifth day after the Secretary of State certifies the election result. In this way, propositions become either part of the constitution – in case it is a proposed amendment – or of the State's statute – if it is a proposed statute – in the same way as if it had been passed by the legislature and signed by the governor. When this occurs, California's legislature can no longer amend or repeal an approved proposition without submitting the change to the voters. There may be cases when provisions approved at the same time conflict one with another. In this case, the measure that receives the highest affirmative vote prevails. Instead, propositions that do not conflict with the winning proposition are passed (Liebert 1998; 33-34).

A less common kind of initiative is the referendum, also known as "petition referendum" or "people's veto," whereby electors approve or reject statutes enacted by the legislatures. Since the first one in 1912, only 89 optional referendums have been proposed, of which 50 qualified for

---

[6] All signatures must be verified in counties where less than 500 signatures have been collected.

the ballot. The process is similar to the one for the *ISS*, with some differences in terms of timing, verification, and circulation calendar.

For example, conversely, from an initiative that must qualify 131 days before the election to appear on a ballot, the referendum can qualify up to 31 days before. Proponents have also only 90 days after the law they aim to question is enacted to submit the request to the Attorney general for the ballot pamphlet, collect signatures, and file the petitions with county elections officials. Finally, there are laws ineligible for optional referenda, such as urgency statutes, statutes calling elections, and those providing for tax levies (Liebert 1998; 29).

Initiatives go through several legislative processes, and they often concern delicate topics so that they may become the subject of litigation either before or after the election. Overall, California Courts prefer seeing whether or not the ballot was successful before reviewing the propositions since they want to defend ballots to preserve the people's will. Nevertheless, there have also been cases when the judiciary intervened concerning the content of the ballot pamphlet (title, summary, language, etc.) and the constitutionality of the proposal. Cases when Courts interfere concern also: the violation of the "single-subject" rule; if propositions revise rather than amending the state constitution; if they violate the federal or state constitution; if they do not only concern legislative matters, but also focus on administrative features; if they violate the rule for which initiative power is limited to the enactment of statutes, and finally if it is redundant (Liebert 1998; 35-36).

Direct initiatives are a constant feature in California's public policy. Instead, due to the long time they took to be approved, indirect initiatives were dismissed in 1966, even though before that date, only 19 initiatives followed this path, of which only 4 received a sufficient number of signatures, and only one was enacted (Stern 2011; 672).

6.4. Indirect Initiatives

In 1911, the California legislature had the power to get involved if the initiative's proponents so desired. The process itself incentivized this measure since proponents had to gather signatures of only at least 5% of the total votes cast at the last gubernatorial election with the legislature's involvement. In comparison, this number increased to 8% for direct initiatives. Nowadays, 10 out of the 24 American states that allow for the initiative include indirect initiatives.

Of these, eight mandate the indirect measure, while the other 2 (Utah and Washington) offer incentives. Legislative sponsored measures may concern constitutional amendments, bond proposals, and measures that would amend or repeal a law already established by the initiative process. Legislation rather than the citizenry sponsors these propositions, and some scholars have suggested that the legislature's involvement could improve in several regards the initiative process (Kashani & Stern 2011; 319-320).

First, a compromise between proponents and legislatures could improve the drafting of an initiative since legislators could use their expertise to help proponents avoiding the mistakes contained too often in the drafts. Second, suppose legislators were given the power to approve the proposal after the confrontation with proponents.

In that case, proposals could be directly enacted, thus saving time and money to the constituents and making the process more transparent. Proponents and legislators are already discussing informally, so this would only be a way to make it public and formal. Finally, as analyzed more in detail in section four, proponents may not properly account for the rights of minorities within the state, so the legislature could help respect minorities' rights (Collins and Oesterle 1995).

At the same time, there are also several arguments against the indirect initiative (Stern 2011; 681-683). First, the initiative process was originally framed on the belief that citizens need a way to bypass corrupt legislators. If legislators intervene, then the whole process becomes a contradiction in terms. Second, legislators could not be the only ones interfering with the indirect process since political elites or interest groups could try to persuade proponents to either drop off the initiative or accept major reviews to let them pass the ballot. Third, initiatives are usually started to address a problem neglected by the legislature, so if the latter were interested in that action, they would have already acted before the initiative process.

Therefore, even though California dismissed indirect initiatives in 1966, these propositions are still in use in other American states, and several scholars propose them as a viable solution to some of the deficiencies of the direct version. To understand more in-depth how a direct initiative is framed, we describe three of the most important propositions in California's initiative history (Proposition 13, Proposition 1a, and proposition 9). Propositions were numbered initially starting from one at each election, but this resulted in certain initiatives getting confused with other ones with the same number in a later year. For this reason, in the November 1982 ballot, legislators decided to continue incrementing the number at every election rather than restarting them from one at each election. This decision yet resulted in a high number of propositions – it reached 200 by the 1996 election – so from the November 1998 ballot, the count was reset back to one, and it is now reset every ten years.[7]

6.5. Examples of Past Propositions

Proposition 13 held in 1978: Proposition 13, titled the "Tax limitation – Initiative Constitutional Amendment", was held on the 6/06/1978 and it was approved with the 64,79% of 'Yes' (4,280,689) against the 35,21% of 'No' (2,326,167). This initiative was proposed by Howard Jarvis and Paul Gann, with the aim to reduce California's tax on properties, and it has since been one of the most debated and analysed proposition in California's Ballot History. This initiative had a significant impact not only on California's public policy, but on American politics on the whole, since it is deemed to have started the movement advocating for tax limitation and a restriction of the spending authority of the state (Sexton et

---

[7]   California LaLawlibrary, retrieved at: https://www.lalawlibrary.org/legal-research/library-materials/propositions

al. 1999; 99-100). Changes proposed by Proposition 13 concerned four main points (Levy 1979).

First, to set a tax on properties at no more than 1% of their full cash value, limiting annual increases of assessed value to the inflation rate of 2%. Before, the property tax rate averaged almost 3% on the market value. Second, upon the transfer, sale, or construction of a property, to reassess tax properties at 1% of the sale price. Third, to prohibit State Legislature from enacting new taxes on the value or sale of properties. Fourth, to authorize the imposition of special taxes by local government by a 2/3 vote of qualified electors. Hence, proposition 13 converted property tax from a local tax to a state tax. With the tax rate at 1%, State's apportionment rules determine how much money each local government received, even though these rules were affected by fiscal crises generated by Proposition 13 and other factors such as judicial mandates and legislative actions (Chapman 1998).

The fact that property taxes had increased significantly over the previous years significantly affected the approval of this initiative. Since property taxes had generated good revenues for the state, voters believed that the approval of this initiative would not have resulted in less public spending but rather in a similar public expenditure with lower taxes and a more stable increase of taxes in the following years. In this way, voters showed that they did not trust State Legislature's fiscal impact on the initiative, according to which such measures would have resulted in annual losses of property tax revenues up to $7 billion in a single fiscal year, with a reduction in annual state costs of only $600 million for the same fiscal year (Ballotpedia, Proposition 13).

Proposition 13 rules are connected to an important aspect of current California's legislation, namely the 'Parcel tax.' This is a form of property tax assessed at a rate based on the characteristics of a unit of property rather than on the assessed value of the property. This tax differs according to the type of property, and in California, it is considered a qualified special tax, namely a tax that a local unit of government can

impose if they obtain a 55% majority vote for approval.[8] Local governments hold elections in this regard when they want to raise revenues,
and over the 2003 to 2020 period, there have been 1189 tax measures,
of which 56.35% were approved (670). This revenue was first placed on
the ballot in 1983, and it is used to fund schools and other public services, namely, two fields that were negatively affected by the decrease in
revenues generated by proposition 13's limit on property tax revenue
(Ballotpedia, Parcel Tax).

Proposition 9 held in 2008: Proposition 9, also called the "Marsy's Law
Crime Victims' Rights Amendment" was an initiative held in California on the 4/11/2008 that focused on the criminal justice system. It was
approved with a 53,84% of 'Yes' (6,682,465), against a 46.16% of 'No'
(5,728,968). This initiative was a combined initiated constitutional
amendment – it amended section 28 of Article I of California Constitution – and a state statute, even though in 2012 judge Kartlon ruled that
the parts that govern the revocation of parole were unconstitutional. This
initiative aimed at improving in several ways Proposition 8 (1982) on
victims' rights (Ballotpedia, Proposition 9).

First, notifying victims and families during all aspects of the judicial
process - including bail, sentencing and parole - especially when offenders
are released from custody after their arrest. Second, giving victims' families
an information card containing resources, rights, and a notification of parole
hearings sooner than it was the case, giving them back also the property
used during investigations and trials. Third, blocking criminal sentences
from being affected by early release policies designed to reduce overcrowding in prisons. Finally, increasing the number of people allowed to attend
and testify on behalf of the victim at parole hearings, while decreasing the
number of parole hearings prisoners were entitled to.

---

[8] Proposition 13 required a 2/3 super-majority in order to approve a local school district bond
measure, but in 2000, proposition 39 reduced this percentage to 55% (Ballotpedia, Parcel tax).

This initiative created a harsh political debate. On the one side, proponents argued that this proposition improved victims' rights. On the other side, opponents such as California's Democratic Party and California's teachers association, argued that Proposition 9 was redundant - it added nothing to what already included in Proposition 8 – and costly, since stopping the early release of criminals would have significantly increased jail operating costs, and changings proposed were doomed to be subject to federal legal challenges. Hence, there was the risk of spending lots of funds to enact laws that would have been going to be dismissed short afterwards (Ballotpedia, Proposition 9).

Proposition 1a in 1966: Proposition 1a was held and approved on the 8/11/1966 – with a 73.49% of 'Yes' (4.156.416) and a 26.51% of 'No' - as a legislatively referred constitutional amendment. Aim of this initiative was to repeal, amend and revise California's Constitution on the branches of government (Ballotpedia, Proposition 1a). First, it revised the system of direct democracy, changing the signatures required to start an initiative statute petition from 8% to 5% of the votes cast at the last election for governor. On top of that, it abolished the indirect initiative system. Second, concerning the legislative branch, it required that legislature would meet in an annual general session unlimited in duration, and as to subjects that could be considered. This was different from what occurred before, when meetings were held in odd-numbered years and fiscal matters were discussed in a separate meeting. Moreover, it required statutes voted by 2/3 of the house rather than by the Constitution to set salaries and expenses of legislators, who could also be charged for conflict of interests and for impeachment.

Third, this proposition brought several changes to the executive: it lowered the age requirement for the office of governor to 21 years; it set technical changes on the pardoning and clemency powers of the governor; it diminished the minimums for statutory salaries of certain elective state officers, and it set provisions for determining questions of succession to the governorship and temporary disability of Governor. Finally,

Proposition 1a modified the judiciary branch, permitting judges to serve superior courts of two or more counties, increasing the experience required for judges of higher courts, preventing names of unopposed incumbent judges from being placed on the ballot for any trial court in the state, and requiring automatic suspension of judges charged with felony.

In sum, these are just three examples of California's proposition-rich history. However, they well exemplify both how initiatives could be used on different and salient issues and how important they could be for shaping the policy framework of a specific state. In the following section, to complete the description of California's procedures of direct democracy, we describe the recall process, namely the power of the voters to remove elected state and local officials before their terms expire.

6.6. California Recall Process

Citizens in California can remove their state and local officials before their term expires, but they cannot remove federal officers, who are instead subject to the US constitution. This process was inserted in California Constitution as a result of a specific conception of local political representation. Whereas federal offices were more independent, because they had to represent the whole country rather than a specific state, local representatives were considered servants of the people of that state, who then had the right to direct politicians in every decision. Hence, State Governments tend to be more directly "people-driven" than the federal government (Amar 2004; 932-933).

Several rules define when the recall procedure cannot be commenced, such as that the officer must not have held office for less than 90 days or be within the last six months of her term, and the officer must not have won a previous recall procedure within the previous six months. If proponents – who must be registered voters for the office they seek to recall - respect these rules, they can initiate the recall procedure (California Office of the Secretary of State 2020; 1-2).

In case proponents aim to recall a 'State Officer,' they must first serve, file, and publish a notice of intention to circulate a recall petition that complies with California law. A petition must contain the name and title of the officer sought to be recalled, the reason for the recall in no more than 200 words, name, and details of each proponent of the recall,[9] and the text of the elections code section 11023 that specifies how the officer sought to be recalled can file an answer. If the petition respects these features, it is then served by personal delivery on the officer.

Together with an affidavit, this notice must be filed with the 'Secretary of State' within seven days of being served. Proponents must publish a copy of the intention in at least one newspaper of general circulation – or at least three public spaces within the jurisdiction – filing a proof of publication. The officer is given the opportunity to address an answer – of a maximum of 200 words – to the proponents and to specify whether or not s/he wants the party affiliation identified in the ballot. Nevertheless, the officer cannot be a candidate to replace his/herself (California Office of the Secretary of State 2020: 3-5).

In the second phase of the process, proponents prepare the recall petition for circulation, following the format given by the Secretary of State. This format includes a request for a recall election, a copy of the notice of intention with the accusation and the answer of the officer sought to be recalled, and a top official funders disclosure. Once the Secretary of State receives the petition, she must notify proponents within ten days specifying whether or not the petition meets the requirements. If it does not, proponents have ten days to comply with the changes required.

Otherwise, the petition gets rejected. If the petition meets the requirements, proponents can start collecting signatures. These latter must be equal to 12% of the last vote for office, must be obtained from five different counties, and in each of the counties, signatures must equal at least 1% of the last vote for office (California Office of the Secretary of State 2020; 6-10).

---

[9] There must be at least ten proponents.

Proponents have then 160 days to collect signatures, and the elections official can check each month how the collection is progressing. Once signatures reach 10% of the total required, the county elections official has 30 days to verify signatures submitted over that period. Once the collection is completed, the Secretary of State has to count and verify the signatures – with the same procedure used to verify signatures for the initiative process - submitted by each county, notifying the department of finance of the results. This latter must, within 30 days, estimate the cost of the recall election, notifying all bodies involved.

Once Governor receives all documents, a notice for the recall election is published not less than 60 days nor more than 80 days from the date of certification of sufficient signatures. The election must take place within 180 days from the same date. At the election, voters decide whether or not to recall the officer and choose a successor if the recall is successful. If the candidate chosen to replace a former officer fails to qualify for the office within ten days after the election, the office remains vacant and is filled according to the law (California Office of the Secretary of State 2020; 12-14).

The procedure for the recall of 'Local Officers' is similar to the one for 'State Officers' since the delivery, publication, drafting, and circulation phase are the same. Instead, the number of signatures required and the deadlines for the submission of the signatures change since they both differ according to the number of registered voters in the electoral jurisdiction. In this case, elections must take place between 88 and 125 days after the date of certification that sufficient signatures have been collected (California Office of the Secretary of State 2020: 21-22).

As for the initiative process, recall procedure has been long debated in the literature since some scholars point out that this process has several defects (Alvarez et al. 2004). First, there are often logistical problems, such as the fact that too few precincts can cause longer lines and upset voters, who may also have difficulties reaching the ballot place and understanding how to enter the premise (Dolan and Guccione 2003). Second, ballots can discriminate against language minorities since it can be difficult to translate the recall question properly in all languages, thus leaving certain minorities confused and unable to vote as they want (Hoffman 2003).

Third, elections always entail problems related to voters' biases, namely the fact that voters tend to votes the names of those who are first on the list, that there may be alignment issues, and that voters may be swayed by the location where they are voting and the circumstances in which they do so (Oppenheimer & Edwards 2012; 39-93; Brennan 2016; 25-53). However, these biases may not be as problematic as argued by critics since citizens can overcome these biases by using heuristic shortcuts, namely pieces of information that voters can draw from their party affiliation, figures of reference, emotional attachments, and others. (Oppenheimer 2012; 177-198). The importance of party cues for voters in ballot elections is yet puzzling since the more parties get involved in the initiative process, the more direct politics assumes the traits of the legislative process it is meant to bypass (Chavez 1998).

Finally, there is a debate concerning the number of signatures required, since some argue that it is too low, and it is thus too easy to start a recall procedure (Amar 2004). This problem is increased because California's constitution generally talks about "misconduct in office," which may open the gates to too many accusations. To resolve this problem, cases, when the procedure can be started should be more precisely defined, and the percentage of signatures required could be increased to 20% or 25%. However, this could, on the other hand, make it too difficult for grassroots movements to gather sufficient signatures to start a procedure.

In sum, the recall process is meant to address two main issues (Amar 2004; 956-958). On the one side, the removal of officials who are no longer acting in the public interest because they have become corrupted by corporate interests. On the other side, the punishment of an official who is not acting as promised during the elections. There are divided opinions on the efficiency of these measures and on which features ought to be improved. Among the several features analyzed, procedures of direct democracy have been criticized regarding one aspect, in particular, namely the influence of money in determining the outcomes of all procedures of direct democracy.

6.7. Impact of Money on Initiative Outcomes

In public imaginary, money has a significant impact on politics on the whole, but especially on the outcomes of the initiative process. Academic research tends instead to downsize this effect, stressing that even though money is necessary, the outcomes of the initiative process are not always those for which oligarchs have invested their economic resources (Bowler 1998). It is then difficult to assess the causal connection between money spent and electoral outcomes since other factors - such as the ballot question and media coverage[10] - play a part in this process. Furthermore, assessing the exact impact of money is complicated because it is impossible to study the counterfactual case, namely, what would have happened had a supporting group not spent money on the side of that initiative.

That said, scholars seem to agree on the fact that contributions from economic groups may be more efficient than those of citizens' groups on the passage rates of an initiative (Gerber 1999). That is, there are certain cases in which investing money is efficient, whereas others where it is not. For example, suppose an incumbent is not contested. In that case, interest groups are not interested in investing money in the ballot, while they are more inclined to intervene in contested elections and balanced ballots. Interest groups thus invest their money strategically where they can change more opinions, leaving aside those who have strong opinions that are hard to change. Important in this regard is the fact that while there are ceilings on contributions to races for federal and local political officers, there are no limits on contributions in ballot campaigns. As a result, initiative campaign spending has risen constantly over the last decades (Stratmann 2005; 1044-1045).[11]

---

[10] Even though Some research has found only little evidence that variation in media market expenditure has a direct impact on opinions (Bowler & Donovan 1998).

[11] For example, in 1992, 117$ million were spent in 21 states on ballot measures, while in 1998 the amount increased to 400$ million. In California alone, 522$ million were spent over the same period (Garret & Gerber 2001).

Money influence seems to change significantly according to whether it is spent in favor of an initiative or oppose it. In particular, when the opposing side outspends the supporting one, the former is more likely to win. Contrary advertisement is more effective than a positive one, and citizens often prefer to vote against an initiative when they are in doubt because they tend to favor the certainty of the status quo to the uncertainty of the change (Bowler and Donovan 1998). This is also why money spent on initiatives campaigning could result less efficiently than it actually is. That is, a simple correlation between money spent and outcomes is not representative of the actual power of money since it shows that more spending is associated with less support, thus making it seem that advertising is ineffective in changing the minds of voters (Levitt 1994).

In sum, academic research supports the view for which even though money is not the only factor influencing initiative outcomes, it can yet sway ballot outcomes on one side or another, especially in contested elections. However, this creates a paradox for direct democracy. Being an expensive process, direct democracy is now subject to economic power even more than regular legislation. However, this is opposite to what initiative procedures are meant for, namely giving citizens a means by which they can govern themselves, thus reducing the power of party bosses and economic interest groups (Schrag 2004).

The importance of money investment in initiative procedures can be well noted by considering the list of the most expensive ballots in California, of which all ten most expensive occurred over the last two decades. As shown by the following table, the most expensive Proposition in California history was Proposition 22 in 2020, which was an initiated statute to define app-based drivers as independent contractors rather than employees or agents. Beforehand, campaigns for four veto referendums against gaming compacts – Proposition 94, 95, 96, and 97 – raised almost 155$ million in contributions.[12]

---

[12] Information retrieved from Ballotpedia at: https://ballotpedia.org/What_were_the_most_expensive_ballot_measures_in_California

Measure	Topic	Years	Total	Support	Opposition	Outcome
1) Proposition 22	App-based drivers as independent contractors	2020	$224,253,017.57	$205,369,249.18	$18,883,768.39	Approved
2) Proposition 30 and 32	Funding education (30); Barring union members' dues (32)	2012	$185,948,365	$127,000,000 (labour)	$59,000.000 (business)	30Approved 32 Rejected
3) Propositions 94, 95, 96, and 97	Veto referendums against gaming compacts	2008	$154,554,073	$115,063,876	$39,490,197	Approved
4) Proposition 87	Tax on oil production to fund alternative energy research	2006	$150,770,683	$58,130,783	$92,639,900	Rejected
5) Proposition 15	Increase large corporations property taxes	2020	$144,006,081.62	$69,208,909.46	$74,735,622.16	Rejected
6) Proposition 8	Kidney clinic rebates to insurers and new taxes on revenue	2018	$130,426,208	$18,943,228	$111,482,980	Rejected
7) Proposition 61	Lower CA agencies payments for prescription drugs	2016	$128,276,770	$19,170,610	$109,106,160	Rejected
8) Proposition 21	Limit rent increases in buildings more than 15 years old	2020	$124,424,013.58	$40,852,356.62	$83,571,656.96	Rejected
9) Proposition 79	Reduce prices for prescription drugs for poor Californians	2005	$121,826,243	$40,516,352	$81,309,891	Rejected
10) Proposition 23	Reconsider Prop. 8 to control dialysis clinics	2020	$111,192,950	$9,000.000	$105,000,000	Rejected

Table 1: 10 Most Expensive Propositions in California's History

In sum, even though academic research has proven that money influence is less efficient than believed by public imagination, the significant amount of money invested in these propositions demonstrates that money does play a part in influencing the outcomes of ballot propositions. For this reason, there have been several reform proposals to the initiative process. In the following section, we describe the primary points of discussion..

6.8. Reform Proposals

Since its adoption, there have been several proposals concerning how to improve each phase of the initiative process. Regarding the drafting phase, one of the criticisms is that there is no public process in the writing process of the initiative. This could result in initiatives containing mistakes that have to be fixed by the legislature afterward, with the risk that the latter is accused of interfering in the process. In this regard, the easiest way to improve the initiative process would be to extend the circulation period of the initiative, allowing the legislature to implement changes for poorly written propositions (Laird and MacDonald 2011; 304-306).

A problem related to the drafting and circulating phase of an initiative is that proponents tend to consider only arguments in favor of their proposal, with the risk that this could neglect other groups' interests and rights. To address this issue, a solution could be – as suggested by the 1992 "California Commission on Campaign Financing" – increasing public debate by conducting public hearings once 25% signatures have been gathered, and once an initiative has qualified for the ballot, allowing proponents to amend the initiative according to the suggestions that emerge (Silva 2000; 14-15). The judiciary could also help to control that an initiative does not hinder minorities' rights since it could establish a judicial or quasi-judicial validation proceeding to determine the constitutionality of a proposal (Eastman 1985).

On top of that, citizens may also find it difficult to understand who is the real proponent of the initiative since interest groups could hide

behind façade groups. In-depth disclosure of significant campaign con-
tributors of the initiative in the media would be required to resolve this
issue. Moreover, voters should be given more insights on the campaign
finance, and the arguments in favor and against the proposition should be
specified better before and during the election. In particular, this could be
achieved by providing a more comprehensive list of endorsements in the
ballot pamphlet, specifying clearly which groups are in favor and which
are against the measure for which citizens are voting (Silva 2000: 15-16):

Finally, some scholars maintain that initiatives should also be subject
to legislative control after they have been enacted (Silva 2000; 19). For
example, the implementation of initiatives could be reviewed every two
years by the legislation. A clearer definition of the single-subject rule in
the constitution would help the review process (Miller 2001) since legislators in California have often interpreted this rule too generally as "rea-
sonably related to a common theme," even though others argue that this
would not be sufficient to decrease voter confusion and avoiding logrolling issues (Lowenstein 1983).

Considering these reform proposals, it may seem that solutions
must require an increase in the legislature's involvement or the judiciary. Nevertheless, this is not the case since some have also argued to
render the initiative process more deliberative. Citizens' direct participation is essential in any democracy, since not only it balances the will of
the majority with the need to protect minority interest, but it also favors
mechanisms for fact-finding, debate, consensus building, and for understanding better what laws imply (Mendelberg 2002). Hence, a problem of
the initiative process could be that it does not allow for sufficient popular
input (Kashani and Stern 2011). For example, the problems related to the
writing of the initiative could be resolved by allowing for a more comprehensive popular participation rather than by increasing the legislature's
involvement.

Adding more deliberation during the drafting phase would thus not
only help citizens understanding better what the initiative implies, but it
would also help proponents to listen and to consider with more attention

both the views of those with opposite political views and minorities' rights (Kashani and Stern 2011; 311-312). The signature phase also lacks deliberation since it often occurs in crowded places where individuals do not want to spend too much time considering what they are signing for. Moreover, ballot measures are difficult to understand.

Most citizens do not even read them until the ballot since one-third of the voters do not see the initiative until they are in the voting booth (Lunch 1998). An online signature-gathering and voting could help in this regard since citizens would have more time to evaluate the measure at home than in a crowded place since they could use the internet to gather the information they require to make an informed decision. On top of that, online procedures would also help diminish the expenses for the signature phase and the following mailing.

Once the proposition gets to the ballot, a lack of deliberation may hinder voters' ability to vote in line with their preferences. Moreover, when voters are uncertain, they tend to vote "no" and privilege the status quo. This means that initiatives that pass are likely to have been well understood by the population, while others may fail because citizens did not understand them.[13] Hence, making sure that citizens are comfortable on the ballot and understand the measure should be the main concern for proponents of an initiative. To resolve this problem, proponents could favor a public hearing on the initiative prior to the election, allowing each side to debate and present their arguments (Kashani and Stern 317-318). Finally, legislatures could be given the power to review the initiative once it is enacted, but only as long as they further the intent and purpose of the law. Citizens should be given the power to review the final version of the measure, debating and afterward voting on the changes made by the legislatures to make sure that the people's will is preserved (Kabat 2009).

---

[13] CTR. For Governmental Studies, Democracy by Initiative: Shaping California's Fourth Branch Of Government, 57 (2d ed. 2008), available at http://www.cgs.org/images/publications/cgs dbiful_book_f.pdf.

In sum, suggestions to improve the initiative process are divided between those who argue in favor of increasing the legislature's role and those who sustain instead that more popular deliberation is required. This difference is the direct consequence of the fact that. In contrast, some scholars are more supportive of direct democracy procedures, others are more skeptical and fear the externalities of this process. The answer to whether or not direct democracy works well is complex, and we cannot fully answer it here. However, in the following section, we briefly present an overview of the arguments in favor and against these procedures so as to clarify the debate regarding California initiatives.

6.9. The Effects of Direct Democracy on Public Policy

Citizens' positive support for direct democracy is expressed in several surveys worldwide (Altman 2010). California follows this trend, since citizens of this State – in all ethnic groups - have greater trust in the initiative process than in their elected officials, with 70% approval for this measure and a 56% that considers better public policy decisions made by voters, than the one made by the governor and the legislature (Public Policy Institute of California 2005). Moreover, 42% of the citizenry would like the initiative process to have more influence than the legislature, and 75% consider the initiative as the best means to address current political problems. The significant support does not mean that citizens think that this process is perfect since only 1 in 5 citizens believe that it is satisfactory, and many believe it is necessary to add changes (Laird and MacDonald 2011; 305-306).

Concerning other aspects of the initiative process, Californians consider useful the information guide mailed to voters by the Secretary of State and also news stories, while they are more suspicious regarding paid political commercials, even though the majority believes that media are the most influential source of information related to voters' decision. On the contrary, only 1 in 4 considers the voters' guide as influential, and even fewer ranks government and independent websites as influential.

Interestingly, 53% believe voters are not receiving enough information, while 15% say there is "more than enough" and 30% "just enough information" (Laird and MacDonald 2011; 307-308).

It is, instead, more difficult to address the effects of direct democracy on policymaking, even though scholars agree that the latter is affected by the former in several ways. First, governments know that an initiative may challenge their policy in the future and thus try to accommodate opposing views before this happens (Hug 2001; 2). In this way, direct democracy pushes policies more towards the median voter (Rowley 1984) and the will of the majority (Matsusaka 2004), even though this is not always respected in a model with imperfect information. That is, some groups may be better than others at mobilizing their supporters to go to the polls (Becker 1983), and there could be deceptive campaigns, so misinformed voters could vote against their interests (Stigler 1971). However, research on voters' behavior proves that citizens do not get fooled easily, also because if they are not sure, they tend to vote to preserve the status quo (Bowler and Donovan 1998).

Second, critics of direct democracy sustain that the initiative process may be more subject to interest groups than the legislative procedure. This is the "populist paradox," namely the idea that special interests can buy influence through the initiative process by affecting information available to make political decisions and having more resources to start initiatives and direct this process. In a nutshell, initiatives may favor oligarchic interests rather than protecting the people's will from special interests (Hug 2001; 20-21).

However, scholars supporting direct democracy argue that initiatives can offer citizens the chance to override the decisions of elected officials so that representatives will be more aware of the different views in society (Gerber and Lupia 1995). Elected officials may have interests different from those of the general public (Niskanen 1971). Rather than distracting elected officials from pursuing the public interest, direct democracy could prevent them from serving their own interests narrowly. Moreover, candidates run for specific decisions in the initiative process, so different groups can find it easier to understand who stands for which values (Besley and Coate 2003). Finally, initiative states tend to adopt shorter term limits than those without initiatives, favoring most of the populace and against that of political elites (Matsusaka 2004).

Economic interests are thus not as efficient in mobilizing voters as maintained by critics of direct democracy since literature has proved that campaign spending by proponents increases only marginally the chance that the initiative passes. In contrast, money spent to oppose the initiative results in more efficient expenditure (Figueiredo et al. 2006). This procedure could also help resolve some of the logrolling problems, namely that legislatures may tend to bundle together different issues as a single package. There are different views concerning how negative logrolling is. However, literature tends to confirm that it leads to high public spending and it is inefficient, so giving citizens the chance to assess specific measures would improve society's welfare (Buchanan and Tullock 1962).

Third, direct democracy has several economic implications. For example, states employing initiative procedures seem to lead to better economic performances (Pommerhene 1983), to have positive economic effects at the municipal level (Feld and Savioz 1997), to have lower government expenditures and more fee-based taxation (Matsusaka 1995; Matsusaka 2000), and also to better levels of "happiness" (Frey and Strutzer 2000). Direct democracy also seems to respond well to criticism that it is too expensive since it leads to increased competition over the policy process that benefits citizens and increases their welfare. Economic interests may indeed put an issue they care about on the ballot, but eventually, this would give citizens the chance to vote the choice that favors them (Matsusaka 2005; 203-204).

Fourth, initiative states seem to adopt more conservative policies, such as the death penalty or abortion restriction (Gerber 1999). In this regard, it may seem that initiatives could be a threat to minorities rights' and could favor groups already better represented by the legislature. However, this argument has received limited support in the literature (Cronin 1989). For example, some research argues that the California initiative process favors white ethnic groups, but at the same time initiative process has also moved the electorate more towards the democratic party, which could thus help to rebalance the political power among ethnic groups (Smith and Tolbert 2007; 433-434).

On top of that, research shows that states with more citizen interest groups (Bohemke 2005), with increased legal professionalism (Banducci 1998), and with a more heterogeneous population (Matsusaka and McCarty 2001) tend to use more initiatives and referendums. Furthermore, even if direct democracy caused negative effects for certain minorities, such externalities would be reduced by the judiciary's role since judges can review ballot measures in cases with clear discrimination of certain social groups (Zimmerman 1999).

Finally, direct democracy is connected to various improvements concerning the citizens' political participation. For example, younger citizens and those more interested in the political process are more supportive of direct democracy (Donovan and Karp 2006), but initiatives increase voters' turnout of the whole population, especially in salient measures (Lacey 2005). This is not only a positive outcome *per se*, but it often leads to an increase in the level of political knowledge and more confidence in government responsiveness (Smith and Tolbert 2004). Therefore, in political systems where information is dispersed, direct democracy could be the best way to collect diversity and produce collective wisdom (Landemore 2013).

In sum, even though describing how direct democracy affects public policy is not a clear-cut answer, and there are several points where this process could be improved, academic research supports the view for which the initiative process results in both instrumental and educative positive outcomes.

6.10. California as a "Hybrid Democracy"

This chapter described that direct democracy plays a significant role in shaping California's public policy. At the same time, it is important to stress that direct propositions do not occur in isolation, but they are always combined with the bodies of the representative system. For this reason, states like California may be described as "Hybrid Democracies," namely regimes neither entirely representative, not wholly direct. Rather, a political system where features of both procedures interact one with another. Above all, three interactions are significant in this political system (Garret 2005).

First, candidates use initiatives to affect turnout and to highlight campaign issues that could help them in the following elections. Candidates are not interested in increasing voters' turnout *per se*. However, they rather want to increase the number of participants who support them, even though it could be difficult to precisely address the topics one wants, without thereby causing potential long-term externalities that could backfire (Tolbert et al. 2001). This strategy is important for California's main political parties since partisanship is the strongest predictor of votes on ballot measures. Hence, parties can use initiatives to advance their political agendas and offset their declining influence in the legislative arena (Smith and Tolbert 2001).

Second, candidates and interest groups can use ballot measures to increase their membership rolls and fill their financial coffers. That is, initiatives are expensive, so one party could use them as a way to drain resources from their opponents, preventing them from using that money in a following electoral campaign. Nevertheless, it is not only about resources, since one candidate could use highly debated initiatives to raise their profile with people sympathetic with their goals, thus increasing their power in future local or state elections (Kousser and McCubbins 2005).

Third, candidates can use initiatives to circumvent financial restrictions on their campaigns. Contrary to electoral campaigns, there are no limits on initiative campaigns, so using the latter to promote oneself in the former may be an efficient strategy. This process has yet often been questioned as a means to corrupt candidates, so in California, the FPCC (California Fair Political Practices Commission) controls funding given to a certain politician in any issue that relates to her. This rendered it easier to control candidate funding. However, at the same time, interest groups preserve other ways to indirectly favor a certain candidate, such as publicizing indirectly a certain position or initiatives that are likely to be crucial in the following campaign (Hasen 2005).

The hybrid nature of democracy is thus puzzling for proponents of the initiative process. Originally, this procedure was meant to render politicians accountable and bypass the legislature if interest groups corrupted this. However, the answer to whether or not citizens are still doing so using the ballot initiative is less clear-cut. On the one side, there are doubts regarding citizens' ability to make decisions competently and fully understand each phase of the initiative process. On the other side, we described several means by which interest groups can sway the process in their favor. Paradoxically then, a procedure meant to counteract economic powers' political power could end up favoring rather than contrasting them.

Acknowledging the hybrid nature of California's democracy does not entail that direct initiatives are just tools in the hands of a few political elites. Research demonstrates that direct democracy is powerful in shaping directly and indirectly public policy in the States where it is used and that direct democracy produces positive outcomes both from the instrumental and the educative point of view. Therefore, as described in section 4, there is space for reforms and improving this process, either by having a more direct involvement by the legislature or increasing popular participation. In any case, the institutional nature of States using processes of direct democracy will always remain that of a "Hybrid democracy," so any reform or discussion about California's politics will have to consider the dual character of its institutional design.

Works Cited

Altman D. (2010), Direct Democracy Worldwide, *Cambridge University Press*, Cambridge.

Alvarez R.M., Goodrich M., Hall T.E., Roderick D, Kiewiet D.R., and Sled S.M. (2004), "The Complexity of the California Recall Election", *Political Science and Politics*, 37 (1), 23-26.

Amar V.D. (2004), "Adventures in Direct Democracy: The Top Ten Constitutional Lessons from the California Recall Experience", *California Law Review*, 92 (3), 927-958.

Ballotpedia, "Proposition 1a", Retrieved at: https://ballotpedia.org/California_Proposition_1A,_the_%22Constitutional_Revision_Amendment%22_(1966)

_____, "Proposition 9", retrieved at: https://ballotpedia.org/California_Proposition_9,_Marsy%27s_Law_Crime_Victims_Rights_Amendment_(2008)

_____, "Proposition 13", retrieved at: https://ballotpedia.org/California_Proposition_13,_Tax_Limitations_Initiative_(1978)

_____, "Parcel Tax", retrieved at: https://ballotpedia.org/Parcel_tax

Banducci S. (1998), "Direct Legislation: When It Is Used and When Does It Pass?", in *Citizens as Legislators: Direct Democracy in the United States*, Ohio State University Press, Ohio.

Becker G. S., (1983). "A Theory of Competition Among Pressure Groups for Political Influence.", *Quarterly Journal of Economics*, 98, 371–400.

Besley T., Coate S. (2003), "Issue Unbundling by Voter Initiatives.", *Working paper*, London School of Economics, London.

Bohemke F. (2005), *The Indirect Effect of Direct Legislation: How Institutions Shape Interest Group Systems*, Ohio University Press, Ohio.

Bowler S, Donovan T. (1998), *Demanding Choices: Opinion, Voting and Direct Democracy*, University of Michigan Press, Michigan.

_____ (2003), "Measuring the Effects of Direct Democracy on State Policy and Politics.", *Working Paper*, UC Riverside.

Bowler S., Donovan T., McCuan D., Fernandez K. (1998), "Contending Players and Strategies: Opposition Advantages in Initiative Campaigns", in *Citizens as Legislators: Direct Democracy in the United States*, 80-92.

Brennan J. (2016), *Against Democracy*, Princeton University Press, Princeton.

Buchanan J. M., Tullock G. (1962), *The Calculus of Consent: Logical Foundations of Constitutional Democracy*, University of Michigan Press, Michigan.

California Office of the Secretary of State (2020), *Procedures for Recalling State and Local Officials*. Available at: https://elections.cdn.sos.ca.gov/recalls/recall-procedures-guide.pdf

California Secretary of State (2021), *Statewide Initiative Guide*. Available at: https://www.sos.ca.gov/elections/ballot-measures/initiative-and-referendum-status/

Chapman, J. (1998), *Proposition 13: Some Unintended Consequences*, Public Policy Institute of California, San Francisco.

Chavez L. (1998), *The Color Bind: California's Battle to End Affirmative Action*, Berkeley, University of California Press, California.

Collins R.B., Oesterle D (1995), "Structuring the Ballot Initiative: Procedures That Do and Don't Work", *University of Colorado Law Review*, 49-94-

Cronin T. (1989), *Direct Democracy: The Politics of Initiative, Referendum, and Recall*, Harvard University Press, Cambridge.

De Figueiredo J. M., Chang Ho Ji, Kousser T (2006), "Do Intiative Backers Waster Their Money? Revisiting the Research on Campaign Spending and Direct Democracy.", *1st Annual Conference on Empirical Legal Studies Paper*, Available at SSRN: https://ssrn.com/abstract=916463

Dolan, M., Guccione J. (2003). "Court Dates Approach for Challenges to Recall.", *Los Angeles Times*, 14 August: A-21.

Donovan T., Karp J. (2006), "Popular Support for Direct Democracy", *Party Politics*, 12 (5), 671-88.

Eastman H. (1985), "Squelching Vox Populi: Judicial Review of the Initiative in California.", *Santa Clara Law Review*, 25, 529.

Feld L.P., Savioz M.R. (1997), "Direct Democracy Matters for Economic Performance: An Empirical Investigation.", *Kyklos*, 50(4), 507-538.

Garrett E. (2005), "Hybrid Democracy," *George Washington Law Review* 73, 5 and 6, 1096-1130.

Garrett E., Gerber E.R. (2001), "Money in the Initiative and Referendum Process: Evidence of Its Effects and Prospects for Reform", in *The Battle Over Citizen Lawmaking*, 73 (M. Dane Waters ed., 2001).

Gerber E. R. (1999), *The Populist Paradox: Interest Group Influence and the Promise of Direct Legislation*, Princeton, Princeton University Press.

Gerber E.R., Lupia A. (1995), "Campaign Competition and Policy Responsiveness in Direct Political Behaviour", *Political Behaviour*, 17, 287-306.

Grodin J.R., Massey C.R., Cunningham R.B. (2016), *The California State Constitution: A Reference Guide*, Oxford University Press, Oxford.

Hasen R.L. (2005), "Rethinking the Unconstitutionality of Contribution and Expenditure Limits in Ballot Measure Campaigns, *California Law Review*, 78, 885-903.

Held D. (2006), *Models of Democracy*, Polity, Cambridge.

Hoffman A., (2003). "Partial Hand-Count of Ballots Reveals Few Irregularities.", *Los Angeles Times*, 16 October, B-4.

Hug, S. (2001), "Direct and Indirect Initiatives.", In *97th Annual Meeting of the American Political Science Association*, San Francisco, 1-36.

Kabat P. (2009), "Till Naught But Ash is Left to See: Statewide Smoking Bans, Ballot Initiatives, and the Public Sphere", *Yale Journal of Health, Polity, Law & Ethics*, 128, 149-50.

Kashani N. H., Stern R.M. (2011), "Making California's Initiative Process More Deliberative", *California Western Law Review*, 47 (2), 311-328.

Kousser T., McCubbins M.D. (2005), "Social Choice, Crypto-Initiatives and Policy Making by Direct Democracy", *California Law Review*, 78, 949-974.

Lacey R. (2005), "The Electoral Allure of Direct Democracy: The Effect of Initiative Salience on Voting, 1990-1996", *State Politics and Policy Quarterly*, 5 (2), 168-181.

Laird J., MacDonald C. (2011), "A.B. 1245 of 2003 - An Attempt at Modest Reform of California's Initiative Process", *California Western Law Review*, 47 (2), 301-310.

Landemore H. (2013), *Democratic Reason: Politics, Collective Intelligence, and the Rule of the Many*, Princeton University Press, Princeton.

Levitt S.D. (1994), "Using Repeat Challengers to Estimate the Effect of Campaign Spending on Election Outcomes in the U.S. House", *Journal of Political Economy*, 102, 777–791.

Levy F. (1979), "On Understanding Proposition 13", *The Public Interest*, 56, 66-89.

Liebert, L. T. (1998), "Researching California Ballot Measures.", *Law Library Journal*, 90, 27-50.

Lowenstein D.H. (1983), "California Initiatives and the Single-Subject Rule, *UCLA Law Review*, 30, 936.

Lunch W.M. (1998), "Budgeting by Initiative: An Oxymoron", *Willamette Law Review*, 34, 663-670.

Lupia A, Matsusaka G. (2004), "Direct Democracy: New Approaches to Old Questions", *Annual Review of Political Science*, 7, 463–82.

Manin B. (1997), *The Principles of Representative Government*, Cambridge University Press, Cambridge.

Matsusaka G. (1995), "Fiscal Effects of the Voter Initiative: Evidence from the last 30 Years.", *Journal of Political Economy*, 103 (3), 587-623.

_____ (2000), "Fiscal Effects of the Voter Initiative in the First Half of the Twentieth Century.", *Journal of Law and Economics*, 43, 619-644.

_____ (2005), "Direct Democracy Works", *Journal of Economic Perspectives*, 19 (2), 185–206.

Matsusaka J., McCarthy N. (2001), "Political Resource Allocation: Benefits and Costs of Voter Initiative", *Journal of Law, Economics and Organization*, 17, 413-448.

Mendelberg T. (2002), "The Deliberative Citizen: Theory and Evidence.", *Political Decision Making, Deliberation and Participation*, 6 (1), 151-193.

Miller K.P. (2001), "Constraining Populism: The Real Challenge of Initiative Reform", *Santa Clara Law Review*, 1037, 1064-68.

Niskanen, W. A. (1971), *Bureaucracy and Representative Government*, Aldine-Atherton, Chicago.

D. Oppenheimer, M. Edwards (2012), *Democracy Despite Itself: Why a System that Shouldn't Work at all Works so Well*, MIT Press, Cambridge.

Pommerehne W. (1983). "Private Versus Oeffentliche Muellabfuhr— Nochmals Betrachtet", *Finanzarchiv*, 41, 466–75.

Public Policy Institute of California (2005), "PPIC Statewide Survey", retrieved at: https://www.ppic.org/content/pubs/survey/S_1105MBS.pdf

Rowley C.K. (1984), "The Relevance of the Median Voter Theorem", *Journal of Institutional and Theoretical Economics*, 140 (1), 104-126.

Schrag P. (2004), *Paradise Lost: California's Experience, America's Future*, University of California Press, California.

Sexton T.A., Sheffrin M.S., O'Sullivan A. (1999), "Proposition 13: Unintended Effects and Feasible Reforms", *National Tax Journal*, 52 (1), 99-111.

Silva J.F. (2000), "The California Initiative Process: Background and Perspective", *Public Policy Institute of California*, California.

Smith A., Tolbert C. (2001), "The Initiative to Party: Partisanship and Ballot Initiatives in California", *Party Politics*, 7 (6), 739-757.

_____ (2004), *Educated by Initiative: The Effects of Direct Democracy on Citizens and Political Organizations in the American States*, University of Michigan Press, Michigan.

Stern R.M. (2011), "California Should Return to The Indirect Initiative", *Loyola of Los Angeles Law Review*, 44 (2), 671-686.

Stigler G. J., (1971), "The Theory of Economic Regulation.", *Bell Journal of Economics and Management Science*, 2, 3–21.

Stratmann T. (2005), "The Effectiveness of Money in Ballot Measure Campaigns", *Southern California Law Review*, 78 (4), 1041-1064.

Tolbert C., Grummel J.A, Daniel A., Smith D.A (2001), "The Effects of Ballot Initiatives on Voter Turnout in the American States", *American Political Research*, 29 (6), 625-643.

Zimmerman J. (1999), *The Initiative: Citizen Law-Making*, Westport, Praeger.

CHAPTER 7

The Executive Branch
of California

7.1. Introduction to the Executive Branch

The Governor of a state or province is the executive head of government in any democratic country and serves as a link between the state and federal governments. The Governor of California is the head of the State's executive branch. They are chosen for a four-year term and may be re-elected by California for a second term (Ferguson). The executive branch of California's government is in charge of executing and enforcing the State's laws, and the Governor leads it. The Governor also appoints members of the State's judiciary.

In practice, when it comes to crafting new laws, the executive branch collaborates closely with the legislative branch. In addition to the Governor, other executive branch members are the Lieutenant Governor, Secretary of State, and Attorney General, to mention a few, who are all elected for four-year terms and, like the Governor, may be re-elected. There are four different sorts of organizations for the executive branch: agencies, which secretaries lead; departments, which directors lead; and boards and commissions, which are led by an executive officer or board member (Ferguson).

The State of California's fundamental governing document is the California Constitution. California's current Constitution was adopted in 1879 and has been revised 516 times as of 2020. The executive branch of the State of California is dealt with under Article V of the Constitution. There are 13 sections in Article v, numbered 1 through 14, with no section 12. The Governor has the supreme executive power in this State, according to Section 1 of the Constitution.

The Governor is responsible for ensuring that the legislation is faithfully carried out. The Governor's tenure is limited in section 2 of the Constitution, as is the electing the Governor of the State. The Governor shall be elected every fourth year at the same time and place as members of the Assembly. He shall occupy office from the Monday after the election until a successor qualifies, according to section 2 of the state constitution. The Governor shall be an elector who has been a United States citizen and a resident of this State for at least five years before the Governor's election. The Governor is prohibited from holding any other public office. A governor may not serve more than two terms in office. Every calendar year, the Governor must report to the Legislature on the State of the State and make suggestions (Costa).

7.2. California Laws

California's laws are administered and enforced by the executive branch. The California executive branch is made up of over 200 state institutions and is led by the Governor. The people of California elect the branch's executive authorities, such as the Governor, Lieutenant Governor, Secretary of State, and Attorney General, to mention a few. Each of these offices is chosen for a four-year term, with a maximum of two terms in each office. There are four sorts of institutions in the executive branch: agencies, which a secretary leads; departments, which a director leads; and boards and commissions, which are led by an executive officer or board member (Morrison, T.W).

The University of California Regents and the Public Utilities Commission, for example, are supposed to be independent of direct supervision by all three parts of the state government. The Governor appoints the majority of these organization's leaders, who the California Senate then confirms. The Governor is also in charge of appointing the secretaries/directors of 11 Cabinet-level state agencies/departments: Business, Consumer Services, and Housing; Corrections and Rehabilitation (Department); Environmental Protection; Finance (Department); Food and Agriculture (Department); Natural Resources; Government Operations; Health and Human Services (Department); Natural Resources; Government Operations; Health and Human Services (Department); Health and Human Services (Department); Health and Human Services (Department); Health and Human Services, Labor and Workforce Development, Transportation, and Veterans Affairs are the four departments that make up the Department of Human Services (Morrison, T.W).

Each Cabinet-level Agency has many departments, the heads of which are likewise nominated by the Governor and are generally subject to Senate approval. The Natural Resources Agency, for example, is part of the Cabinet.

7.3. The State's Governor

The Governor of California is the most influential figure in the State's executive branch. The Governor of California is elected by the people of California and is limited to two four-year terms. The following are some of the roles and duties.

The State Address is delivered to members of the Legislature at the start of each legislative session. The annual budget is presented to the Legislature, together with projected revenue and cost statements. The ability to veto any bill enacted by the Legislature and return it to the house of origin with his concerns. Appropriation legislation is subject to line-item veto power.

The requirement is that an itemized budget be submitted to the Legislature within the first ten days of each calendar year. The judiciary has the authority to fill vacancies in government executive departments and appoint people to those posts. The Governor has the authority to serve as the State's Commander in Chief and represent the State's informal dealings with other states and the federal government. Governors are elected by popular vote for a four-year term, with a two-term limit if elected after November 6, 1990.

"I (Governor) solemnly swear that I will support and defend the Constitution of the United States and the Constitution of the State of California against all enemies foreign and domestic, that I will bear true faith and allegiance to the Constitution of the United States and the Constitution of the State of California, that I take this obligation freely without reservation," says the Governor (California's Constitution).

The Governor's responsibilities are outlined in the California Constitution. They include delivering the State's annual State address to the California State Legislature, submitting the budget, and ensuring that state laws are followed. In 1849, the year before California became a state, the office was founded. California's current Governor is Democrat Gavin Newsom, who took office on January 7, 2019.

7.4 California Legislative Power

Governors have various responsibilities in the office, but there are two primary responsibilities concerning state legislatures. First, they may have the authority to call extraordinary legislative sessions, provided that the purpose and schedule for the sessions are established ahead of time in most situations. Second, the Governor collaborates and collaborate with state legislators in the approval of state budgets and appropriations.

The Governor is also responsible for enacting state legislation. Any state or society's backbone is the judiciary. In California, the Governor appoints all of the State's judicial and executive officials. Last but not least, the Governor's authority over executive branch duties in the State is subject to legislative review (Kaskla).

Governors frequently explain their legislative platforms in State of the State statements, and many governors prepare particular legislative proposals to be introduced on their behalf. Additionally, state departments and agencies may seek gubernatorial support for legislative projects.

Governors and other executive branch leaders are frequently summoned to speak on legislative initiatives. They will attempt to organize public opinion and interest groups in support of or opposition to specific legislative ideas. In conjunction with department heads and staff, governors may endeavor to influence the progress of legislation through regular meetings with legislators and legislative officials to garner support for legislative measures.

7.5. Budget Powers

For consideration and approval by the Legislature, Governor prepares and submits annual or biennial budget proposals to the Legislature for consideration and approval. Governors in several states, commonwealths, and territories have the authority to exercise "reduction" veto power (also known as "line-item" or "line-item" veto power), which allows them to remove appropriations from budgets that they oppose.

The use of these tools allows governors and their budget staff to significantly impact the establishment of priorities for the allocation of state resources in a variety of ways (Kaskla).

7.6 Budget Oversight

During oversight hearings and other legislative activities, governors interact with their legislatures to help ensure that their priorities, goals, and achievements are accurately presented and positively received. These activities include examining and evaluating the implementation of legislatively mandated programs and services by the executive branch.

7.7. Chief Security

Californians have a long and proud tradition of military service that dates back more than two centuries to when Alta California was a Spanish colony and later a Mexican province when the State was known as California. More than any other state, California has contributed more citizens to our national defense since joining the Union. Californians have always been there, whether in the isolated colonial presidios of the El Real Ejército de California (Royal Spanish Army of California) in the 18th century or the mountains of Afghanistan, or protecting our citizens from natural disasters. They have continued the tradition of selfless service.

The California State Guard is an integral part of the State's integrated disaster and emergency response system in today's world. The National Guard provides a trained military force with unique capabilities. It collaborates seamlessly with our National Guard counterparts, federal agencies, State and local governments, and non-governmental relief organizations to provide critical assistance when required.

The missions of today are as diverse as the missions of California. It does not matter if they are screening people for the coronavirus, evacuating residents from a wildfire, rescuing people from floodwaters, delivering critical food and medical supplies to those in need, or providing emergency shelter for displaced residents, the men, women, and children of the California State Guard keep their motto, "Ready to Respond," in mind every single day.

7.8. The Constitutional Executive Officers

The Governor, Lieutenant Governor, Secretary of State, Attorney General, State Controller, State Treasurer, Insurance Commissioner, and State Superintendent of Public Instruction are the eight constitutional officers who serve statewide. These officers are elected concurrently in a General Election and are eligible for re-election for a maximum of two four-year terms.

In the event of a vacancy in the Governor's office, the Lieutenant Governor shall succeed to the Governorship. In the event of a vacancy in either the Governor or Lieutenant Governor offices, the succession order is as follows: first, the last duly elected Senate President Pro Tempore; second, the last duly elected Assembly Speaker; third, the Secretary of State; fourth, the Attorney General; fifth, the State Treasurer; and finally, the State Controller.

7.9. The California Governor

The Governor of the State of California has supreme executive authority, and it is his responsibility to ensure that the law is faithfully executed. The Governor is the State's Commander-in-Chief. The Governor serves as the State's official liaison with the federal government and other states in the United States. The Governor is responsible for supervising the official conduct of all executive and ministerial officers and ensuring that all positions are filled and duties are performed.

The Governor's appointment authority encompasses a sizable portion of state government. First, the Governor has the authority to fill judicial vacancies (i.e., in the Municipal, Superior, Appeals, and Supreme Courts) and create new judgeships. Second, the Governor has the authority to appoint a large number of positions throughout the executive Department, subject to confirmation by the State Senate.

Throughout the calendar year, the Governor communicates with the Legislature about the State's condition and makes recommendations. Within the first ten days of each year, the Governor submits an itemized budget to the Legislature. The Governor has the authority to veto any bill passed by the Legislature and return it to the house of origin with his objections. Additionally, the Governor may reduce or eliminate one or more appropriation items while approving other provisions of a bill.

Along with his immediate staff, the Governor appoints a cabinet consisting of the secretaries of ten major state agencies (Business, Transportation, and Housing; Corrections and Rehabilitation; Environmental

Protection; Food and Agriculture; Health and Human Services; Labor and Workforce Development; Resources; State and Consumer Services; and Veterans Affairs), as well as the Director of Finance. This group serves as the Governor's chief policy advisory body, and each member implements and coordinates the Governor's policies throughout the State in their respective capacities. The Cabinet provides the Governor with a comprehensive overview and up-to-date history of state operations and serves as a resource for long-range planning.

7.10. The California Lieutenant Governor

In the event of a vacancy, the Lieutenant Governor becomes Governor, according to the Constitution. In the Governor's absence from the State, temporary infirmity, or impeachment, the Lieutenant Governor will function as acting Governor. According to the Constitution, the Lieutenant Governor is also President of the Senate, although solely with a casting vote. A casting vote is used to break a tie in a vote. Only the casting vote may be utilized if it will produce the requisite majority.

The Lieutenant Governor is an ex-officio member of the Board of Regents of the University of California and a voting member of the Board of Trustees of California State University. As chair of the State Lands Commission, he alternates with the State Controller. The Lieutenant Governor also chairs the California Commission for Economic Development.

7.11. The Secretary of State

The Secretary of State is California's chief elections officer, in charge of overseeing and certifying elections and inspecting and certifying voting technology for use in the State. She enforces election laws, maintains a voter database, certifies official candidate lists for each election, certifies initiatives for inclusion on the state ballot, publishes the Voter Information Guide before each statewide election, compiles election returns, publishes the official Statement of Vote, and certifies election results. By giving the public access to a wide range of corporate, Uniform Commercial Code, campaign finance, lobbying, and election data, the Secretary of State plays a significant role in making government transparent and accessible. The California Lobbyist Directory and the California Roster of federal, state, and local government officials are both available online through the Secretary.

The California Business Portal, run by the Secretary of State, provides businesses with online information, resources, and services. The Secretary of State receives, reviews, and approves articles of incorporation for new California corporations and qualifies out-of-state and international corporations to conduct business in the State. The Secretary's Business Programs Division also approves and registers trademarks, trade names, service marks, and fictitious names, as well as amending the records of domestic and qualifying foreign corporations. The Secretary is in charge of commissioning and appointing notaries public and administering oaths of office to non-civil service officers and workers. The Domestic Partnership Registry, the Advance Health Care Directive Registry, and the Safe at Home initiative are managed by the Secretary of State. Safe at Home's discreet mail forwarding program assists survivors of domestic abuse, sexual assault, and stalking, as well as those who work in reproductive health care clinics, to protect their identities.

The Secretary of State maintains a detailed record of all official acts of the state legislature and executive departments. The Secretary is in charge of the enrolled copy of the Constitution, all acts and resolutions approved by the Legislature, each house's Journals, the Great Seal of California, and all books, documents, deeds, parchments, maps, and papers retained or deposited in the office subject to the law. As custodian of the public archives, the Secretary maintains and adequately equips safe and secure vaults to preserve materials entrusted to her. The Secretary of State affixes the Great Seal on commissions, pardons, and other public papers that require the Governor's signature, along with her attestation.

7.12. The California Attorney General

The Attorney General is responsible for implementing California's laws consistently and fairly and assisting district attorneys, local law enforcement, and federal and international criminal justice agencies in administering justice.

The Attorney General's constitutional responsibilities are carried out through the Department of Justice's programs. The Department's legal programs represent the people in civil and criminal cases before California and federal trial, appellate, and supreme courts. The Attorney General defends Californians from fraudulent, unfair, and illegal acts that harm consumers or endanger public safety, as well as enforcing environmental and natural resource protection laws.

The Attorney General also serves as legal counsel to state officers and governmental agencies, boards, and commissions, with a few exceptions. Central law offices for the Department's legal program are located in Sacramento, Fresno, San Francisco, Oakland, Los Angeles, and San Diego. The Division of Law Enforcement of the Department of Justice conducts forensic services, narcotic investigations, criminal investigations, intelligence, and training. Using cutting-edge computer technology, the Division of California Justice Information Services promotes the sharing of accurate, fast, and entire criminal justice intelligence.

7.13. The State Controller

The State Controller is the State's chief financial officer. The State Controller's primary responsibilities include: (1) providing sound fiscal control over both public fund receipts and disbursements; (2) reporting on the financial operations and condition of both state and local governments regularly; (3) ensuring that money owed to the State is collected through fair, equitable, and effective tax administration; (4) providing financial guidance to local governments; and (5) providing financial guidance to local governments.

No money can be taken from the Treasury unless it is by a lawful appropriation and on warrants issued by the State Controller. The State Controller oversees the State's financial affairs, makes recommendations for improving and managing public revenues, keeps all accounts in which the State has an interest, and keeps a separate account for each appropriation, showing the appropriation's balance at all times. The State Controller is in charge of overseeing the State's finances and auditing all claims against it. The State Controller is in charge of collecting all monies owed to the State and is permitted to go to court if required to retrieve the property or money owed. The State Controller oversees the general procedure for tax sales, tax deeds, and redemptions and enacts essential fiscal rules and regulations.

7.14. The State Treasure

The State Treasurer is the government's banker, investor, and asset manager. The Treasurer invests money on behalf of the State, cities, counties, schools, and other local governments. The Treasurer is in charge of selling and administering the State's bond program, which includes voter-approved infrastructure bonds. The Treasurer is a member of the California Public Employees' Retirement System (CalPERS), the State Teachers' Retirement System (CalSTRS), and the California Housing Finance Agency's boards of directors (CalHFA).

The Treasurer heads and supervises authorities that fund various programs, including education, health care, affordable housing, transportation, economic development, alternative energy, and pollution cleanup. The California Alternative Energy and Advanced Transportation Financing Authority, the California Debt and Investment Advisory Commission, the California Debt Limit Allocation Committee, the California Educational Facilities Authority, the California Health Facilities Financing Authority, and the California Healthy Food Financing Initiative are just a few of the boards, commissions, and authorities that the Treasurer chairs.

7.15. The Insurance Commissioner

The Insurance Commissioner is in charge of supervising the insurance sector in California and ensuring that the State's insurance consumers are protected. California's insurance sector is worth $123 billion each year and contributes considerably to the State's economy. The Insurance Commissioner leads the California Department of Insurance. The California Department of Insurance (CDI) guarantees that customers are protected. The insurance market is dynamic and stable, and the law is adequately enforced in an open and equitable regulatory environment.

As the head of the State's biggest consumer protection agency, the Insurance Commissioner is responsible for enforcing the California Insurance Code and promulgating rules to put it into effect. The Commissioner has the authority to regulate auto, homeowners, and other property and casualty insurance rates and has saved consumers and businesses tens of billions of dollars in premiums. However, the Commissioner does not have the authority to approve or disapprove health insurance rates or premiums.

The Insurance Commissioner licenses more than 200,000 agents, brokers, solicitors, and bail bond agents in the State and insurance and title firms to do business in California. Consumers with insurance-related inquiries or difficulties can call CDI's statewide toll-free hotline, which functions as an information clearinghouse. Insurance specialists staff the service, which receives roughly 200,000 customer Requests for Assistance each year. The Department investigates firms and licensees suspected of insurance code breaches, including fraud, based on these Requests for Assistance, and the result is the restoration of tens of millions of dollars to customers each year, as well as the punishment of individuals who break the law.

7.16. The State Superintendent

Of California's eight statewide constitutional officials, the State Superintendent of Public Instruction is the only one who is nonpartisan. The

Superintendent is responsible to the people of California for enforcing and implementing education laws and regulations and continuing to reform and enhance public elementary and secondary schools, adult education, and some preschool and child care program. The State Board of Education's executive officer and Secretary and the director of the California Department of Education are the Superintendent (CDE). The California Department of Education (CDE) runs the State's public education system. The objective of the CDE is to guarantee that all students in California, from early childhood through maturity, get a world-class education. The CDE supports our State by innovating and partnering with educators, schools, parents, and community partners to ensure that children are prepared to live, work, and prosper in a globally linked society.

The Superintendent is in charge of the CDE's day-to-day operations and two deaf schools, one blind school, and three neurologically impaired diagnostic clinics. The Superintendent is an ex officio member of the California State University and California Commission on Teacher Credentialing boards of trustees and an ex officio member of the University of California Board of Regents. More than 100 boards, commissions, and committees formed by the Department, the Legislature, or the Executive Branch include the Superintendent as an ex officio member or with representation.

7.17. Super Agencies of The State of California

Many agencies in California are providing their services to the people of California and helping the Executive Branch of California. The Business, Consumer Services, and Housing Organization (BCSH) is a cabinet-level California government agency that aids and educates consumers about professional and business licensing regulations and enforcement. Nine departments make up this organization, and they all work for the people of California. These departments are:

The California Department of Consumer Affairs (DCA) : The California Department of Consumer Affairs (DCA) is a California Department of Business, Consumer Services, and Housing division. DCA's declared purpose is to protect California consumers' interests by assuring a high level of professionalism in critical industries and encouraging educated consumer behavior. To safeguard the public from unethical or untrained persons who advertise misleading products or services, the DCA offers safe consumer practices.

The Department of Fair Employment and Housing: The California Department of Fair Employment and Housing is a state organization tasked with protecting residents against discrimination in employment, housing, and public accommodations, as well as hate violence. It is the United States' largest state civil rights agency. It also provides legal counsel to hate crime victims. DFEH was established in 1980 as a different agency from the Department of Industrial Relations. DFEH is led by a director nominated by California's Governor, and it operates five offices and five instructional clinics around the State.

The Department of Housing and Community Development (HCD): The California Department of Housing and Community Development (HCD) is a division of the California Department of Business, Consumer Services, and Housing that develops housing policy and building codes (such as the California Building Standards Code), regulates manufactured homes and mobile home parks and administers housing finance, economic development, and community development programs.

The Department of Financial Protection and Innovation (DFPI): The California Department of Financial Protection and Innovation (DFPI) is a division of the BCSH that regulates a wide range of financial services, products, and professions.

The Department of Real Estate (DRE): The California Department of Real Estate (DRE) is the state agency in charge of administering real estate license exams, issuing real estate licenses and specific mortgage loan originator endorsements to those who pass them, regulating and disciplining real estate licensees, and qualifying specific residential subdivision offerings.

The Department of Alcoholic Beverage (ABC): The California Department of Alcoholic Beverage Control (ABC) is a governmental organization that governs the manufacturing, distribution, and sale of alcoholic drinks in California. The Agency is led by a director nominated by California's Governor, and its two divisions are organized into districts depending on demographic and geographic demands.

The Alcoholic Control Appeals Board: The California Alcoholic Beverage Control Appeals Board is a quasi-judicial administrative court and constitutional office in the U.S. state of California. The Board hears appeals from final decisions of the Department of Alcoholic Beverage Control regarding the issuance of alcoholic beverage licenses, license conditions, protests against the issuance of licenses, and violations of law by licensees.

The California Horse Racing Board (CHRB): The California Horse Racing Board (CHRB) was founded in 1933 as an autonomous body of the California State Government. The CHRB is in charge of regulating horse racing and parimutuel betting at California race tracks licensed. The CHRB's job is to keep an eye on approved California horse races to safeguard the public from scams. It is a division of the Business, Consumer Services, and Housing Agency.

The Seismic Safety Commission: The Seismic Safety Commission was created in 1975 to enact the Seismic Safety Act to advise the Governor, Legislature, and state and municipal governments on methods to minimize earthquake risk. The Commission examines earthquakes, researches earthquake-related topics and reports, and makes policy and program recommendations to the Governor and Legislature to decrease earthquake risk.

Natural Resources: The California Natural Resources Agency (CNRA) is a cabinet-level state agency of the California government. Sections 12800 and 12805, et seq. of the California Government Code establish the Natural Resources Agency and define its authority. Seven departments, ten conservancies, seventeen boards and commissions, three councils, and one urban park in Los Angeles with two museums, the California Science Center and the California African American Museum, make up the Agency.

The Natural Resources Agency is responsible for protecting prehistoric history, natural landscapes, and cultural sites, monitoring and stewarding state lands and waterways, regulating fish and game use, as well as private lands and the intersection with federal lands and waters, through its 25 departments, conservancies, and commissions. Wade Crowfoot, the current Secretary of Natural Resources, is a member of Governor Gavin Newsom's Cabinet.

Departments: The Natural Resources Agency is the parent department to several other departments:

The Department of Conservation: The California Department of Conservation is a division of the California Natural Resources Agency and is part of the state government of California. The Department of Conservation manages several programs vital to California's public safety, environment, and economy with the help of a staff of scientists, engineers, environmental experts, and other professionals.

The purpose of the Agency is to manage California's working lands. It oversees the regulation of oil, natural gas, and geothermal wells, the research and mapping of earthquakes and other geologic phenomena, the mapping and classification of mineral deposit areas, the reclamation of mined land, and the administration of agricultural and open-space land conservation programs.

The CALFED BAY-Delta Program: The CALFED Bay-Delta Program, or CALFED, is a California government agency managed by the California

Resources Agency. The Agency serves as a consortium, combining the actions and interests of California's state government and the federal government to concentrate on linked water issues in the Sacramento-San Joaquin River Delta. Following a decade of fierce conflicts between California, the federal government, environmental organizations, agricultural interests, and municipal water utilities, Governor Pete Wilson and federal Interior Secretary Bruce Babbitt established the coordinating program in 1994.

The California Department of Fish and Wildlife (CDFW): The California Department of Fish and Wildlife (CDFW), previously known as the California Department of Fish and Game (CDFG), is a California Natural Resources Department state agency. The State's animals, wildflowers, trees, mushrooms, algae (kelp), and natural habitats are managed and protected by the Department of Fish and Wildlife (ecosystems). Regulatory enforcement and administration of associated recreational, commercial, scientific, and educational applications are the responsibility of the Department.

California Department of Forestry and Fire Protection: Cal Fire (California Agency of Forestry and Fire Protection) is a fire department in California, United States, part of the California Natural Resources Agency. It is in charge of fire prevention in a total of 31 million acres under state control and the management of the State's private and public forests. In addition, the agency contracts with local governments to offer a variety of emergency services in 36 of the State's 58 counties. Thom Porter, the Department's head, was appointed by California Governor Gavin Newsom.

California Department of Parks and Recreation: The California State Parks system is managed by the California Department of Parks and Recreation, commonly known as California State Parks. Over 280 miles (450 km) of shoreline, 625 miles (1,000 km) of lake and river frontage, over 15,000 campgrounds, and 3,000 miles (4,800 km) of hiking, bicycling, and equestrian paths are managed by the system, which spans 1.4 million acres (570,000 hectares).

California Department of Water Resources: The California Department of Water Resources (DWR), which is part of the California Natural Resources Agency, manages and regulates water use in the State. Following catastrophic floods in Northern California in 1955, Governor Goodwin Knight established the Agency in 1956, combining the Department of Public Works Division of Water Resources with the State Engineer's Office, the Water Project Authority, and the State Water Resources Board.

California Conservation Corps: The California Conservation Corps, or CCC, is a state government agency that reports to the California Resources Agency, part of the state cabinet. The CCC is a volunteer job development program for men and women aged 18 to 25 (up to 29 for veterans), including environmental conservation, fire prevention, land management, and natural disaster response.

Government Operations: The California Government Operations Agency (Cal Gov Ops) is the state agency in charge of state operations such as procurement, real estate, information technology, and human resources. Governor Jerry Brown named Marybel Batjer as the Agency's first secretary in June 2013. Batjer was appointed head of the California Public Utilities Commission by Governor Gavin Newsom on July 12, 2019. Batjer will leave CalGovOps in late July or early August.

Departments, Boards, and Offices: The Government Operations Agency oversees 12 departments, boards, and offices:

Office of Administrative Law (OAL): The California Office of Administrative Law (OAL) is the state agency responsible for enforcing the California Administrative Procedure Act's rulemaking provisions. The California Government Operations Agency is in charge of it. The OAL is in charge of producing the weekly California Regulatory Notice Register and the California Code of Regulations that results from it (CCR).

Complete Count Committee (CCC): The Governor of California appoints the California Complete Count Committee (Committee), tasked with developing and implementing a statewide outreach and awareness campaign to guarantee that all Californians are tallied in the decennial census. The U.S. Census Bureau and Complete Count Committees form cooperation. More than $435 billion is awarded to states based on census data in whole or in part.

Department of FISCAL: The California Department of Financial Information System for California (FISCal) is a state government department that is part of the California Government Operations Agency, which is part of California's executive branch. The Department is trying to have its FISCal system fully managed and operated. Since the Department's official designation in July 2016, current director Miriam Barcellona Ingenito has headed it.

The California Franchise Text Board (FTB): The California Franchise Tax Board (FTB) collects the State's personal and corporate income taxes. The California Government Operations Agency is in charge of it. The California State Controller, Director of the California Department of Finance, and Chair of the California Board of Equalization make up the Board. The Franchise Tax Board's executive officer is the Board's top administrative official.

Department of General Services (DGS): The California Department of General Services (DGS) is a state government department part of the California Government Operations Agency, which is part of the executive branch of California's government. It performs a similar function to the General Services Administration for the United States federal government in providing a wide range of services to other California government departments.

Department of Human Resource (CalHR): The California Department of Human Resources (CalHR) is the state department in charge of state employee human resource management, including salary and benefit problems, job classifications, training, and recruiting. The Government Operations Agency oversees it. CalHR was established in 2012, combining the previous Department of Personnel Administration (DPA) with most of the State Personnel Board's functions.

State Personnel Board (SPB): The California State Personnel Board (SPB), a constitutional office, is one of the two California bodies in charge of administering the merit-based civil service employment system for state agencies. The other is the California Department of Human Resources. The Board establishes and enforces rules for state civil service appointments and exams and maintains a staff of administrative law judges to resolve a variety of human resources issues, including whistleblower complaints, disability and medical condition discrimination complaints, reasonable accommodation denials, and appeals from unfavorable human resources decisions (e.g., reprimand, salary reduction, suspension without pay, demotion or dismissal). The Board itself hears appeals from the Board's administrative law section.

Transportation: The California State Transportation Organization (CalSTA) is a cabinet-level state agency in charge of transportation-related departments. The Agency was established in 2013 by Governor Jerry Brown when the portfolio of the former Business, Transportation, and Housing Agency was reorganized. Following Governor Gavin Newsom's nomination in April 2019, David S. Kim became the third Secretary of the California State Transportation Agency (CalSTA) on July 1, 2019.

Organizations: CalSTA consists of the following transportation-related entities

Board of Pilot Commission (BPC): The California state body responsible for licensing and regulating pilots inside one of the world's biggest ports and the downstream Sacramento River delta is the Board of Pilot Commissioners for the Bays of San Francisco, San Pablo, and Suisun. The San Francisco Bar Pilots Association licenses and controls up to 60 pilots. They are known as "bar pilots" because they navigate ships over a vast and hazardous sand bar at the entrance of San Francisco Bay, right outside the Golden Gate.

The California Highway Patrol (CHP): The California Highway Patrol (CHP) is a law enforcement organization that serves the State of California in the United States. The CHP, commonly known as the state police, has patrol authority over all California roads. They also have control over city streets and have the authority to carry out law enforcement operations there. With legislation approved by Governor C. C. Young on August 14, 1929, the California State Legislature created the California Highway Patrol as a Department of Public Works Division of Motor Vehicles component.

The California Transportation Commission (CTC): The California Transportation Agency (CTC) was formed in 1978 as an independent government transportation commission. The California Highway Commission, the State Transportation Board, the State Aeronautics Board, and the California Toll Bridge Authority were all replaced by the CTC, which took over their duties.

Department of Motor Vehicle (DMV): The California Department of Motor Vehicles (DMV) is the state agency in the United States that registers automobiles and watercraft and provides driver licenses. It supervises new vehicle dealers, commercial freight carriers, private driving schools, and private traffic schools (via the New Motor Vehicle Board). The DMV collaborates with California's superior courts to quickly register convictions against driver licenses and then suspends or revokes licenses when a motorist collects too many convictions.

Department of Transportation (Caltrans): Caltrans (California Agency of Transportation) is a state executive department in the United States. The Department is part of the California State Transportation Agency, a cabinet-level agency (CalSTA). Sacramento is the headquarters of Caltrans. [4] Caltrans is responsible for managing the State's highway system, which includes the California Freeway and Expressway System, and funding and oversight for three state-supported Amtrak intercity rail routes, which are collectively known as Amtrak California.

The California High-Speed Authority (CHSRA): The California High-Speed Train Authority (CHSRA) is a California state organization charged with developing and implementing high-speed intercity rail service, namely the California High-Speed Rail project, under the California High-Speed Rail Act.

New Motor Vehicle Board (NMVB): The California Department of Motor Vehicles (DMV) is the state agency in the United States that registers automobiles and watercraft and provides driver licenses. It supervises new vehicle dealers, commercial freight carriers, private driving schools, and private traffic schools.

Office of Traffic Safety (OTS): The California Office of Traffic Safety aims to efficiently administer traffic safety funds to provide innovative programs and reduce traffic deaths and injuries on California roads.

Health and Human Services: The Human Relations Agency was established in 1961 under Government Code section 12800, was changed to the Health and Welfare Agency in 1972, and then to its present name in 1998.

The California Health and Human Services Organization (CHHS) is a state agency in the United States responsible for the administration and supervision of "state and federal programs for health care, social services, public assistance, and rehabilitation." The Secretary of the California Health and Human Services Agency is in charge of the Agency, based in Sacramento. It is responsible for enforcing several of the California Health and Safety Codes.

Governor Gavin Newsom nominated Mark Ghaly, MD, MPH, to be Secretary of CHHS on March 6, 2019. On June 17, 2019, the California State Senate overwhelmingly approved Ghaly. Ghaly formerly worked for Los Angeles County as the director of health and social impact, deputy director of the Los Angeles County Department of Health Services, and medical director of the Southeast Health Center of the San Francisco Department of Public Health. Ghaly graduated from Harvard Medical School with a doctorate in medicine and the Harvard T.H. Chan School of Public Health with a master's degree in public health.

The California Department of Health Services was established due to a restructuring of several California organizations, notably the California Health and Welfare Agency.

Organizations: The Agency is divided into various departments and boards:

California Department of Aging: The California Department of Aging (CDA) is the state agency in charge of enforcing the Older Californians Act and the Older Americans Act in California. It is ostensibly run by the California Department of Health and Human Services. Sacramento is the company's headquarters. Director Kim McCoy Wade has been in charge of the California Department of Aging since Fall 2019. Governor Newsom's Master Plan on Aging is being implemented by McCoy Wade, the former head of the California Department of Social Services' CalFresh and Nutrition Branch.

California Department of Child Support Services: Child support and medical support orders are established and enforced by 47 child support agencies throughout California. Whether or not there is an existing child support order, any parent or guardian of a child may start a child support case, and a case is automatically filed when a kid gets public assistance. Any case services are handled at the county or regional level, and all child support issues should be directed to the Agency in one's county or area of residence first.

California Department of Community Services and Development: CSD works with a network of commercial, non-profit, and local government community service providers committed to assisting low-income families in achieving and maintaining self-sufficiency, meeting their home energy requirements, and living in lead-free homes.

California Department of Developmental Services: The California Department of Developmental Services is a state organization located in Sacramento, California. California with developmental impairments, such as autism, cerebral palsy, epilepsy, intellectual disability, and disorders linked to intellectual disability, are served by the organization. It does it via regional centers, which are non-profit organizations. In the State of California, there are 21 regional centers.

California Emergency Medical Services Authority: The California Emergency Medical Services Authority (EMSA or EMS Authority) is a state government organization in California. The California EMS Authority is one of the California Health and Human Services Agency's thirteen departments. A physician with extensive expertise in emergency care is needed as the director. The current Director is Dr. Dave Duncan. The California EMS Authority aims to provide high-quality patient care by coordinating a statewide emergency medical care system, injury prevention, and disaster medical response.

California Department of Health Care Services: The California Department of Health Care Services (DHCS) is a division of the California Health and Human Services Agency that funds and manages various healthcare delivery programs, including Medi-Cal, which helps low-income individuals get health care. The California Department of Health Services was renamed the DHCS and the California Department of Public Health when it was restructured. Jennifer Kent, Director of the Department of Health and Human Services, announced her retirement on September 10, 2019, effective September 30, 2019. Governor Gavin Newsom named Richard Figueroa, Jr. as Acting Director on September 25, 2019.

California Department of Managed Health Care: In California, the Department of Managed Health Care (DMHC) is the regulatory agency that oversees managed health care programs, often known as Health Maintenance Organizations (HMOs). Mary Watanabe is the DMHC's acting director at the moment. The DMHC is a division of the California Department of Health and Human Services. It was founded in 2000 to enforce the Knox-Keene Health Care Service Plan Act of 1975 and other associated laws and regulations.

California Managed Risk Medical Insurance Board: The California Managed Risk Medical Insurance Board is committed to improving Californians' health by expanding access to affordable, comprehensive, and high-quality health care. Access for Infants and Mothers (AIM), Healthy Families, and the Major Risk Medical Insurance Program are also under its jurisdiction (MRMIP). It is in charge of the state SCHIP program, including the Healthy Families and Access for Infants and Mothers (AIM) program and the state high-risk insurance pool.

California Department of Public Health: The California Department of Public Health (CDPH) is the governmental agency in charge of the State's public health. It is a branch of the California Department of Health and Human Services. It is responsible for enforcing parts of the California Health and Safety Codes, particularly those relating to certain health-care institutions' licensing. One of its responsibilities is to supervise vital records activities throughout the State.

California Department of Rehabilitation: The California Department of Rehabilitation (DOR) is a governmental agency that oversees vocational rehabilitation programs in California. It offers vocational rehabilitation programs and advocacy to people with disabilities in over 100 sites throughout California, intending to help them find work, independence, and equality. On October 1, 1963, the DOR was created.

California Department of Social Services: The California Department of Social Services (CDSS) is a state organization that oversees many of the programs that make up the United States' social safety net. It is part of the California Health and Human Services Agency. This Department distributes federal and state funds for adoptions, the nation's most extensive SNAP program (CalFresh, formerly led by current Department of Aging Director Kim McCoy Wade), CalWORKs, foster care, disability assistance, family crisis counseling, subsistence payments to low-income families with children, child welfare services, and many other initiatives.

California Department of State Hospitals: The California Department of State Hospitals (DSH) is in charge of a statewide progressive in-patient mental health treatment program that draws the best and brightest in the profession of psychiatry and is a patient-centric, treatment-first environment managed by psychiatrists. The DSH system comprises five separate facilities throughout California: the Central Coast, Napa Valley, Los Angeles, Inland Empire, and Central San Joaquin Valley.

California Office of Statewide Health Planning and Development: Californians now have easier access to high-quality healthcare, thanks to the OSHPD. It maintains the safety of hospital structures, provides financial support to people and hospitals, and collects and publishes healthcare data. California's Office of Statewide Health Planning and Development (OSHPD) is the industry leader in data collection and dissemination on the State's healthcare infrastructure.

OSHPD supports a more evenly dispersed healthcare workforce and disseminates valid data on healthcare outcomes. OSHPD also oversees the building, remodeling, and seismic safety of hospitals and skilled nursing homes and provides loan insurance to help California's not-for-profit healthcare organizations meet their capital requirements.

California Office of Health Information Integrity (CalOHII): The California Office of Health Information Integrity (CalOHII) ensures that the Health Insurance Portability and Accountability Act (HIPAA) and other relevant State and federal regulations are followed by all California state agencies. CalOHII serves as a HIPAA resource for all state agencies, assisting them in protecting their citizens' protected health information from unlawful access or disclosure.

California Office of Law Enforcement Support: The Office of Law Enforcement Support (OLES) aspires to be the primary investigative and legal monitoring resource for the Department of State Hospitals and the

Department of Developmental Services, promoting progress and instilling responsibility. Through continuous supervision, investigations, and collaborative collaborations, the OLES protects the safety and security of patients and residents in California's state hospitals and developmental facilities, resulting in systemic changes in policies, procedures, and relationships.

California Office of the Patient Advocate: The Office of the Patient Advocate assigns a score to health plans and medical organizations based on the quality of medical treatment and the patient experience. Consumers may use this website to compare health plans and physician groups, monitor consumer complaints, and learn about patient rights and health care options. It was founded in 2000 and offers consumer education, scorecards for quality of treatment, and reporting on customer inquiries and complaints.

California Office of Systems Integration: The California Office of Systems Integration is a division of the California Department of Health and Human Services that oversees a portfolio of significant, complex health and human services I.T. projects.

Office of the California Surgeon General: California's Surgeon General is the State's primary spokesman on public health issues. The Surgeon General of the United States is one of only four State Surgeons General in the country. Governor Gavin Newsom established the position on January 7, 2019, and it does not need confirmation by the California State Senate. Dr. Nadine Burke Harris, the current Surgeon General, assumed office on February 11, 2019. The Governor's "California for All" plan, which includes a projected $1.7 billion in financing for increased early childhood education and early intervention, includes the Surgeon General as a significant component.

Environmental Protection: CalEPA (California Environmental Protection Organization) is a state cabinet-level agency under the California government. CalEPA aims to safeguard public health, environmental quality, and economic viability by restoring, protecting, and enhancing the environment. Governor Pete Wilson established the California Environmental Protection Agency (CalEPA) in 1991 by Executive Order W-5-91, following a "Big Green" initiative Wilson proposed during the 1990 state gubernatorial elections, promising a cabinet-level agency to oversee state environmental regulations and research. On July 17, 1991, the Agency became a cabinet department due to inter-agency reorganizations initiated by the Governor and reviewed by both chambers of the California State Legislature. The Agency was established by statute under Government Code section 12800 as of 2019.

CalEPA, via its departmental California Air Resources Board, was a strong proponent of the Global Warming Solutions Act of 2006, which became California the first state in the U.S. to impose a limit on all greenhouse gas emissions from large enterprises.

CalEPA stated in June 2008 that new global warming performance badges would be required on all new vehicles beginning January 1, 2009. The stickers will display two scores: a smog score and a global warming score, both of which will be graded on a scale of one to ten, with the higher the rating, the more environmentally friendly the car.

Departments

California Air Resources Board (ARB): The California Air Resources Board (CARB or ARB) is the State of California's "clean air agency." CARB is a department under the cabinet-level California Environmental Protection Agency established in 1967 when then-governor Ronald Reagan signed the Mulford-Carrell Act, which combined the Bureau of Air Sanitation and the Motor Vehicle Pollution Control Board. CARB's stated objectives include achieving and maintaining healthy air quality, safeguarding the public from harmful air pollutants, and developing new ways to comply with air pollution laws and regulations.

Department of Pesticide Regulation (DPR): The California Department of Pesticide Regulation, commonly known as DPR or CDPR, is one of the

California Environmental Protection Agency's (Cal/EPA) six boards and departments. DPR's declared goal is to "protect human health and the environment by regulating pesticide sales and usage, as well as encouraging low-risk pest management." DPR is widely considered the most critical U.S. agency for pesticide control, as well as a peer to the U.S. Environmental Protection Agency and Health Canada. It is also regarded as a worldwide authority in the area.

California Department of Resources, Recycling, and Recovery (Cal Recycle): CalRecycle (California Department of Resources, Recycling, and Recovery) is a division of the California Environmental Protection Agency in charge of the State's waste management, recycling, and waste reduction initiatives. CalRecycle took over from the California Integrated Waste Management Board in 2010. It is renowned for, among other things, managing the California Redemption Value (CRV) program.

Department of Toxic Substances Control (DTSC): The California Department of Toxic Substances Control (DTSC) is a state government department in California. The DTSC's goal is to safeguard human health and the environment from hazardous exposure. DTSC is a California Environmental Protection Agency (Cal/EPA) with over a thousand employees and a Sacramento headquarters. DTSC also maintains field offices in Sacramento, Berkeley, Los Angeles, Chatsworth, Commerce, Cypress, Clovis (Fresno), San Diego, and Calexico and two environmental chemistry labs throughout the State.

Office of Environmental Health Hazard Assessment (OEHHA): The Office of Environmental Health Hazard Assessment (OEHHA) is a specialist department under the cabinet-level California Environmental Protection Agency (CalEPA) responsible for assessing health hazards from environmental chemical pollutants. CalEPA's scientific advisor, OEHHA, conducts health impact evaluations that aid regulatory decision-makers at CalEPA, the California Department of Public Health, and other government and non-government organizations.

State Water Resources Control Board (SWRCB): The State Water Resources Control Board (SWRCB) is one of the California Environmental Protection Agency's six branches. The State Water Board is in charge of allocating California's water resources to various entities and for a variety of purposes, ranging from agricultural irrigation to hydroelectric power generation to municipal water supplies, as well as ensuring the cleanliness and purity of Californians' water for everything from bubble baths to trout streams to ocean beaches.

The California Integrated Trash Management Board, which focused on waste reduction and recycling, ended operations in 2010. It was replaced by the California Department of Resources Recycling and Recovery—CalRecycle, which is now part of the California Environmental Protection Agency.

Labour and Workforce: The California Labor and Workforce Development Agency (LWDA) is a cabinet-level California state agency that oversees seven central departments that deal with benefits administration, labor law enforcement, employee benefits appellate functions, workforce development, tax collection, and economic development activities. Governor Gray Davis conceptualized it, and it was officially established in 2002.

Organizations: The Agency oversees multiple departments and programs:

California Agricultural Labor Relations Board: The Agricultural Labor Relations Board (ALRB) is a California state body that oversees the implementation of the California Agricultural Labor Relations Act, which provides collective bargaining for farmworkers in the State. The ALRB has two primary responsibilities: conducting, overseeing, and certifying representation elections, as well as investigating and pursuing remedies for unfair labor practices (ULPs). The majority of cases are decided by administrative law judges and agency employees, with the five-member Board acting as the ultimate arbitrator.

Employment Development Department: The Employment Development Department (EDD) in California is a government agency that offers a range of services to companies, employees, and job seekers. The administration of the Unemployment Insurance (U.I.), Disability Insurance (DI), and Paid Family Leave (PFL) programs, which give benefits to employees who are eager to work but are jobless, disabled, or must care for family members, is the EDD's primary responsibility. The Department also administers job assistance programs and gathers labor market and employment statistics for the State.

California Public Employment Relations Board: The Public Employment Relations Board (PERB or Board) is a quasi-judicial administrative agency charged with enforcing collective bargaining laws that apply to employees of California's public schools, colleges, and universities, as well as employees of the State, local public agencies (cities, counties, and special districts), and the trial court, employees.

California Unemployment Insurance Appeals Board: The California Unemployment Insurance Appeals Board is a quasi-judicial administrative court in the United States that handles appeals from the Employment Development Department's decisions on unemployment insurance claims and taxes. It is administered by a five-member Board, with the Governor appointing three members, the Speaker of the Assembly one, and the Senate President pro tempore one. The Board of Directors was established in 1943.

California Workforce Development Board: The California Workforce Development Board (CWDB) is charged with helping the governor carry out the federal Workforce Innovation and Opportunity Act of 2014's duties and obligations. The Governor appoints all members of the Board. They represent various interests in workforce development, including business, labor, public education, higher education, economic development, youth activities, employment and training, and the Legislature. The Board meets regularly, and members of the public are welcome to attend. A collaborative approach is used to make decisions.

California Department of Industrial Relations: The California Agency of Industrial Relations (DIR) was established in 1927 as a State of California government department. It is now part of the California Labor and Workforce Development Agency, part of the Cabinet. Its present headquarters are at Oakland's Elihu M. Harris State Office Building. California provides frequent updates on COVID-19, including Coronavirus information collected by the Labor & Workforce Development Agency for California businesses and employees. Due to local shelter in place orders, several DIR offices are closed. For the most up-to-date information on closures and alternate service alternatives, go to the DWC and DLSE websites.

Employment Training Panel: Employers may get money from the Employment Training Panel (ETP) to help them upgrade their employees' abilities via training that leads to good-paying, long-term employment. The ETP was established by the California State Legislature in 1982 and is financed by a special payroll tax levied on California businesses. The ETP is governed by a three-tiered system, with appointed Panel members representing industry, labor, and state government. The ETP is a financing organization, not a training organization. Businesses set their training requirements and how they will be met. ETP personnel may help with funding applications and other elements of involvement.

Works Cited

Aberbach, Joel D., and Mark A. Peterson. The executive branch. Oxford University Press on Demand, 2005.

Brown Jr, Edmund G. "Attorney General." State of California, "Comments on Draft Environmental Impact Report for Coyote Canyon Specific Plan," June 19 (2007).

Brown Jr, Edmund G. "Governor of California." Health of People, Health of Planet and Our Responsibility (2018): 371.

Costa, Nicola, "Civics for Citizens: The Executive Branch." The Andrew Goodman Foundation, September 21, 2017.

Fairlie, John A. "The Veto Power of the State Governor1." American Political Science Review 11.3 (1917): 473-493.

Ferguson, Margaret Robertson, ed. The executive branch of state government: people, process, and politics. ABC-CLIO, 2006.

Ferguson, Margaret Robertson, ed. The executive branch of state government: people, process, and politics. ABC-CLIO, 2006.

Glaser, Jason. California. Capstone, 2003.

Goyette, Don, Statecraft Sheryl White, and Statecraft Joe Lyaix. "State of California, Secretary of State." (2000).

Kaskla, Edgar, "California's Governor and Challenges to the Plural Executive System: Gubernatorial Competence and Political Personality." Sage Knowledge.

Lindler, Vanessa, and Susan Chapman. "Workforce in California." (2003).

Micheli, Chris, "An Overview of California's Executive Branch." California Lawmaking. 2o May, 2019.

Morrison, Trevor W. "Constitutional Avoidance in the Executive branch." Colum. L. Rev. 106.

"The Executive Branch." YouTube, Uploaded by Citizen Genius, May 21, 2003, https://www.youtube.com/watch?v=OUFuujbqSYA Accessed July 12, 2021.

Wells, Roger H. "The item veto and state budget reform." American Political Science Review 18.4 (1924): 782-791.

CHAPTER 8

California court system

8.1. Introduction: The Three Tiered Court System

The judiciary in the United States has a dual court system, with courts at both the national and state levels. Both levels have three basic tiers consisting of trial courts, appellate courts, and finally courts of last resort, typically called supreme courts, at the top. However, as a state itself creates each state's court system, each one differs in structure, the number of courts, and even name and jurisdiction. Thus, the organization of state courts closely reflects the system at the federal level but not in a clear-cut manner.[14]

The state court system in California has two types of state courts, trial courts (also called "superior courts") and appellate courts, made up of the Courts of Appeal and the California Supreme Court. The California Constitution also founded the Judicial Council, which is the governing body of the California courts and is led by the California Supreme Court Chief Justice.[15]

---

[14] Bureau of International Information Programs, United States Department of State. Outline of the U.S. Legal System. 2004.

[15] See California Courts – The Judicial Branch of California, https://www.courts.ca.gov/998.htm?rdeLocaleAttr=en (last visited July 4, 2021).

8.2. Trial courts

Trial courts are also known as "superior courts." In the trial or superior court, a judge, and sometimes a jury, hears testimony and evidence and decides a case by applying the law to the facts of the case. In the whole state of California, there are 58 superior courts, 1 in each county (California Constitution, Article VI, §§ 4).

While some counties may have several courthouses in different cities, they are all part of the same superior court for that county. This type of court handles such issues as all civil cases (e.g., family law, probate, juvenile, and other civil cases), all criminal cases (e.g., felonies, misdemeanors, and infractions, like traffic tickets), small claims cases, and appeals of small claims cases, appeals of civil cases involving 25 000 dollars or less, and appeals of the infraction (like traffic) and misdemeanor cases.

Trial court judges are elected at a general election by voters of the county on a non-partisan ballot (Shortell, 2013). The term of the office of a trial judge is six years. The potential judge of a trial court needs to be certified by an attorney to practice law in California or have a 10-years-record as a judge.

8.3. Courts of Appeal

When a defendant loses a case or part of a case in the trial court, one can appeal this decision in a higher court (an appellate court) to review the trial court's decision. Appeals of family law cases, probate cases, juvenile cases, felony cases, and civil cases for more than $25 000 are heard in Courts of Appeal.

In each Court of Appeal, a panel of 3 judges (justices) decides appeals from trial courts. Each district (or division) has a presiding justice and two or more associate justices (California Constitution, Article VI, §§ 3). Appellate justices are appointed by the Governor and confirmed by the Commission on Judicial Appointments. The same rules that govern the selection of Supreme Court justices apply to those serving on the Courts of Appeal.

However, the Courts of Appeal only review the record in the trial court case (except death penalty cases that they cannot review) to decide if a legal mistake was made and if that mistake affected the outcome of the trial court case. They do not provide new trials. On the other hand, the Courts of Appeal have to provide a mandatory review of jurisdiction. There are 6 Courts of Appeal, and each of them covers a specific number of counties in California (California Government Code § 69100). The district headquarters for Courts of Appeal is located in San Francisco, Los Angeles, San Diego, Fresno, and San Jose.

8.4. California Supreme Court

The Supreme Court is the state's highest court. It can review cases decided by the Courts of Appeal. Also, certain kinds of cases go directly to the Supreme Court. They are not heard first in a Court of Appeal, such as death penalty appeals and disciplinary cases involving judges (California Constitution, Article VI, §§ 10, 11). There are seven justices on the Supreme Court, and at least four must agree to decide. The 7 includes 1 Chief Justice and six associate justices, are appointed by the Governor, confirmed by the Commission on Judicial Appointments, and confirmed by the public at the next general election (California Constitution, Article VI §§ 2).

A justice also comes before the voters at the end of his or her 12-year term. To be eligible for an appointment, a person must have been a member of the State Bar of California or a court judge in this state for at least ten years. All other state courts must follow a decision of the Supreme Court in California. Decisions of the Supreme Court are published in the California Official Reports. Based on the official statistics of the judiciary in California, the Supreme Court deal with approximately 9 000 cases per year.[3]

8.5. Federal courts and state courts

In parallel to state courts, in each state function, federal courts deal with cases that refer to the U.S. government, the U.S. Constitution, or federal laws. Federal courts are also involved when a case is between 2 parties from two different jurisdictions (i.e., states). However, federal courts usually do not deal with cases related to divorce and child custody, probate and inheritance, real estate, juvenile matters, criminal charges, contract disputes, traffic violations, or personal injury. On the other hand, bankruptcy cases are only handled by federal courts

Alternative Dispute Resolution (ADR): Most civil disputes are resolved without filing a lawsuit, and most civil lawsuits are resolved without a trial. The courts and others offer various Alternative Dispute Resolution (ADR) processes to help people resolve disputes without a trial. ADR is usually less formal, less expensive, and less time-consuming than a trial. There are different types of ADR[16], such as:

Mediation: In mediation, an impartial person called a "mediator" helps the parties try to reach a mutually acceptable resolution of the dispute. The mediator does not decide the dispute but helps the parties communicate to try to settle the dispute themselves. Mediation leaves control of the outcome with the parties. This method of dispute resolution may be particularly useful when parties have a relationship they want to preserve, for instance, between family members, neighbors, or business partners. On the other hand, mediation may not be effective if one of the parties has a significant advantage in power over the other (e.g., a history of abuse or victimization).

Arbitration: In arbitration, a neutral person called an "arbitrator" hears arguments and evidence from each side and then decides the outcome of the dispute. Arbitration is less formal than a trial. The arbitration may be either "binding" or "nonbinding." Binding arbitration means that the parties waive their right to a trial and agree to accept the arbitrator's decision as final. Overall, there is no right to appeal an arbitrator's decision. Nonbinding arbitration means that the parties are free to request a trial if they do not accept the arbitrator's decision.

---

[16]   See, California State Courts – ADR Types & Benefits, https://www.courts.ca.gov/3074. htm?print=1 (last visited July 4, 2021).

Arbitration is best for cases where the parties want another person to decide the outcome of their dispute for them but would like to avoid the formality, time, and expense of a trial. It may also be appropriate for complex matters where the parties want a decision-maker who has training or experience in the subject matter of the dispute.

Neutral Evaluation: In neutral evaluation, each party gets a chance to present the case to a neutral person called an "evaluator." The evaluator then gives an opinion on each party's arguments' strengths and weaknesses and how the dispute could be resolved. The evaluator is often an expert in the subject matter of the dispute.

Although the evaluator's opinion is not binding, the parties typically use it as a basis for trying to negotiate a resolution of the dispute. Neutral evaluation fits the best cases with technical issues and requires special expertise to resolve, or the only significant issue in the case is the number of damages.

Settlement Conferences: Settlement conferences may be either mandatory or voluntary. In both types of settlement conferences, the parties and their attorneys meet with a judge or a neutral person called a "settlement officer" to discuss the possible settlement of their dispute. The judge or settlement officer does not decide the case but assists the parties in evaluating the case's strengths and weaknesses and negotiating a settlement. Settlement conferences are appropriate in any case where settlement is an option. Mandatory settlement conferences are often held close to the date a case is set for trial.

Collaborative courts: Collaborative courts (also known as problem-solving courts) combine judicial supervision with rehabilitation services that are monitored and focused on recovery to reduce recidivism and improve offender outcomes. The key components of collaborative justice include:

1. They integrate services with justice system processing.

2. They aim to achieve the desired goals without using the traditional adversarial process.

3. Early and prompt identification of eligible participants for the program.

4. They provide access to a variety of services, such as treatment and rehabilitation services.

5. Frequent monitoring of compliance and interaction with collaborative justice court participants, including continuing interdisciplinary education.

6. The court's responses to participants' compliance use a system of sanctions and incentives to foster compliance.

7. It includes the system that evaluates the achievements of the program.

8. Partnerships forge the effectiveness of the program among collaborative justice courts, public agencies, and community-based organizations.

9. Awareness of and responsiveness to diversity and cultural issues.

Examples of collaborative justice courts for adults are:

1. Community and homeless courts - therapeutic justice courts offering strengths-based support and services for homeless and housing-insecure program participants

2. Drug courts - provide an alternative to traditional criminal justice case adjudication for high-risk/high need individuals struggling with substance use disorders.

3. DUI (driving under the influence) courts - a type of collaborative court that provides individualized treatment and supervision to defendants with repeat DUI (driving under the influence) or DWI (driving while impaired) charges.

4. Mental health courts - a form of a collaborative court that provides specific services and treatment to defendants dealing with mental illness.

5. Reentry courts - a type of collaborative justice court for individuals who have been released from prison, have violated their terms of community supervision, and have a history of substance abuse or mental health issues.

6. Veterans courts – a form of collaborative justice court that targets the root causes of veterans' criminal behavior.

Examples of collaborative justice courts for the underaged are:

- Youth domestic violence courts (dating courts) - focus on youth who have committed violence in the context of a specific relationship, i.e., an intimate partner, such as a spouse, girlfriend/boyfriend, or someone in a dating relationship, or acts of abuse directed at a close family member, such as a parent or sibling

- Juvenile drug courts – this type of court is designed to fill this gap by providing immediate and continuous court intervention in the lives of children using drugs or involved in family situations in which substance addiction is present.

- Juvenile mental health courts – are dedicated to minors who have a mental health diagnosis.

- Peer (youth) courts – they serve teenagers arrested on misdemeanor charges or a minor felony. Teens in youth courts act in traditional courtroom roles such as an attorney, clerk, and bailiff and serve on the jury.

- Girls' courts and CSEC (commercially sexually exploited children) courts – are dedicated to girls who have a history of trauma or exploitation or may be at risk for these things. The goal of a girls' court is to have a different track from a traditional delinquency court that recognizes these girls' unique and gender-specific risks and needs.

8.6. Diversity in the court system[17]

According to demographic statistics of the judicial branch of California (2020), 37.4% of all judges in the state were women, and 62.6% were men. However, the ratio between male and female judges was significantly lower in the Supreme Court (42.9% to 57.1%) than in Trial Courts (37.4% to 62.6%). Moreover, it is important to mention that the total number of female judges increased from 28.3% in 2008 to 37.4% in 2020.

In terms of racial variations, differences are depending on the court level. In the Trial Courts, 65.2% of all judges were declared to be White, 11.2% had Hispanic or Latino origins, and respectively 7.9% and 7.6% were Asian or Black/African American. In the Court of Appeal, the ratio of judges reported as White grew to 73.5%. The second group on this court level were Black or African American (8.8%), and then respondents that declared to be Asian or Hispanic/Latino (5.9% each). Finally, on the level of the Supreme Court, White and Asian judges (two judges each) represent 28.6% each. Three other judges declared to be either Black/African American, Hispanic/Latino, or Some Other Race. Over time the total ratio of judges that declared to be White decreased from 72.5% in 2008 to 65.6% in 2020. In contrast, between 2008 and 2020, the total ratio of judges that declared to be Hispanic/Latino, Asian, and Black/African American increased from 6.7% to 10.9%, 4.4% to 7.9%, and 4.8% to 7.7%, respectively.

In terms of variation regarding gender identity/sexual orientation, respondents declared to be Heterosexual at each level. The least at the Trial Court level (71.3%) and the most at the Supreme Court level (100%). In terms of the other respondents, at the Trial Court level, 1.5% declared to be Lesbian, 2% to be Gay, and 0.1% to be either Bisexual or Transgender.

---

[17] See, California State Courts – Demographic Data Provided by Justices and Judges Relative to Gender, Race/Ethnicity, and Gender Identity/Sexual Orientation (Gov. Code, § 12011.5(n)), As of December 31, 2019, https://www.courts.ca.gov/documents/2020-JO-Demographic-Data.pdf (last visited July 4, 2021).

25.1% did not provide an answer. At the Court Appeal level, 2% declared to be Lesbian (2 respondents), 1% to be Gay (1 respondent). 18.6% of respondents did not provide an answer.

The other data provides a question on veteran or disability status. At the Trial Court level, 7% of respondents were declared veterans, and 3% of respondents declared a disability status. At the Court of Appeal level, these ratios dropped to 5% and 2%, respectively.

8.7 A case in the California court system

"Civil" cases are court cases that aren't about breaking a criminal law (called a violation of criminal law). There are many different kinds of cases in this category. One files a civil case, or "action" in Civil Court if this person has been hurt, financially or physically. When one is hurt, it's usually called a "tort." The Civil Court deals with things like car accidents and contract disputes.

Among the most common things that the Civil Court deals with are car accidents or contract disputes. Civil cases also refer to property damage, family cases (i.e., divorce, child support, child custody), juvenile cases (child abuse and neglect, or when someone under 18 breaks the law). Landlord and tenant cases refer to renting or leasing real property. Small claim cases are civil cases that are worth 5 000 dollars or less. In such civil cases, the people represent themselves. Finally, probate cases refer to personal affairs (e.g., guardianship, name changes, adoption, elder abuse).

When one file to the Superior Court is worth more than 25 000 dollars (limited or unlimited jurisdiction case), a case goes through 5 steps. Firstly, one fills out the papers to start a court action. Afterward, one needs to wait for the other person to default and answers. Thirty days after the other person answers starts a step called discovery. During this time, the other person exchanges information about the cases. A pretrial starts about 90 days before the trial if one is unable to settle its case.

During this time claimant must make decisions if he/she needs an expert witness and have settlement conferences with the judge. The length of the trial depends on how complicated the case is. During post-trial, the claimant can appeal or collect the judgment.

If the state thinks one has committed a crime, the District Attorney's Office, representing the State, may bring criminal charges against this person. The difference between criminal and civil cases is that only the state can charge you with a criminal violation. There are three different kinds of criminal cases: **infraction**s, misdemeanors, and **felonies**.

An **infraction** is a minor violation. For instance, some traffic violations are infractions. A misdemeanor is a more serious crime that can be punished by up to 1 year in jail or fined with 1 000 dollars (California Penal Code § 19). Among examples of misdemeanor violations are: petty theft, driving on a suspended license, vandalism, or drunk driving. Finally, a **felony** is the most serious kind of crime. If one is found guilty, one can be sent to state prison for at least a year or receive the death penalty. Examples of felony violations include murder, possession of dangerous drugs for sale, robbery, rape.

The criminal cases are usually start being processed when the defendant is arrested by the police and taken to jail. Afterward, there are three options. The first of them is that the jail lets the defendant out without filing charges. The second of them is that the defendant posts bail or is released on his/her recognizance. In this case, the authorities tell the defendant when to go to court for arraignment. The final option is that the defendant stays in custody (jail) and is transported to the court for arraignment.

During the arraignment, the defendant appears in front of the court for the first time. A judge or judicial officer explains what the charges are, about the defendant's constitutional rights, and if the defendant can hire a lawyer (otherwise, the court appoints a lawyer). The defendant enters a plea of guilty, not guilty, or no contest. If the defendant pleas being guilty, that means that he or she committed the crime. In such a case, the judge finds the defendant guilty and enters a conviction in the court record. If the defendant does not contest (disagree with) the charge, the defendant is considered guilty, but the conviction cannot be used against the defendant in a civil lawsuit. In some cases, the judge will let the defendant out of jail on his/her Recognizance or, the judge will set bail and send the defendant back to jail.

The next step depends on whether the case refers to a misdemeanor or felony crime. In the case of the former, the defendant goes through the pretrial period. During this time, the prosecution and the defense exchange information (discovery). Either side can file pretrial motions to set aside the complaint, dismiss the case, or prevent evidence from being used at trial. The defendant can change his or her plea to guilty or no contest. The judge and lawyers of both parties may talk about whether and how the case could be resolved without going to trial. Suppose the defendant faces charges for a felony crime at the preliminary hearing. In that case, the judge will decide if there is enough evidence that the defendant committed the crime to "hold the defendant over" for trial. If the judge holds the defendant "to answer," the prosecutor will file a document called the Information. Then, the defendant will be arraigned on the Information. At that time, the defendant will enter a plea and proceed to trial.

The next step is a trial. Defendants in criminal cases (other than infractions) have the right to have a jury of their peers decide their guilt or innocence. Therefore, before trial, defendants need to decide whether to have a jury trial (where the jury decides if the defendant is guilty or not) or a **court trial** (where the judge decides). Everyone accused of a crime is legally presumed to be innocent until they are convicted, either by being proved guilty at a trial or by pleading guilty before trial. Therefore, it is the role of the prosecutor to convince the jury that the defendant is guilty and must provide proof. The defendant has the right to remain silent, and that silence cannot be used against him or her.

The law also defines the date of the trial. In case of a misdemeanor case, if the defendant is in custody at the arraignment, the trial must start within 30 days of arraignment or plea, whichever is later (California

Penal Code § 1382). If the defendant is not in custody at the arraignment, the trial must start within 45 days of arraignment or plea, whichever is later (ibid.). There is also a possibility to have a trial after the required deadline (known as "waiving time"). If the defendant waives time, which an attorney advises, the law states that the trial must start within ten days after the trial date is set (ibid.). In case of felony cases, the prosecutor must file the Information within 15 days of the date the defendant was "held to answer" at the preliminary hearing. The trial must start within 60 days of the arraignment on the Information. If the defendant agrees to waive time, the trial after 60 days (ibid).

Before the trial starts, the lawyers choose a jury. The process for choosing a jury is called "voir dire." During this process, the attorneys on both sides ask questions of the potential jurors to verify if the jurors will remain impartial. Before the lawyers of both parties can present evidence and witnesses, both sides have the right to give an opening statement about the case. During the trial, lawyers present evidence through witnesses who testify about what they saw or know. After all the evidence is presented, the lawyers of both parties give their closing arguments. The jury must find the defendant guilty beyond a reasonable doubt. Finally, the jury decides if the defendant is guilty or not guilty.

The defendant is released if the jury finds the defendant not guilty. The defendant can never be tried again for the same crime. However, it is important to note that finding not guilty is not the same as a finding of innocence. In other words, the jury was not entirely convinced that the defendant was guilty beyond a reasonable doubt. On the other hand, the arrest will still show on the defendant's record, along with the acquittal. If a defendant was wrongfully arrested and charged, and this person wants to get the arrest removed from her or his record, a hearing to determine the factual innocence of the defendant must be held in front of a judge. It is often much harder to prove factual innocence than to raise a reasonable doubt about guilt. If the defendant is found guilty, the defendant will be sentenced.

Both criminal and civil cases can be appealed. One or more plaintiffs or defendants can appeal a Trial Court's judgment to a Court of Appeal. However, the appeal can be dismissed if the deadline is missed (California Rules of Court, Rules 8.821-8.843, 8.880-8.891). For instance, for misdemeanor cases, one must file a Notice of Appeal within 30 days of the date of the judgment or order. In the case of felony cases, a Notice of Appeal needs to be filled within 60 days of the date of the judgment or order.

One can appeal in situations when plaintiffs or defendants believe that there was not enough evidence in the trial to justify the verdict or judgment or when there were mistakes of law during or before the trial that hurt your case. Then the Appellate Court will decide if there was any irregularity or mistake that prejudiced (hurt) your case. If the Appellate Court finds the Superior Court made a mistake in the verdict, it can reverse the decision or send it back to the Trial Court for further action.

8.8. Administration of Californian courts

The Judicial Council is the governing body of the California courts. The California Supreme Court Chief Justice chairs it. The California Constitution directs the Judicial Council to provide policy guidelines to the courts, make recommendations annually to the Governor and Legislature, and adopt and revise California Rules of Court in the areas of court administration, practice, and procedure. The council performs its constitutional and other functions with the support of its staff.

New judicial members of the council and its committees are selected through a nominating procedure intended to attract applicants from throughout the legal system and result in a diverse membership in experience, gender, ethnic background, and geography.

The council has 21 voting members, including 14 judges appointed by the Chief Justice, four attorneys appointed by the State Bar Board of Trustees, one member from each house of the Legislature, and two non-voting members who are court administrators (California Rules of Court,

Rule 10.2). The council performs most of its work through internal committees and advisory committees, and task forces.

The State Bar of California is California's official attorney licensing agency. The role of this agency is to manage the admission of lawyers to the practice of law, investigate complaints of professional misconduct, prescribe appropriate discipline, accept attorney-member fees, and distribute sums paid through attorney trust accounts to fund nonprofit legal entities. The board is directly responsible to the Supreme Court of California. All attorney admissions are issued as recommendations of the State Bar, which are then routinely ratified by the Supreme Court.

The full 13-member Board is comprised of five attorneys appointed by the California Supreme Court, who will serve four-year terms, two attorneys appointed by the Legislature, one by the Senate Committee on Rules and one by the Speaker of the Assembly, six "public" or non-attorney members, four appointed by the Governor, one by the Senate Committee on Rules and one by the Speaker of the Assembly.[6] The Board meets approximately six times a year, alternating between the State Bar's San Francisco and Los Angeles. Meetings are open to the public except for closed sessions that are allowed by law. All attorney admissions are issued as recommendations of the State Bar, which are then routinely ratified by the Supreme Court. Membership in the State Bar of California is mandatory for most practicing lawyers in California (with exceptions in very specific instances).

8.9. Juries

To be qualified for a jury member during a jury trial, one needs to: be a U.S. citizen, be at least 18 years old, can understand English enough to understand and discuss the case, be a resident of the county where the trial takes place, have not served on a jury in the last 12 months, be not on a grand jury or another trial jury, be not under a conservatorship, have civil rights restored if the person was previously convicted of a felony or malfeasance while holding public office (California Labor Code, §§ 230,

230.1). However, since January 2020, individuals with criminal records that meet certain criteria are eligible to serve as a juror.

The service as a jury in California takes one day. This means that there are no obligations to come to a courtroom for more than one day of jury duty unless this person is assigned to a courtroom for jury selection, or serve on a trial, more than once every 12 months. If one was not chosen for a jury selection or when it is after the trial, the service is completed for at least a year.

When a jury trial is about to begin, the trial court judge requests a panel of potential jurors to be sent to the courtroom from the jury assembly room so that the jury selection process can begin. After reporting to a courtroom, the prospective jurors are first required to swear that they will truthfully answer all questions asked about their qualifications. At first, the judge presents the details of the case and, together with the attorneys, asks jurors questions to determine if the jurors can be fair and impartial -"voir dire" (California Rules of Court, Rule 4.30).

The law considers situations when the judge and the lawyers can excuse individual jurors from service (California Rules of Court, Rule 2.1008). The juror can be excused from the service using so-called "challenges" for cause or peremptory. When jurors are excused for cause, there is usually a specific reason that a person may not be part of a particular jury because they may not be a fair and impartial juror for this case. For instance, a juror has a family or professional relationship with one of the parties. On the other hand, peremptory challenges are several situations when one party can excuse the juror from the service without reason. According to the law, each side has ten peremptory challenges in criminal cases and six in civil cases. The process of questioning and excusing jurors continues until 12 persons are selected.

During jury deliberations[7], a presiding juror is selected who is responsible for moderating the discussion and ensuring that every juror is allowed to participate. All jurors should deliberate and vote on each issue to be decided in the case. In addition, the presiding juror has to supervise that the voting proceeds properly. In a civil case, the judge will tell you how many jurors must agree to reach a verdict. In a criminal case, the unanimous agreement of all 12 jurors is required. If the required number of jurors have an agreement, the presiding juror will sign and date the verdict, with the advice of the bailiff or court attendant, and return with the signed verdict and any unsigned verdict forms to the courtroom.

If there are reasons that a selected juror may request to be excused from jury service, this person needs to report that he is qualified and has not been excused or had his/her service postponed. Any person who fails to respond may be fined up to 1 500 dollars, incarcerated, or both. Among reasons why one may be excused from jury service are no means of transportation, and excessive travel distance to the courthouse, a physical or mental impairment, the person provides care for a dependent, service would be an excessive financial burden.

The Constitution of the State of California requires every county to impanel a Grand Jury each year. This body has existed in California since the adoption of the original constitution from 1849-1950. The Grand Jury serves as a part of the judicial system but acts independently. In California, the Grand Jury system consists of 58 separate grand juries -one in each county (California Penal Code § 905) and they are convened on an annual basis by the Superior Court. Many of the statutory provisions relative to the Grand Jury have been reviewed and interpreted by the California Supreme Court and the Courts of Appeal. Their written opinions, known as "case law," clarify the powers and duties of the Grand Jury. Because of the complexity of state law, the Legislature has provided legal assistants for each county grand jury: A judge of the Superior Court, the District Attorney, the County Counsel, and under certain circumstances, the state Attorney General.

The main function of the Grand Jury (California Penal Code, § 888) is to review the operations of city and county governments as well as other tax-supported agencies and special districts. Moreover, the Grand Jury can inquire into the willful or corrupt misconduct in office of public officers and submit a final report of its Findings and Recommendations no later than the end of its term to the Presiding Judge of the Superior Court.

The term of Grand Jury members is one year. A person is qualified to be a grand juror if he/she (California Penal Code, § 893 – 894): is a citizen of the United States, is at least 18 years old, has been a resident of the county for at least one, possesses the ability of sound judgment, and knows the English language enough to communicate both orally and in writing. No particular background, training, or experience is necessary to be a grand juror. In addition, the law requires the Superior Court to ensure that each incoming grand jury receives training to help it understand these laws.

However, there are also four reasons why a person can be considered as ineligible to act as a grand juror if her or she: is serving as a trial juror in a state court at the time of selection, has been discharged from grand jury service within the preceding year, has been convicted of malfeasance in office or any felony or other high crime, or is serving as an elected public officer.

In terms of monitoring a local government's activities, the Grand Jury has a platform to serve as a watchdog because it serves as an independent body that operates separately from other entities. Moreover, the Grand Jury has access to public officials, employees, records, and information that allows them to make their assessments. The findings of the Grand Jury, which are aimed at identifying problems, are published at the end of the term. The report also includes recommendations on improving the quality of local governance and enhancing responsiveness (the role of a "watchdog").

The local governmental entity must answer the findings and recommendations in writing within a specified period: 60 days for officials or agencies' heads and 90 days for governing bodies. Copies of the Grand Jury Final Report are made available to all public libraries, county and city officials, and the news media. The findings of the Grand Jury also are reported in the local newspapers. Overall, this means that the grand jury acts as a representative of county residents in promoting government accountability.

The Grand Jury also considers criminal indictments based on the presented evidence. The Grand Jury can investigate accusation cases of a public official's corrupt or willful misconduct in office, and if the juries believe that the evidence is convincing, it may be filed indictments against the suspect. The accusation process is considered to be "quasi-criminal" in nature. However, accusations, which are also filed and taken to trial by the District Attorney, are filed infrequently.

In these criminal proceedings, the Grand Jury can be an economic tool that can efficiently assess without lengthy preliminary hearings. The Grand Jury carefully reviews the evidence and listens to testimonies. Its role is to determine whether there is probable cause to believe that the defendant may commit the crime. However, the Grand jury does not have the power to judge and convict people. This is solely the function of a court of law. The Grand Jury can investigate complaints from private citizens, both local government and government employees.

Each California county determines the specific procedures for creating grand juries. The criminal proceedings of the Grand Jury take place before the defendant appears for an arraignment. The defendant is not permitted to be present at these proceedings and may not even be notified that the proceeding is going on. The criminal Grand Jury is also closed to the public. Despite the efficiency of the criminal Grand Jury in California, the majority of felony charges are brought through the preliminary hearing.

The likelihood that district attorneys will use the Grand Jury indictment process increases if: there is a high public interest in the case, a preliminary hearing would take more time than a grand juror hearing, the prosecution plans to call witnesses who are minor or who for other reasons would not do well under the cross-examination that would occur at a preliminary hearing, the case against the defendant seems unconvincing - and the prosecutor wants a chance to "test" it out before jurors, the case involves wrongdoing by a public officeholder, and/or the witnesses are incarcerated in state prison.

8.10. Criminal Justice and Prison System in California

The prison system in California includes various types of facilities like prisons, fire camps, contract beds, reentry programs, and other programs administered by the state-owned agency - California Department of Corrections and Rehabilitation (CDCR), with its headquarter in Sacramento. CDCR owns and operates 34 prisons throughout the state and operates one prison leased from a private company.

Type of facilities in California:

- **City and Country Jails** - short-term facilities where inmates are held while going to court, being sentenced, or serving time for a minimal crime. These crimes are mostly misdemeanors or parole violations, and typically, the sentence is less than a year. The average county jail term is 30 days. Almost all counties in California have a jail.

- **State Prisons**- There are 34 state prisons in California, run by the CDCR. Inmates are assigned to state prison after being sentenced to serve time, usually convicted of felonies and violent crimes such as robbery with a weapon, rape, arson, etc. These crimes generally earn the inmates a sentence of more than one year. Inmates may be released with no supervision, parole supervision, or to a community program after being in prison.

- **Federal Prisons**- The Federal Bureau of Prisons (FBOP) houses inmates that are sentenced because of federal crimes, including bank robbery, kidnapping, money crimes, multistate drug crimes, and others. There are 11 FBOPs in California, 121 nationwide. Federal prisons operate under different security levels: low, medium, and high and can be run by FBOP or by private "for-profit" prison groups.

- **ICE Detention Centers**– Immigration and Customs Enforcement (ICE) facilities house inmates who are caught illegally living or working in the United States. The inmates remain in the facility until they are deported to their home country, and their stays range from 24 hours to a year. If the ICE detainee has been convicted of an additional crime in this country, they may be sentenced to serve time in county jail, state prison, or federal prison depending on the type of crime they commit and then are deported once they have completed their stay.

- **Juvenile Facilities**- County Juvenile facilities house inmates are under the age of 18 for various nonviolent crimes. Juveniles that commit violent crimes are sent to state juvenile corrections where they can stay until the age of 25.

- **Camps**- Prison camps are mostly connected to the state prison system, and they house low-security level inmates. Many of these inmates fight fires thorough out or state.

CDCR additionally staffs California City Correctional Facility, which was leased from CoreCivic in 2013 as part of attempts to reduce state prison overcrowding. Two facilities are designated for women, and additionally, one prison is designated for both men and women in separate facilities.

California has two death row locations for men at San Quentin State Prison and Corcoran State Prison. There is one death row location for women being Central California Women's Facility. While capital punishment is still legal in California, the last execution was in 2006, and Governor Gavin Newsom issued a moratorium on executions in 2019.

8.11. Three Strikes Sentencing Law

The original Three Strikes sentencing law in California was originally enacted in 1994. The essence of the Three Strikes law was to require a defendant convicted of any new felony, having suffered one prior conviction of a serious felony, to be sentenced to state prison for twice the term otherwise provided for the crime. If the defendant was convicted of any felony with two or more prior strikes, the law mandated a state prison term of at least 25 years to life.

However, in 2012 the voters approved Proposition 36, which substantially amended the law with two primary provisions: the requirements for sentencing a defendant as a third strike offender were changed to 25 years to life by requiring the new felony to be a serious or violent felony with two or more prior strikes to qualify for the 25 years-to-life sentences as a third strike offender; and the addition of a means by which designated defendants currently serving a third strike sentence may petition the court for reduction of their term to a second strike sentence if they would have been eligible for second strike sentencing under the new law (Couzens & Bigelow 2017).

However, this law also faces strong criticism as it may lead to lower efficiency of the court system as defendants can take cases to trial to avoid or postpone life sentences. In addition, it is criticized for its contribution to overpopulated jails as defendants who must be detained while waiting for these trials because the likelihood of a life sentence makes them a flight risk. Moreover, life imprisonment is an expensive and inefficient option because it requires additional health care services for the elderly among life-sentenced prisoners. Relatives and dependents of life-sentenced prisoners may also be problematic for welfare services in the long run. The other reason against the three-strikes sentencing law is that prosecutors avoid using it by processing arrests as parole violations rather than new offenses or by bringing misdemeanor charges when a felony charge would have been legally justified.

Similarly, potential witnesses may refuse to testify, and juries refuse to convict if they are against convicting a defendant for a life sentence. As a result, this can introduce discrepancies in punishments among third-time offenders. Finally, three-strikes laws have also been criticized for imposing disproportionate penalties and putting too much emphasis on street crime rather than white-collar crime (Shichor 1997).

According to the National Registry of Exonerations, 2800 documented exonerations' have occurred in the United States since 1989, with 241 coming from California.9 Based on the national data, the leading causes of wrongful conviction in California are mistaken witness identifications, false confessions, bad or misleading forensic evidence, perjury or false accusations, and official misconduct.

One factor contributing to wrongful convictions is a variation of criminal justice systems (Brooks & Brooks 2016). Each state has its criminal penal code, where criminal activities in one state are often legal in another. There can also be dramatic differences at the county level because resources allocated to criminal defense are decided at the county level, jurors are drawn from within the county, and people elect prosecutors.

8.12. California Innocence Project

California Western School of Law (San Diego) has established in 1999 a nonprofit organization – the California Innocence Project (CIP) to deal with wrongful convictions. This organization has three missions: "free the wrongfully convicted from prison, work to reform the criminal justice system, train law students to become zealous advocates." Overall, CIP provides pro bono legal services to individuals claiming to be innocent of the crime they have been convicted of. As an advocate for wrongfully sentenced convicts, CIP can also ask the court to reopen the case through an evidentiary hearing if there is strong evidence of innocence. In case of providing enough evidence of innocence, the client of CIP is exonerated.

Each year, CIP reviews more than 2000 claims of innocence from inmates convicted in Southern California. Moreover, CIP lobbies for law reforms that aim to prevent wrongful convictions, freeing the innocent, and helping exonerees.

According to The Sentencing Project, the prison population has increased from 23 264 inmates in 1980 to the peak of 173 942 inmates in 2006. Since 2012 the number of inmates started decreasing again (see 4.6. Realignment policy (2011 act) below). In 2020, the prison population

(122 417) reached approximately the same level as in 1994. Despite the decrease of the prison population in California, prisons in this state face overcrowding, which makes the whole system less efficient and threatens the health of prisoners.

According to the Legislative Analyst's Office, the average cost to incarcerate an inmate in prison in California is about 81 000 dollars per year. Over three-quarters of these costs are for security and inmate health care. Since 2010-11, the average annual cost has increased by about 32 000 dollars or about 58 percent. Significant drivers of this increase in costs were employee compensation, activation of a new health care facility, and additional prison capacity to reduce prison overcrowding.

8.13. Privatization of prisons in California

As maintenance of prison facilities and the cost of incarceration are expensive, states have an incentive to cut prison costs, and one of the means to do it is privatization. Suppose a state hinges its willingness to contract with a private corporation upon the corporation's ability to offer a bid 5 to 10% lower than current state expenditures. In that case, it is difficult to see how the state would not save money (TafollaYoung 2007). Moreover, some researchers show that privatization of state prisons, generally implemented through a Corrections Corporation of America (CCA) company, has already saved some states considerable expenses (Blumstein & Cohen 2003).

Despite fiscal benefits, the privatization of state prisons receives mixed opinions among experts and scholars (Austin & Coventry 2001). Some scholars point out that private companies can provide constructions more quickly (Cripe & Pearlman, 1997) because they do need to be accountable to the public (Robbins 1997). On the other hand, one of the central concerns raised by critics of prison privatization is that companies are motivated by financial gain and can make thus decisions that are at the expense of the rights and well-being of inmates (Durham 1994). As a result, it also affects public safety per se because it is mainly a government domain (Durham 1993).

According to The Sentencing Project, the number of incarcerated inmates in private prisons has dropped in California from 4547 in 2000 to 1134 in 2019. In fact, in 2019, Governor Gavin Newsom signed a law that ended the use of private prisons and federal immigration detention centers in California. Since Jan 2020, CDCR cannot enter into or renew a contract with a private company to run a state prison unless needed to meet court-ordered inmate housing limits.

As a response to the overpopulation of prisons in California, the Public Safety Realignment Act (Assembly Bill 109) was signed into law by the Governor on April 5, 2011, and amended by Assembly Bill 117 on June 30, 2011. This bill shifted to counties the responsibility for monitoring, tracking, and incarcerating lower-level offenders previously bound for state prison. It was a response to shortfalls in medical and mental health care for the state's prison population. This legislation specifies new responsibilities for managing adult offenders in California. It obligates counties to develop and recommend a Realignment Plan through the Community Corrections Partnership (CCP), a group created in connection with prior criminal justice legislation. While the legislation is comprehensive and complex, three major groups are affected by Realignment Act. First of all, felony offenders who have never been convicted of a "serious" or "violent" crime or an aggravated white-collar crime and are not required to register as sex offenders (referred to as the "triple-nons") will now serve their sentences in local custody. Second, released prisoners whose current commitment offense qualifies them as "triple-non" offenders are diverted to the supervision of county probation departments under Post Release Community Supervision (PRCS). Third, if persons on PRCS violate the technical conditions of their supervision (rather than committing a new crime), they can no longer be returned to state prison but must be sanctioned in local (county) jail or community alternatives, including house arrest, drug treatment, or flash incarceration.

All parole revocations, other than those for inmates with life terms, will be served in county jail and be limited to 180 days. Additionally, the legislation mandates the Court as the body responsible for parole and PRCS revocation hearings, rather than the Board of Parole Hearings.

One important element of the criminal justice system is the bail process. When someone is arrested, this person has a right to post bail to be released while awaiting trial. The Court keeps the bail as a guarantee to make sure that the defendant appears. The defendants can either pay the cash themselves or use a bail bonds person to post the amount. However, the bail process has been criticized for not being based on public safety and whether the person is a flight risk. In contrast, the bail process is based on whether the person can afford the cost of bail. Another issue is the predatory nature of the for-profit bail system.

In California, the efforts to reform the bail system gained public attention in 2018 when an appellate court in California held that the state's bail system was unconstitutional. Simultaneously, legislators were developing laws to modernize the system. Already in 2017, the bill known as The California Money Bail Reform Act was originally proposed in the Legislature, where it was obstructed. The new and reworked version of this legislation passed one year after.

The California Money Bail Reform Act (Bonta, 2018) planned to eliminate cash bail and establish an alternative system based on risk assessment and the probability that a defendant will return to court for appearances. The main aim was to narrow the economic gaps in the criminal justice system.

Under the law, those charged with certain nonviolent misdemeanors may be automatically released within twelve hours of booking without requiring a risk assessment. However, others will face a risk assessment based on their specific charges, prior history, safety concerns for victims, and other factors at a judge's discretion. Under the category of low risk, defendants would be released with the least restrictive non-monetary conditions possible.

Under the medium risk category, it would depend on local standards if a defendant could be released or be held. Under the category of high risk, a defendant would stay in custody until their arraignment. Defendants with prior failures to appear, recent felony convictions, or a history of domestic violence allegations would be characterized as higher risk and therefore unlikely to face release.

On the other hand, this act got strong opposition from advocacy groups such as American Civil Liberties Union and Human Rights Watch. One of the reasons behind their criticism is the level of decisiveness given to judges in assessing a suspect's detainment before trial. Moreover, in their view, the criminal justice system can be highly discriminatory, especially against marginalized communities. As a result, individual biases and the reliance on potentially biased statistical data could lead to unfair results for certain communities. Another concern is that with the shuttering of the bail industry and the millions of dollars needed to implement the law, there are also potential economic ramifications.

While some other states like Washington D.C. and New Jersey have made changes in their law to de-emphasize cash bail, California was supposed to be the first state to pass legislation that eliminated cash bail. However, in the referendum in 2020, voters rejected this idea (only 56.41% was against).

8.14. Criminal justice reform California

Over many years, California lawmakers and voters adopted a series of laws that prioritized punishment over rehabilitation. This process led to overcrowding in state prisons and also disproportionately impacted Black and Latin communities (Gavers, 2020). The situation began to change at the beginning of the previous decade when Californian authorities were reconsidering when prison overcrowding reached crisis proportions. The state faced lawsuits filed on behalf of incarcerated adults.

State-level reforms that were enacted into law through either voter approval of ballot propositions or through legislative action have focused on reducing incarceration, promoting more effective pathways to rehabilitation, and addressing the disparate impacts of criminal justice policies on people of color, particularly Black and Latinx communities (Garves, 2018). These reforms contribute to the decline of the prison population and crime rates in California.

Finally, major reforms to California's criminal justice system take effect from January 1, 2021. They refer to clearing criminal records and restoring rights, law enforcement practices, sentencing, and youth offenders. These reforms intend to shift the criminal justice system's focus from punishment and systematic bias to rehabilitation, reducing recidivism and equal treatment regardless of race or income. These acts include:

- **Misdemeanor diversion** (AB 3234): allows judges to offer misdemeanor diversion to most offenders. If terms are complied with, the criminal action will be dismissed and the record erased. Some domestic violence charges, stalking, and registrable sex offenses are not eligible for being dismissed.

- **"Clean Slate Act" automatic criminal record expungement** (AB 1076): gives automatic record clearance for individuals arrested after January 1, 2021. The bill applies to Californians that are eligible to clear their criminal records under Penal Code 1203.4 as follows: committed a misdemeanor or felony that did not result in incarceration in state prison, fulfilled all terms of their probation. The defendant was not convicted for any of the specified crimes that make someone ineligible to receive a California expungement.

- **Reduced sex offender registration** (SB 384): could reduce those required to register for life by up to 90%. The new three-tier system defines registration requirement terms of 10 years, 20 years, or a lifetime, depending upon the severity of the offense.

- **Banning chokeholds** (AB 1196): bans chokeholds and carotid holds by law enforcement.

- **Restoring felon voting rights** (Proposition 17): approximately 50 000 felons on probation receive the right to vote.

- **False reports and harassment** (AB 1775): make false 911 calls based on someone's race, gender, religion, or other types of discrimination a hate crime.

- **Capped probation terms** (AB 1950): proposes a maximum 1-year probation term for misdemeanor offenses and two years for felony offenses, with some exceptions.

- **Problem juveniles in school** (AB 901): changes punishment of insubordinate, disorderly students from probation programs to community-based programs. Additional changes also aim to remove problematic students from court supervision.

- **Phasing out juvenile prisons** (Juvenile justice realignment bill SB 823): replaces the remaining juvenile prisons with the Office of Youth and Community Restoration.

- **Hiding juvenile records** (AB 2425): protects the records of juvenile offenders from public inspection.

- **Sheriff oversight board established** (AB 1185): empowers the establishment of a sheriff oversight board and inspector general in each county with subpoena power to help oversee the sheriff.

- **California Racial Justice Act** (AB 2524): allows persons charged or convicted of a crime to challenge racial bias that may have occurred in their case to pursue a new trial or re-sentencing.

- **Transgender Respect, Agency, and Dignity Act** (SB 132): requires the California Department of Corrections and Rehabilitation (CDCR) to ask inmates to specify their gender identity and whether they identify as transgender, nonbinary, or intersex. Inmates must then be housed in a correctional facility designated for men or women based on the individual's preference.

Works Cited

The Amendment of The Three Strikes Sentencing Law, Proposition 36 (2017).

Austin, J., & Coventry, G. (2001). *Emerging Issues on Privatized Prisons.* Bureau of Justice Assistance.

Bonta, R. (2018). The California Money Bail Reform Act: Ensuring Pretrial Justice and Public Safety. UCLA *Criminal Justice Law Review*, 2(1).

Brooks, J., & Brooks, Z. (2016). Wrongfully Convicted in California: Are There Connections Between Exonerations, Prosecutorial and Police Procedures, and Justice Reforms. *Hofstra Law Review, 45,* 19.

California Constitution, §§ 4 Article IV (1879).

California Constitution, §§ 3 Article VI (1879).

California Constitution, §§ 10, 11 Article VI (1879).

California Constitution, §§ 2 Article VI (1879).

California Government Code, § 69100 (2021).

California Labor Code, §§ 230, 230.1 (2020).

California Penal Code, § 888 (1983).

California Penal Code, § 893 – 894 (1983).

California Penal Code, § 19 (1983).

California Penal Code, § 905 (1983).

California Penal Code, § 1382 (1983).

California Rules of Court, Rule 2.1008 (2009).

California Rules of Court, Rule 4.30 (2009).

California Rules of Court, Rule 10.2 (2009).

California Rules of Court, Rules 8.821-8.843 (2009).

California Rules of Court, Rules 8.880-8.891 (2009).

County board of supervisors: Sheriff oversight, Assembly Bill No. 1185 (2020).

Criminal justice alignment, Assembly Bill No. 109 (2011).

Criminal justice alignment, Assembly Bill No. 117 (2011).

Criminal procedure: Discrimination, Assembly Bill No. 2542 (2020).

Criminal records: Automatic relief, Assembly Bill No. 1076 (2019).

Cripe, C. A., & Pearlman, M. G. (1997). *Legal aspects of corrections management.* Aspen Publishers.

Durham, A.M., III (1993). "The Future of Correctional Privatization: Lessons From the Past. G. Bowman, S. Hakim, and P. Seidenstat (eds.) *Privatizing Correctional Institutions.* New Brunswick, NJ: Transaction Publishers.

Durham, A.M., III (1994). Crisis and Reform: Current Issues in American Punishment. Boston, MA: Little, Brown, and Co.

False reports and harassment, Assembly Bill No. 1775 (2020).

Graves, S. (2018). *State Corrections in the Wake of California's Criminal Justice Reforms: Much Progress, More Work to Do.* California Budget & Policy Center.

Graves, S. (2020). *Criminal Justice Reform Is Working in California: Advancing Reform Efforts Is Critical for Black and Latinx Californians and Their Families* (Criminal Justice) [Ballot Propositions]. California Budget & Policy Center.

Juvenile justice realignment: Office of Youth and Community Restoration, Senate Bill No. 823 (2020).

Juvenile police records, Assembly Bill No. 2425 (2020).

Juveniles, Assembly Bill No. 901 (2020).

Peace officers: Use of force, Assembly Bill No. 1196 (2020).

Probation: Length of terms, Assembly Bill No. 1950 (2020).

Public Safety, Assembly Bill No. 3234 (2020).

Robbins, I.P. (1997). The Case Against the Prison-Industrial Complex. *Public Interest Law Review*, Winter: 23–44.

Sex offenders: Registration: Criminal offender record information systems, Senate Bill No. 384 (2017).

Shichor, D. (1997). Three Strikes as a Public Policy: The Convergence of the New Penology and the McDonaldization of Punishment. *Crime & Delinquency*, *43*(4), 470–492.

Shortell, C. (2013). Voting in Trial Court Elections: Ballot Roll-Off in Partisan, Nonpartisan, and Retention Elections in High-Population Counties. *The Justice System Journal*, *34*(2), 153–170.

TafollaYoung, K. (2007). The Privatization of California Correctional Facilities: A Population-Based Approach. *Stanford Law & Policy Review*, *18*(438).

The Transgender Respect, Agency, and Dignity Act, Senate Bill No. 132 (2020).

Voting Rights Restoration for Persons on Parole Amendment, California Proposition 17 (2020).

CHAPTER 9

California Legislative Branch

9.1 Introduction to California Legislative Branch

The First California Legislature planned to meet in San Jose in 1849. There were 16 Senators and 36 Assemblymen present in the first California legislature assembly. There is an exciting story of the first meeting suggested on December 15, and that was a rainy day. Because of so much rain on December 15, meeting day, out of 52 legislatures, only 20 members of the legislatures were present. On December 17, the quorum was accomplished, and the regular session was started that day (Waggoner).

9.2 The California Legislature

The Legislature is a body of members with the power to make laws for political entities such as the country's state. Legislature forms an essential part of the government. In the separation of power model, which Montesquieu gave, they are often compared with the executive branch and the judicial branch of parliamentary government. The Legislature has four core functions to perform well for a political entity, country, or state. These functions are; electoral representation of the particular area, authorization of budget for country or state, policymaking to run that political entity, and last but not least to oversight of the assessment, monitoring, and implementation process relating to the laws and government policies (Calvo).

The California State Legislature is a bicameral legislature consisting of the lower house, The California Sate Assembly, 80 members (2021), and the upper house, The California State Senate, 40 members (Squire, P.). The California State Legislature is one of ten complete legislature assemblies in the United States of America.

9.3 The Process of Policymaking in California State Legislature

All legislations begin with an idea or thought. These ideas or thoughts may come from a variety of sources. The process began with any legislation when Senator or Assemblymember decided to author a bill. A legislature sends his/her idea to Legislature Council, where this idea is drafted into a bill. Then returned to the Legislature for introduction in assembly. If the bill's author is Senator, then the bill will initiate in Senate, and if the author is a member of the Lower house, then the bill is presented to the lower house as well.

A bill is introduced in assembly when the name of the author is read in the assembly. In all assemblies of the world, bills are sent to the printing branch of the assembly for printing copies of the bill. In California, also this procedure is being used for the process of making laws in assembly. There would be no other bill be initiated in the assembly in 30 days after a bill is introduced in California Assembly. The introduced bill then goes to the Rules Committee of the assembly, where it is assigned to the appropriate Committee for the first hearing to make this bill into law. There is categorization in the house for bills in California State Assembly. If Senate bills dealing with health care facilities would first go to Senate Health and Human Service Committee for policy review.

Any bill requires an expenditure of state fund must also be introduced for hearing in house's fiscal Committee, Senate Appropriate or

Assembly Appropriate. Both houses have their own policy committee and fiscal Committee. When the Committee hears the bill, the bill author gives an argument in favor of the bill, and the Committee hears the opposite views about the bill. The Committee then votes by passing the bill. The Committee can amend the bill or reject the bill by votes (Musso, Graddy & Grizard,). This is a purely democratic way to pass or reject the bill by the votes of the Committee.

Before introducing a bill in Committee, there is an analysis of existing laws about those matters, required laws, and some background information about the bill. If the Committee passes the bill, the bill will be introduced again in assembly for the second and third hearings. When the bill was introduced in assembly the third time, then the author of the bill read it, and members of the assembly discussed it before giving a vote in favor or against it.

If the original house passes the bill, then for further process, it will be presented in another house. The second house may pass it or may amend it if necessary. If the second house wants an amendment in the bill, then it will send back to the first house for amendment. If the first house did not agree to amend the bill and there is a disagreement between both houses, then the bill will go to a special committee of both houses, Three members from the Senate and three members from the Lower House, for the compromise bill. If compromise is reached, then the bill is returned to both houses for a vote.

For making law in any state or country, the final approval is required from the constitutional head of the state or country. In the California State Assembly case, the bill was sent to the Governor of California for final approval. The Governor of California has three choices. Governor can sign the bill to become law, allow it to become law without his/her signature, or veto it. Governor's veto can be overthrown by the vote of a two-thirds majority in the house. In California, the bill normally goes into effect on January 1, but in some urgent cases, the bill becomes law after the consent of the Governor.

9.4. How Annual Budget is Made in the California State Legislature

The fiscal year of California started on July 1 and end on June 30. A budget is a financial plan of expenditure and income in a given set of periods. In any budget, a state, country, or entity gives an outline for its expenditure in a given period, usually a year. If a state is giving a budget, then it will propose all its expenditure that where its money will be spent throughout a year. The budget also includes a state's income than how the state will generate its money to spend a year—a budget than proposed in front of the assembly to be approved. After approving a budget, then a state's fiscal year started.

California is the largest state in the United States of America population-wise. The size of its economy is large than most of the countries of the world. According to the official budget reports, California is the 5th largest economy globally (state-wise). Its budget size is 54.3 billion dollars which are more than most of the countries in the world.

Preparing a budget and introducing it in assembly is a lengthy and intelligent process. In California, it takes almost four to months to prepare a state budget and outline its expenditure and income for one year. The annual state budget, next to the state constitution, is the most crucial document in California. A budget reflects the society of that country or state. California's budget also reflects how the state will generate income by imposing taxes and which services will provide to its people in a given year. In California, the legislative must submit its budget to the Governor of California on January 10. The five-month period (January–June) is critical for considering and passing a multi-billion-dollar budget for California (Musso, Graddy & Grizard).

Both houses must be incorporate Governor's proposals in the budget. The court and The Constitution constrain California's large portion of budget spending. A State budget runs from July 1 to June 30 after went through all necessary processes. Budget discussed in both house's committees on the proposal of expenditure and income of a state. In California, The Senate budget committee, also known as Committee on Budget and Fiscal Review, starts its hearing in February. The Committee divided the budget into different sections like Education, Resources, Health, and more. To discuss and send it to the concerned department and state agency of these subcommittees, and these subcommittees started hearing in March. The staff of these sub-committees prepare all necessary details and prepare the alternative that is put on the official website of the budget committee.

In California, people of the state are given importance on budget. If anyone has a reservation about budget, he/she can tell his/her Legislature by mail or call the office staff or direct contact to the Legislature. After hearing the subcommittee, each subcommittee proposed changes and sent them to the full Senate committee for final approval. Full Committee may propose changes or accept it as it is.

Each house discusses the budget and proposes amendments in the house. A single member of the house can propose an amendment to the budget. Then budget refers to a budget conference committee of both houses to resolve differences, if any (Musso, Graddy & Grizard). The budget conference committee discusses all differences and the proceeding of the conference committee is live broadcast for the general public. During the conference committee meetings, no public testimony is heard, and the Legislature's role is to accept or reject or amend the budget. After all discussion on budget, the conference committee votes on the proposed version of the budget, and any conference committee change must have a majority from each house. If any difference in the conference and cannot pass from the conference committee, the legislative leaders meet the Governor privately or discuss any impasse. When compromise is reached, both houses' leadership requests the conference committee to conclude the budget review.

The final process to implement the budget is the Governor's signature on the budget. Governor has 12 working days to sign on the budget bill or using his/her authority to "blue pencil" (reduce or eliminate) any appropriate constrain in the budget. The Legislature has authority to override veto any blue pencil item of Governor by giving 2/3 vote (Musso, Graddy & Grizard).

9.5. How California Constituency influence the Legislature

It is vital to maintain a balance between a representative's ideology and the will of his/her constituency in legislation. The relationships between constituency and a legislator have presented not classical theorists such as Edmund Burke and John Stuart Mill. However, contemporary scholars also presented their research about the relationship between the legislator and the constituency of the legislator (Jewell).

Before modern democracies, the lawmakers or legislators were accountable to his/her constituency from where they have elected to represent. However, nowadays, it has become a reality that people of the constituency influence their legislators to make laws and work according to their will and choice. In modern democracies, the influence of constituency on legislators has become common practice. The Legislature, in a modern democracy, has to be responsive to what citizens of his/her constituency want (Jewell).

In California, the role of constituency in legislation is observed. People from different constituencies give their opinion about legislation, and even they influence their legislators to act like what they want in assembly. The process to influence may differ in different constituencies, but their role has been little increased in modern times to influence the legislators (Bishin. B. G). People influence legislator through local meetings during election campaigning and let their legislator know what their community or constituency want and give their opinion. People follow the law-making process through media and get involved in giving their opinion on any law or legislation.

9.6. Executive Branch of California State Legislature

In any democratic country, Governor, in a state or province, is the executive head of government and is the bridge between the state government and federal government. In California, Governor is the head of the state's executive branch. He/she is elected for four years term and may be elected for the second term by the people residing in California State (Ferguson). Under the leadership of the Governor of California State, the executive branch is responsible for administering and enforcing the laws of the state.

The California Governor also makes appointments in the judiciary of the state. In practice, the executive branch works closely with the legislative branch in shaping proposed legislation. The executive branch also consists of other people than the Governor, such as the Lieutenant Governor, Secretary of State, and Attorney General, to name a few, who are also elected for four years terms and, as Governor, may be elected for another term as well. If one talks about the executive branch in detail, there are four types of entities; agencies, which are sectary's heads; departments, directors heads; and boards and commissions headed by an executive officer or board member (Ferguson).

9.7. Leadership and structure of the Legislature. California Government.

State Legislature in California consists of two houses, the lower house, California State Assembly, 80 members; and the upper house, California State Senate, with 40 members. The meeting point of both houses is in Sacramento, the Capital of California state.

The Speaker is the most crucial person in the State Assembly in California. The assembly members usually elect him or her at the start of the two-year legislative term. He or she presided over floor sessions and constitute committees in the assembly. Speaker is followed by Speaker pro Tempore, appointed by the speaker himself/herself, and presided the session in the absence of the speaker.

The majority party caucus elects the majority Floor leader. It also represents the speaker on the floor, starts the assembly procession through parliamentary procedures. Minority leader floor leader is elected by minority party caucus. Some other important people in an assembly are the Majority Whip, Minority Whip, Assistant Majority Whip, Assistant Minority Whip, and more.

The President of the Senate is the Lieutenant Governor under the state constitution. He or she presided over the session in limited time. He or she may be invited periodically to preside ceremonial occasions, such as the session's opening. However, he or she must be present when there is a tie in the assembly on any law to cast a vote. President pro Tempore served as Chair of the Rule Committee and the actual leader of the Senate. He or she is the presiding officer on the floor, the appointment of committee members, assignment of bills, etcetera. Then there is a majority leader chosen by the majority party and a minority leader chosen by minority members of the Senate. Majority whip and minority whip are also present in the Senate by majority and minority, followed by Assistant majority whip and assistant minority whip.

California is divided into 53 congressional districts. Each district elects a representative to serve in the United States House of Representatives as part of California's congressional delegation. California's current districts were drawn in 2011 by a California Citizens Redistricting Commission (Phillips).

9.8. Important Terms Used in California State Legislature

These are some important terms that are regularly using in the California State Legislature.

Bipartisanship: The political cooperation between and among political parties is known as bipartisanship. Political parties sit together to define rules of engagement in order to enhance consensus in the country. For instance, in the United States, the Republican Party and the Democratic party cooperate, especially in national security matters.

Gerrymandering: It is a political process in which one faction of society gets benefits from the particular laws enacted in the Legislature. In this process, the game rules are set in a manner in which one party or faction dominates the political scene. For instance, in the United States, Jim crow laws were enacted to benefit white voters at the expense of black voters.

Caucus: Caucus is taken from the Algancon language, which means a gathering of tribal leaders to discuss any matters. It is a meeting of registered voters in a particular region to nominate the candidates for Presidential elections in the USA. Voters gather at a school or any hall to eliminate some candidates and choose some over the others. In the United States, the process is followed strictly by both political parties: Republican and Democratic. However, each has its own way of choosing the candidates. For instance, Democrats directly vote and get the most votes to go to the second stage, while Republican members convince each other to select a candidate.

Statute: Any law passed by a legislature of a country is known as a statute. Statutes are often legislated through consensus. Both houses of the Legislature are involved in such activity. Statutes are a fundamental part of international law as well.

Party caucus: Caucus is taken from Alingcon language, which means a meeting of Trible leaders. The process is defined as meeting voters to choose candidates in the United States. The process is used in selecting US President. Moreover, only the Democratic party uses this process to elect a Presidential candidate. The republican party, on the other hand, uses primaries for the same purpose.

Trifecta: *Trifecta* is a situation in which one party controls the executive and both houses of the Legislature to dominate the entire political scene. It happens strictly in bicameral legislatures. In this situation, a government can pass any laws in the Legislature and implement those laws through the executive quickly as the same party controls both elements of government. Mostly, it happens in single-party states. China is the supreme example of a trifecta.

Supermajority: A supermajority or qualified majority is a specified majority to gain voters' support more than fifty percent. In other words, it is a process in which more than fifty percent is required to legislate a law or define something. It is to curb the power of the majority so that the former does not erode the rights of the latter. For instance, in 2006, the State of Florida changed its constitution with a supermajority as sixty percent of voters voted to change the constitution.

Redistricting: It is a process in which huge districts are redrawn to discourage the disparities popping up from small districts in terms of representation in the Legislature. In other words, it is to redraw the borders of voting districts for equal and productive representation of people in the Legislature. In the USA, during the 1960s, a series of suits were filed to redefine and redraw the map of huge districts, as they were trampling on the rights of small districts in California.

Stakeholder: "A person or group of people who own a share in a business. A person such as an employee, customer, or citizen is involved with an organization, society, and more. Furthermore, therefore has responsibilities towards it and an interest in its success" (Freeman. R. E). In politics, all people living in a country and participating in the political process are stakeholders in a country. In California, people of the state, politicians, business people, Federal Government officials, law enforcement agencies officials, and stakeholders.

The fiscal year in California: The fiscal year is when the government or any other organization announces its revenue and expenditure throughout a year. It is an outline of accounting for an entity. In California, the fiscal year started from July 1 to June 30.

Incumbents: It is official persons who were currently taking responsibility to run any organization or a country. In California, people who are in government and making decisions are incumbents such as Gavin Newsom, Democratic Party, is incumbent Governor. Gavin Newsom took his charge in 2019 as Governor of California.

Law-making: The process of making an idea of any law into law is called Law-making. This process has to pass many stages, from an idea to Committee, special Committee, Assembly and then lastly, from the signature of Governor, this idea becomes a Law. This whole process is called law-making.

Works Cited

Bishin, Benjamin G. "Constituency influence in Congress: Does subconstituency matter?." *Legislative Studies Quarterly* (2000): 389-415.

Calvo, Ernesto. "The responsive legislature: Public opinion and law making in a highly disciplined legislature." *British Journal of Political Science* (2007): 263-280.

Dye, Thomas R. "A comparison of constituency influences in the upper and lower chambers of a state legislature." *Western Political Quarterly* 14.2 (1961): 473-480.

Ferguson, Margaret Robertson, ed. *The executive branch of state government: people, process, and politics.* ABC-CLIO, 2006.

Freeman, R. Edward. "Stakeholder theory." *Wiley encyclopedia of management* (2015): 1-6.

Jewell, Malcolm E. "Legislator-constituency relations and the representative process." *Legislative Studies Quarterly* (1983): 303-337.

Musso, Juliet, Elizabeth Graddy, and Jennifer Grizard. "State Budgetary Processes and Reforms: The California Story." *Public Budgeting & Finance* 26.4 (2006): 1-21.

Phillips, Daniel Wesley. *Defining the Community of Interest as a Criterion for Boundary Drawing of Electoral Districts.* Diss. UC Santa Barbara, 2016.

Squire, Peverill. "The theory of legislative institutionalization and the California assembly." *The Journal of Politics* 54.4 (1992): 1026-1054.

Waggoner, Philip D. *Legbranch.org.* 03 April 2018. 18 June 2021.

Zander, Michael. *The law-making process.* Bloomsbury Publishing, 2015.

CHAPTER 10

The California budget process

10.1. Chapter Summary

The state budget is probably the most crucial piece of legislation that the California state can enact. Passing the budget is essential to run the projects that keep things working as expected. It expresses on the spending side a set of priorities for the use of public resources. At the same time, it provides a variety of incentives and disincentives for various activities on the tax side. Compared with other states, the personal income tax in California relies more on capital gains than on taxes on wage earners. Wage-earners with families have a substantial personal exemption, sufficiently high that families with children do not pay personal income tax until their income is between $40,000 and $50,000.

Almost every state public policy in California is in some way embedded in the budget. Optimal and healthy democratic functioning requires that all citizens' views, opinions, and interests are represented in political decisions and social policy in California. The budget should reflect what Californians think, desire, and pursue. The extreme polarization in regional political cultures across the state makes legislative compromise and consensus building difficult, as illustrated by the stark differences in partisanship, political tolerance, and voting tendencies observed in San Francisco, Los Angeles County, and San Diego County. Politically speaking, the Republican Party has not been able to recover significant ground. Given the current blue state politics in California, the Democrats greatly influence the state policy making process in the state.

10.2. Introduction to the California budget process

Successfully passing the budget is at the center, both in difficulty and scope, of what the state government does each year. The overall California tax structure, compared with other states, is more dependent on volatile taxes. While most states that rank high on the scale of taxes per $1,000 of personal income are low-income states like South Carolina, California is generally considered a rich one. The California state budget includes economic assumptions, revenues, and expenditures.

Even though California does not have the filibuster that thwarts majority rule in the United States Congress, it does have two fundamental checks on effective majority governance. One is that the California Legislature and the Governor are elected separately and they both can represent different parties. The second is that a two-thirds majority is needed to get budget or appropriation measures passed or taxes raised, requiring, in the hypothetical absence of an overwhelming one-party majority in the state, that the two parties work together to produce a budget.

The California state legislature is also different from the United States Congress. It is term-limited, and the Governor has a line-item veto, which allows him to cut or eliminate any item in a budget bill without rejecting the whole bill. It is worth considering that both houses are based on population, and California also has the initiative process that allows the legislative process to be bypassed, most often by interests with deep pockets.

Bills are introduced by members and sent to appropriate committees. They must pass the floors of both houses with identical wording before they are successfully sent to the California governor for his signature. If he vetoes a bill, it takes a two-thirds vote of each House to override it. Budget, tax bills, and appropriation also require a two-thirds vote, giving the minority party immense power in the Legislature and making it difficult for the majority party to govern.

10.3. Basics of drafting a California state budget

Passing the budget implies various challenging decisions and trade-offs and includes economic assumptions, revenues, and expenditures. The budget in California is formed in four fundamental steps. The Governor formulates his state budget with the support of the Department of Finance. He then sends the budget to the Legislature each January. Each May, he publishes the May revision, which contains any changes made to the state budget since its publication in January. Unlike the January budget proposal mandated by the California constitution, the Governor's May Revise budget is a traditional but not mandated practice. The May Revise takes account of whatever new information on revenues and spending has developed in the following months and the political response to the original January budget proposal.

The Legislature later adopts the budget and passes it, including any tax increases by a two-thirds majority in each house. It is very common that the Assembly and Senate drafts of the budget differ, so a budget conference committee, with members from each side, attempts to resolve the differences. Third, the governor signs or vetoes the budget. If he signs the budget, he still can use his line-item veto to lower any line item. Finally, the agencies implement the budget as passed, including any control language with directions for studies that have to be presented to the Legislature.

Like a checking account, it is possible to distinguish between flows and stocks. Flows occur over specified periods in a place. In the case of California, the budget is enacted for fiscal years beginning each July 1. So, when talking about state spending, what is generally being discussed is the annual outflow from the General Fund planned for a fiscal year. State revenue is mainly the inflow of taxes and fees - understood as user charges for various state services-. However, revenue can also flow into the General Fund from interest payments received by the California state and other miscellaneous sources.

Nevertheless, a checking account may have a reserve or balance in it at any moment in time. Banks will generally require that there be enough money in the account at all times so that any expenditures (checks) can be safely covered. Some specific accounts may come with overdraft privileges so that if the balance goes negative, the bank can lend sufficient funds to cover any excess outflows from the account. The General Fund is similar because the state must have money available to meet expenses as they occur.

If the balance goes negative in the General Fund, the state must obtain added funds by borrowing money to cover its ongoing and future projects. Through external borrowing, it can do so by obtaining the funds from "Wall Street" or through internal borrowing from other funds that California operates outside the General Fund. The California state already has many earmarked funds set up by the Legislature for particular purposes. These funds may have specific tax or fee sources, and they will likely have positive cash balances in them at any moment in time. In the case of cash deficiency in the General Fund, the state controller can temporarily borrow from these other funds to cover the deficiency adequately. However, if this practice is used poorly excessively, these special funds may not fulfill their dedicated purposes.

Under certain circumstances during a budget crisis, the fiscal year may end with a deficiency. For example, if planned revenues turn out to be insufficient to cover outflows for the entire period. When such developments happen, the state can issue "Revenue Anticipation Warrants," short-term securities that cross from one fiscal year into another. In highly severe budget crises, the state may find itself unable to borrow to cover a cash deficiency. On those occasions, it may Registered Warrants to those to whom it owes money. The last time they were issued was in the summer of 2009 in the aftermath of the Great Recession. They are usually understood as involuntary loans from those to whom the state owes money. In 2009, most lenders were state-income taxpayers to whom refunds were due and some suppliers of goods and services to the California state.

The government process by which bills are considered and laws are enacted is known as the Legislative Process, which starts when an Assembly Member or Senator decides to write a bill and later passes the idea for the bill to the Legislative Counsel where it is drafted into the actual bill. The draft of the bill is then returned to the Legislator for the introduction process. If the author is a Senator, then the bill is introduced in the Senate. If he is an Assembly Member, it is introduced in the Assembly. A bill is read or introduced the first time when the bill number, the author's name, and the descriptive bill title are read on the house floor. The bill is later sent to the Office of State Printing. It is worth mentioning that no bill may be acted upon until 30 days have passed from the date of its introduction.

After that, the bill should go to the Rules Committee of the origin house. There it is assigned to its policy committee for its first hearing. Bills are assigned to the policy committee according to the subject area. Bills that require the expenditure of funds also have to be heard in the fiscal committees: Senate Appropriations or Assembly Appropriations.

Fiscal committees in each house are those that consider appropriations: Appropriations and Budget Committees. All fiscal bills are referred to a fiscal committee. Fiscal bills are any measure that contains an appropriation of funds or needs a state agency to spend money for any purpose or results in a substantial loss of revenue to the state. The budget bill is referred only to the Budget Committee. Usually, other fiscal bills are heard by the Appropriations Committee after the approval of policy committees. If the fiscal committee approves the bill, it usually then moves to the House Floor.

Each house has a specific number of policy committees and one fiscal committee. Each committee is composed of a specified number of Senators or Assembly Members. The author presents the bill to the relevant committee during the hearing, and testimony can either support or oppose the bill. After that, the committee votes by passing the bill, passing the bill as amended, or defeating it. Bills can be amended at various times. Letters of support or opposition are needed. These letters should be mailed to the author and committee members before the bill is scheduled to be heard in the appropriate committee. The system requires a majority vote of the full committee membership for a bill to be passed by the committee. Each house maintains a rigorous schedule of legislative committee hearings. Before the bill's hearing, an analysis is prepared that explains current law, what the bill is intended to do, and some other relevant background information. Usually, the analysis also lists organizations that support or oppose the bill.

The California State Legislature comprises two Houses: the Senate and the Assembly. In California, there are 40 Senators and 80 Assembly Members representing the people (California State Association of Counties, 1). The Legislature has a legislative calendar containing relevant dates of activities during its two-year session. California's constitution requires a two-thirds vote of the total membership— not just those present and voting—in each Legislature house to pass the budget. The two-thirds requirement intends to ensure that a more significant majority than 50 percent agrees on the size and distribution of the budget, assuming that this number reflects a consensus in society. However, since neither party has had a two-thirds majority in either the Assembly or the State Senate in decades, the majority party must make accommodations with some minority party legislators to obtain the necessary votes. The price these legislators have demanded in the past has supported programs and projects of interest to them.

Three essential and well-regarded groups of staff are non-partisan and work for the entire California Legislature. The first is the Legislative Analyst's Office, which analyzes budget proposals and the fiscal impact of ballot propositions. The second is the Legislative Counsel of California, which helps write bills, prepare digests for each bill, analyze ballot propositions, and provide proper legal advice to the Legislature. The third is the Auditor General's office, which does management and fiscal audits of the California executive branch.

In California, as in most states in the United States of America, the Governor has a line-item veto in appropriations, including those in the state budget. This special power allows the Governor to reduce or even eliminate a specific spending item, although he cannot increase items. This provision means that the Legislature cannot force the Governor to include an item that he opposes in a larger bill, most of which he supports. A veto is the governor's formal action disapproving a measure by returning it to origin, and a two-thirds majority vote of each House can override it. The Governor can also use a line-item veto, where the amount of an appropriation is reduced or eliminated, and the rest is approved. A two-thirds vote in each House can also override a line-item veto.

Bills that immediately take effect or require an appropriation usually require 27 votes in the Senate and 54 votes in the Assembly to be passed. There are other bills that generally have 21 votes in the Senate and 41 votes in the Assembly. If a bill is defeated, the Member can seek reconsideration and another vote. Once the house has approved the bill of origin, it proceeds to the other house, where the procedure is repeated.

According to many observers, the irony is that the requirement designed to produce a budget that reflects a strong consensus in society and is smaller than what a simple majority would pass results in a bigger budget, with more waste. Nevertheless, when offered the opportunity to reduce the two-thirds requirement to 55 percent or a majority, the voters have opted to stay with the two-thirds requirement.

The state budget is prepared and sent to the California Legislature by January 10, with revisions later in the spring as the financial outlook becomes clearer. The Governor then faces the challenge of getting the budget approved by the Legislature, where a two-thirds majority of each house is required. To reach this two-thirds majority, the Governor must gain support not only from the majority party, but from the minority party as well. This may require some expensive trade-offs for some recalcitrant legislators who withhold their support until they receive an offer they will likely accept.

10.4. The mechanics of budgets: Revenue

One of the critical determinants of the condition of the California state budget is the general state of the state economy. Economic growth brings in more tax revenue. Recession cuts revenue, mainly because of the heavy dependence of state revenue on the fates of top income earners (personal income tax). For many utilities, one can consider residential customers to be the lifeblood of their operations. So, if customers choose to substitute away from utility-provided tap water, there will likely be less revenue available for quality monitoring and essential distribution infrastructure.

The best a state government can do to eliminate or reduce the impact of a recession is to build up a considerable budget reserve. State or local governments function like a household. As a household, state governments have saving reserves to adequately cushion the impact of a sharp drop in state income. In the household case, a job loss might trigger a family income crisis, for example. In the government case, it is generally a recession that cuts into tax revenue. Jerry Brown, in his first iteration as Governor, managed to build up a considerable reserve. However, that same reserve had, unfortunately, when combined with a different type of political failing, produced a fiscal crisis in California.

As is typical of state budgets, California divides its budget into various "local funds." The most significant is the General Fund which can be understood as a state checking account from which ongoing day-to-day bills are paid. Generally, expenditures from the General Fund account for about 69% of all state expenditures (excluding spending from the various state pension funds). Outside the General Fund account, special funds account for approximately 28% of the overall state budget. Finally, various bond funds account for the remainder. The California state borrows by issuing bonds for various capital purposes. Once the funds are raised, expenditures for those purposes are made as required. At the California state level, the most significant source of expenditure is education, about 51% of the General Fund in Newsom's first budget. At the K-14 level, state spending for education is mostly a passing of funding to local school districts and community college districts. It is worth mentioning that the University of California and California State University systems are directly funded by the state and are state government entities. The state has other relevant responsibilities apart from education. Twenty-eight percent of the California General Fund goes to Health and Human Resources. About 9% of the General Fund goes to prison and incarceration-associated purposes.

When citizens refer to the state budget, they are actually referring to the General Fund in most cases. The truth is that the California state budget has many funds that are earmarked for various purposes outside the General Fund. For example, the most significant external funds deal with transportation. The gasoline and motor vehicle-related taxes go into funds that provide for roads and local public transit. Nevertheless, many less visible funds exist -but receive less attention-, such as the Illegal DrugLab Cleanup Account, the San Joaquin River Conservancy Fund, the Medical Waste Management Fund, and the Marine Invasive Species Control Fund, only to name a few ones.

The government also lobbies the government itself. Taxpayer protection groups have called these interests—education, health, special districts, local government, state agencies—"the spending lobby" since they are motivated by the desire to maintain or increase their revenue. In 2005, for instance, the government was the highest spender among the nineteen categories of lobbyist employers registered with the secretary of state (Anagnoson, 131).

Successfully passing the budget is at the center, both in difficulty and scope, of what the state government does each year. Since the passage of Proposition 13, the state government has considerably received less revenue, which has since then become more volatile, rising and falling with the state economy. The California constitution clearly states that the Legislature is to pass the budget by June 15. Since the year 1990, the Legislature has only met the deadline four times, and two of those were budget surplus years.

What are the sources of revenue in California? The largest single source of revenue is the personal income tax, which provides almost half the general fund (which can be thought of as a checking account used for ongoing services, and California education is its most prominent component). Personal income tax is highly progressive[18] in California (Anagnoson, 162). The sales tax is the next largest source, providing almost 30 percent of the budget.

Local governments are allowed to add one-eighth to one-half percent for local uses to the sales tax. The state returns a portion of the sales tax to each locality, which has become very significant in the era since Proposition 13, as localities have sought to add sales tax- producing businesses, like big-box shopping centers and automobile dealerships, to their communities. The bank and corporation tax is the third significant source of revenue for the budget. Smaller revenue supplies come from insurance, tobacco, motor vehicle fuel, and alcohol taxes[19] (Gerston and Christensen, 113). California's tax system is not rated highly compared to other states' systems, partly because it is highly dependent on the economy, producing more significant surges than the economy in good times and substantial deficits in needy times.

Today, revenue for the General Fund more or less comes primarily from three taxes: the personal income tax (70%), the sales tax (19%), and the bank and corporation tax (9%). These percentages may slightly differ over the years, but proportions mostly stay the same. Through a careful combination of discretionary allocation and formula, some General Fund revenue is taken off the top and diverted to another fund, known as the Budget Stabilization Account. Although the Budget Stabilization Account ("rainy day fund") was created during the Schwarzenegger period, former Governor Schwarzenegger was never able to make much

---

[18] For more information on the most significant sources of revenue in California, see Anagnoson.

[19] California also gets a small but growing portion of its revenue from fees and charges for services. For example, 90 percent of the operating costs of state parks were funded by taxes in 1982-1983, but within a decade, only 40 percent came from tax revenues, whereas 57 percent came from fees and concessions. For more information on this topic, see Gerston and Christensen.

use of it. Under Brown, however, the BSA was given real-life importance in California politics by a formula that takes revenue off the top before it goes to the General Fund and other allocations made by the Legislature.

As shown in the Introduction and Revenue Estimates chapters for the period 2021-2022, revenues are up considerably over the Governor's Budget forecast. Since the beginning of the year, the situation seems to result from two major federal relief bills, solid cash trends, continued stock market appreciation, and a significantly upgraded economic forecast. California will also receive $27 billion Coronavirus State Fiscal Recovery Funds from the American Rescue Plan Act of 2021 (ARPA). The total amount of federal stimulus funds for California state programs is today close to $275 billion. The improved revenue forecast allows for the elimination of $2 billion in proposed program suspensions that were previously delayed at the Governor's Budget.

10.5. Explaining California Expenditures, Deficits, and Debt

Within the first ten days of the calendar year, the governor must submit to the Legislature a unified budget that is carefully balanced, contains a reasonable explanation for each proposed expenditure, and is accompanied by a budget bill itemizing each recommended expenditure. This is how the budget is formed in California.

Politically speaking, one can consider the budget a statement of priorities. State budgets tend to express the fiscal priorities of some groups over others. Many politically-oriented groups have an interest in budget outcomes and state policy more generally. For example, a group that has been very influential among the Democrats in California in the Legislature is public-sector unions.

Respective appropriations chairs introduce the budget bills immediately in each House. The Legislature should pass the budget by June 15 of each year. Nevertheless, there is no penalty for not reaching the deadline. Appropriations from the general fund should be passed in each House by two-thirds of the membership, not just those present and voting. It is worth mentioning, however, that education funding (K-12) is exempted from the two-thirds rule, but in practice, the entire budget is approved as a whole by a two-thirds vote majority. He can reduce or even eliminate an item of appropriation when he signs the budget bill. This very potent tool is the line-item veto.

Education is the most significant single expenditure in California; expenditures for K-14 education are required by Proposition 98 to be 40 percent or more of the general fund. If one includes higher education, education constitutes approximately half the state budget. Health and human services is the next largest category, followed by the courts and corrections. Recent California state budgets have had huge gaps between revenues and expenditures because revenues plunge when the economy goes into recession and expenditures stay the same or increase. Balancing budget revenues and expenditures has not always been easy for state leaders. Between 1991 and 1995, the state budgetary process was hobbled by an unrelenting recession and its by-product, inadequate revenues. During this period, California suffered annual budget shortfalls of anywhere between $5 billion and $14 billion, often forcing Governor Wilson and the recession-weary legislature to raise taxes and borrow billions from banks to make ends meet. Fortunately, the state recovered in 1996, leading to the enormous surpluses of 1999 and 2000.

In recent years, California policymakers, lawmakers, and the governor have closed the budget gap with the standard techniques such as incremental tax increases; cuts in education, health, and social services, and enormous parts of the budget; and borrowing through bond issues that will be repaid over a five- to ten- year period to cover a portion of the yearly deficit. It is worth considering that the economy of California is the fifth or sixth-largest economy among the nations of the world. On a global stage, its closest comparison is probably India. However, it is essential to note that California has a labor force of 19.5 million compared to India's labor force of 519 million.

When ordinary citizens think of a budget deficit, they generally think about a situation in which the yearly outflows exceed the inflows. When they think of a "surplus," they likely have in mind a situation in which, in California, more money is flowing in than flowing out. When someone hears of the federal deficit, it is with these flow concepts in mind. However, it is worth mentioning that there is much muddier language, at least at the state level, and a tendency to mix up stocks and flows. The language also appears to be loose about what time is being discussed.

It is worth considering that the California state has long featured sloppy budgetary language when it comes to deficits and surpluses. Specifically, the use of the terms deficit and surplus has historically been loose. As Mitchell points out, this language looseness has involved fundamental policymaking sins. Surpluses and deficits are flow concepts. Nevertheless, they have been sometimes confused with stock concepts such as reserves in California budget-speak.

On the other hand, as flow concepts, they inherently involve a period, typically the fiscal year. It is very challenging to properly evaluate fiscal policy if there is confusing descriptive language and the past errors were bad enough. For example, using the term surplus to describe discretionary spending is not considered a good practice.

Over time, California has experienced several budget crises. By February 2004, for example, the state's budget deficit had grown massive and out of control.[20] Throughout the time, observers had trouble even finding the words to describe it. When the state faced a severe deficit in 1992, legislators had to find ways to balance the state budget, ideally without cutting spending or raising taxes, and comply with Proposition 98. Consequently, they deposited a significant portion of the collected local property tax revenues, especially from the counties, into educational revenue augmentation funds and directed that these funds be spent on schools to meet the obligations imposed by Proposition 98.

---

[20] Herb Wesson Jr., Speaker of the State Assembly, said in 2013: "That's a hole so deep and so vast that even if we fired every single person on the state payroll, we would still be billions short."

However, compared to a projected budget deficit of $54 billion in 2020, the state now has a projected $75.7 billion surplus. In addition, combined with over $25 billion in federal relief, this supports a $100 billion California Comeback Plan. Even though it is unreasonable to believe this growth in economic resources will continue at the current pace over the long term, the truth is that the combination of the state's surplus and federal relief funds are allowing California to make a once-in-a-lifetime investment in the future of the state. (California Government)

Most United States states, including California, require a balanced budget. Even if California has no law limiting the amount of public debt the state can accumulate, its policymakers should carefully monitor the state debt growth. From $60 billion in 2008, the California state debt has risen to $152 billion. California today carries the largest state debt burden in the country and is also among only a few states that have borrowed close to a budget gap.

10.6. Political problems with Budgeting

Three major kinds of problems confront California's various local governments. The extreme polarization in regional political cultures across the state makes legislative compromise and consensus building difficult, as illustrated by the stark differences in partisanship, political tolerance, and voting tendencies observed in San Francisco, Los Angeles County, and San Diego County. The second is the challenge posed by internal conflicts and secessionist movements in some local jurisdictions, as illustrated by the recent attempt of the San Fernando Valley to secede from Los Angeles. The third is the crisis in local government finance and the threat to effective home rule caused by the worsening state budget deficit and the state government's efforts to solve it by seizing property tax revenues from county and city governments.

Given the current blue state politics in California, the Democrats greatly influence the state policy making process. For example, by the time Newsom made that second run some years ago, California had adopted its non-partisan top-two primary system. From the start, it was clear that Newsom would come in first, and the only question that remained to be answered was whether the candidate who would come in second place in the June 2018 primary would be a Democrat or a Republican.

During the second decade of the XXI century, there was no doubt that the eventual gubernatorial winner would likely be a Democrat. Nevertheless, there were still two Republicans in the non-partisan race heading for the June 2018 primary and four Democrats. From the beginning of the polling process, it was clear that in that "top-2" primary, Lieutenant Governor Gavin Newsom would be the top vote-getter. Considering that it would be very tough to win, both national and state Republicans wanted one of the two Republicans - Travis Allen or John Cox - to be on the gubernatorial ballot in the California November general election. This goal was based on the impact on Republican voters and not on any idea that either one could win against Newsom or any other Democrat. It was thought that if there were no Republicans at the top of the ticket, Republican turnout in the election would be reduced, and Republican congressional candidates and legislative candidates could ultimately be hurt.

Even though Allen was probably the most loyal Trump supporting candidate since Cox reportedly did not vote for Trump in 2016, President Trump eventually endorsed businessman Cox as the stronger of the two candidates. However, Cox still came in second place and knocked out Allen and the Democrats competing with Newsom. Once the primary was finally over, Cox was given only nominal support by the Republican national establishment. There was only one perfunctory radio debate between Cox and Newsom and little to no political advertising because of his very limited chances of winning. In the end, the 2018 California general election was a repeat of 2014. Newsom received just under 62%; Cox received just over 38%. Democrats won supermajority control of the two houses of the California Legislature. After the election, Republicans in California commented that California's "one-party rule" is to stay unless Republicans separated from President Trump or some new third party was formed.

This situation suggests that the "Old Grand Party" days are over in California since the Republican influence in the state is very limited nowadays. However, even if things are unlikely to change in the near future, it is worth considering that Republicans still received 40% of the vote in the 2014 gubernatorial election, which is not an insignificant percentage. If Republicans are later able to take advantage of changes in state election law, they may have a chance of winning. In 2016, Democrats were better able to benefit from these changes than the Republicans.

Considering that, it came as no surprise that Newsom would inherit Brown's tensions with the Trump administration. Wildfire fighting had budgetary implications for California state, and President Trump constantly threatened to cut back on FEMA assistance based on the idea that California was doing a poor job of forest management. Much of those threats were only tweets and not actual policy. California Republican legislators opposed Trump's threats. Newsom did acknowledge state mismanagement in the DMV with its long lines and other problems, and he announced that a dramatically named "strike force" would be appointed to study what needed to be done.

There are five relevant players in the budget game in California: the governor and the four leaders of both parties in both houses of the Legislature[21]. The need for one or two marginal votes may create even more fundamental players. Because of his role at both ends of the budgetary process, considering that one person is required to broker the deal, the Governor is usually the key player. However, even he can be held hostage by other recalcitrant legislators.

In its present-day political configuration, the California Legislature is mostly dominated by Democrats. The Democratic leadership and the California governor will confer on what is acceptable to the latter. One should consider that only a simple majority in the Legislature is needed

---

[21] Even as Republican representation shrank in the last years, ,there remained a two-thirds vote requirement to pass a budget, giving the minority party a significant voice in the process. For more information on that, see Mitchell, 2019.

to pass a budget. Nevertheless, if any tax increases are part of the budget, a two-thirds majority in both houses is needed. In the past, this supermajority requirement gave Republicans some limited leverage in the state. However, the Democrats have ultimately had the two-thirds needed to prevail in the last years. So, Republicans have lately tended to be bystanders in the California budget process.

The California constitution vests supreme executive power in the Governor, and even though limited, the formal powers of the California governor are still formidable. The Governor has special powers, most important the line-item veto that is denied to the United States president. Yet impressive as this list of powers is, these powers are most important as vantage points upon which the Governor bases his informal powers or powers to politically and socially persuade. A governor who expects to use only his formal powers to govern will not accomplish much. He must use those powers as a basis to persuade other political actors to support his goals. For instance, he can use his appointment power to persuade a relevant legislator to support his budget by promising to appoint one of the legislator's supporters to a vital state commission. To this date, Jerry Brown is the only former Governor who could serve four terms in total as Governor of California. Unless term limits are abolished, no future governor will surpass this record.

It is worth mentioning that even though the governor has the power to veto the entire budget, that scenario is thought to be unlikely to happen. Throughout history, California governors have exercised the line-veto power more frequently than the full veto power. However, since there is eventually a three-way deal among the California leaders, even line-veto vetoes are also very limited. Still, both have occurred in different periods of California state history.

The governor appoints members to approximately 325 boards and commissions. Once appointed, individuals do not directly have to answer to the governor, although political pressure and lobbying, including budget pressure, can exist. He also has several staff advisory agencies, including the Department of Finance, the Office of Planning and Research, and the Department of Personnel Administration. Perhaps the most important of all these is the Department of Finance, which prepares the governor's state budget.

The governor's powers are constitutionally restricted by the Legislature but he can act independently of it in certain cases. There are actions permitted by the California constitution or under laws passed by the Legislature. These actions are most significant in times of need and emergency. The governor's most significant power is probably that of preparing the budget, along with the line-item veto of budget provisions. At the federal level, the United States president presents Congress with a budget proposal, but it is just a proposal since the House of Representatives has constitutional authority over fiscal matters.

The California constitution grants the power of preparing the budget to the governor. All budget requests from executive branch agencies must pass through the California governor. The Department of Finance does all actual work on this process. Agencies implement the budget as passed. The Department of Finance states that agencies and departments are expected to operate within their budgets and comply with any provisions enacted by the Legislature.

The California Legislature adopts a budget based on the Governor's proposal. Both the Assembly and the State Senate should adopt the budget by a two-thirds majority of the entire membership of the legislative body. The California Assembly and Senate budget committees and their subcommittees hold hearings on the budget bills, receiving relevant testimony and input from individuals and groups, including associated departments and agencies, the Department of Finance, the Legislative Analyst's Office, committee staff, and interest groups.

The Legislative Analyst's Office provides a non-partisan and independent review of the entire budget, offering alternative and useful ways to accomplish the same goals and objectives. Although the Legislative Analyst's Office seldom makes specific budget proposals, it produces what one can consider as a workload budget in mid-November, indicating what the budget for the coming fiscal year would be if no significant programmatic changes were made. If nothing extraordinary happens, one might expect that the January budget plan would look like the LAO's workload budget at least on the spending side, but probably including a more restrained revenue projection.

It is worth mentioning that even though the Governor has the power to veto the entire budget, that scenario is thought to be unlikely to happen. Throughout history, California governors have exercised the line-veto power more frequently than the full veto power. However, since there is eventually a three-way deal among the California leaders, even line-veto vetoes are also very limited. Still, both have occurred in different periods of California state history.

The Legislature constitutionally restricts the Governor's powers, but he can act independently of it in some instances. There are actions permitted by the California constitution or under laws passed by the Legislature. These actions are most significant in times of need and emergency. The Governor's most significant power is probably that of preparing the budget, along with the line-item veto of budget provisions. At the federal level, the United States president presents Congress with a budget proposal, but it is just a proposal since the House of Representatives has constitutional authority over fiscal matters.

The California Legislature is fragmented. There are eighty members of the California state assembly and forty members of the California State Senate. These 120 legislators have staff support. But particularly with term limits and turnover, there is usually more expertise in the hands of the governor. To balance the process back in the 1940s, the legislature had to create the Legislative Analyst's Office (LAO), which provides insightful commentary on, and critiques of, the budget outlook forecast and the specifics of the governor's proposal.

Commonly, the Assembly budget and the Senate budget differ in certain aspects, resulting in the appointment of a Budget Conference Committee to work out the differences, with an eye on compromises that will maximize the probability of receiving a two-thirds vote on the final budget passage. Suppose the conference committee cannot resolve an issue. In that case, the Big 5 group consisting of the Governor, Assembly Speaker, Senate president pro tempore, and the Assembly and Senate minority leaders meet to resolve the budget issue.

California has a winner-take-all system of voting. The candidate receiving the highest vote wins the election. Social scientists have long known that such a system promotes two dominant political parties. Consequently, two major political parties dominate the political process in California: the Republicans and the Democrats.

Third parties, which are defined as any party other than the Republicans and Democrats, play only a limited role in California politics. However, several third parties are considered qualified and are entitled to appear on the California ballot. Those parties are the American Independent Party, the Natural Law Party, the Peace and Freedom Party, the Green party, and the Libertarian Party. Since the Legislature in California is dominated by the Republicans and the Democrats, it is not easy for third parties to successfully qualify to get on the ballot. Consequently, California politics is almost totally dominated by the Republicans and Democrats, which is the general rule in the United States of America.

Throughout California history, the tendency toward ideological extremism in Democratic and Republican parties, combined with the effects of term limits on legislators' knowledge and the need to obtain a two-thirds majority to pass the budget, has led to a late budget on various occasions, especially during the 1990s.

Interest groups have proposed self-serving initiatives or opposed what many feel changes that would strengthen politics and policy. For example, Proposition 98 requires that 40 percent of the state budget, at a minimum, fund the elementary and secondary schools and community colleges. Each year, it is clear that this is a tightly specified area of the budget. Within the 40 percent are over 100 categorical programs, each designed to achieve a specific goal with a specific amount of money aimed at a specific population of schools or pupils. School officials must spend the money as specified.

Former Governor Gray Davis once advised eliminating sixty-four of the special programs and combining the money into one grant that school districts could spend pretty much as they chose. In an article in the Sacramento Bee, Dan Weintraub described the ensuing melee as a flurry of criticism from the narrow interests served by each of the dozens of special programs. There was little support from the wider public that would benefit from the change but does not even know the debate exists." Governor Arnold Schwarzenegger has recommended the same change. Related situations complicate any number of policy areas in California.

10.7. California Taxation: Why so high?

The overall California tax structure, compared with other states, is more dependent on volatile taxes; they go up and down with the economy (income tax and sales tax) and less dependent on taxes that do not vary with the economy (the property tax), because of the Proposition 13 limits. Although the sales tax of approximately 8 percent is high, it is less than the sales taxes paid in nine other states. The average state obtains 29 percent of its total state and local tax funds from the property tax, but because of Proposition 13's limits, California obtains only 22 percent. Yet though the public and elected officials may agree on the need and importance of taxes, they often disagree on how much should be collected and where it should be spent. When policymakers seem to stray from public values concerning budgetary issues, the voters are not shy about using the tools of direct democracy to reorder the state's fiscal priorities. With the annual state budget at more than $100 billion, one can say that much is at stake in California. States as California can only spend as much money as they collect and have.

While most states that rank high on the scale of taxes per $1,000 of personal income are low-income states like South Carolina, California is generally considered a rich one. Compared with high-income states of its league like New York and Massachusetts, California's tax burden is sixth-highest, with some of the other high-income states ranked much lower. California's tax system is not rated highly compared to other states' systems, partly because it is highly dependent on the economy, producing more significant surges than the economy in good times and substantial deficits in needy times.

Until the Great Depression of 1929-1933, the relatively small state government relied on minor taxes on businesses and utilities for funds. No economic downturn since the Great Depression of the 1930s had a steep and long-lasting impact on city revenues and expenditures. As was the case for cities throughout the nation, the adverse spillover effects of foreclosure on cities in California were stifling. During the Great Depression, state aid fell by about 11.5 percent, and property taxes fell by 8.5 percent. California history teaches that, after the economic crash, the state was forced to develop new tax sources to cope with hard times. The first of these was a 2.5 percent sales tax, adopted to provide permanent funding for schools and local governments. Today the Legislature temporarily adjusts the sales tax upward or downward in response to economic conditions. Such an adjustment last occurred in December 1989, in response to the major earthquake in northern California.

A second significant revenue source in California, the personal income tax, was modeled after its federal counterpart to collect larger amounts of money from those residents with greater earnings. Today the personal income tax varies between 1 and 9.3 percent, depending upon one's income. State lawmakers and Governor Wilson increased the tax on the highest incomes to 11 percent in 1991, but Wilson argued for and won a reduction to 9.3 percent beginning in January 1996. The personal income tax is currently the most important and fastest-growing revenue source in California. Because the tax goes up with increasing incomes, it has filled the state coffers with the dramatic economic recovery since 1998.

California's local governments used the biggest single source of money once to be the property tax, an annual assessment based on the value of land and buildings (Gerston and Christensen, 131). However, in 1978, local voters approved Proposition 15, a statewide initiative that cut property tax revenues by 57 percent. Cities in California adjusted to Proposition 13 in various ways. Some cut jobs and services to save money. Others introduced or increased charges for services such as sewage treatment, trash collection, building permits, and the use of recreational facilities. Such charges are now a very significant source of income for most cities, followed by the sales tax, which returns one percent of the state's basic 7.25 percent tax to the city where the sale occurred (or the county). Utility taxes also help some cities.

In California, financial industry and corporation taxes contribute much less than sales and personal income taxes. It is a fact that taxes on corporations and banks did not exceed 5.5 percent until 1959 when the Legislature enacted a series of upward rate changes. A significant increase occurred in 1980. In response to local governments' losses from Proposition 13, the California Legislature boosted the bank and corporation tax from 9.6 percent to 11.6 percent.

Even though it is a fact that Californians pay high taxes, it is a controversial topic to argue that Californians are overtaxed. One should consider that the state has cut taxes several times in the last decade, not raised them, as the state received more revenues than it expected. The tax is low for middle-class families that have little or no tax until they earn more than $45,000; the tax load from the state and local governments in California is about average among the fifty states, and sometimes, even below average. The highest-income Californians continue to pay a considerable share of California's personal income tax. For the 2018 California tax year, the top one percent of income earners paid around 46 percent of personal income taxes.

It is essential to consider that those California top earners tend to derive significant incomes from financial markets. Consequently, the ups and downs of the stock market can strongly affect personal income tax collections. As a result, budget forecasting ultimately involves projecting trends in the real economy and financial booms, cycles, and busts. The volatility of the California tax system, mainly because of its dependence on financial markets and general economic trends, is a significant motivation for building up reserves to handle fiscal uncertainties adequately. The more money there is in reserve, the more potential protection there is against some future financial downturn. It is relevant to note that the top earners have constantly been contributing more than 40 percent of the monies collected by the personal income tax.

Utility affordability is one of the top priorities for California policymakers. Thus, low-income rate assistance programs (LIRAs) offer discounts on utility bills for low-income California customers and can provide direct or indirect benefits to eligible households. In California, it is also worth highlighting that a way to better provide utility affordability assistance to low-income customers in the future might be through water rate restructuring indirectly, by fixed or variable rates. Water is equally, if not more, vital to households than natural gas and electricity.

Compared with other states, the personal income tax in California relies more on capital gains than on taxes on wage earners. Wage-earners with families have a substantial personal exemption, sufficiently high that families with children do not pay personal income tax until their income is between $40,000 and $50,000. Meanwhile, the capital gain surge of 1999-2000 came from the sales as the stock market surged. With the recession of the early 2000s, such sales have dwindled.

Works cited

Anagnoson, J.T. *Governing California in the Twenty-First Century: The Political Dynamics of the Golden State*. New York: W.W. Norton & Co, 2013. Internet resource.

California Budget Summary 2021-2022. California Government, May 2021, www.ebudget.ca.gov/2021-22/pdf/Revised/BudgetSummary/Full-BudgetSummary.pdf. Accessed 25 June 2021.

Mitchell, D. *California Policy Options 2019*. UCLA Luskin School of Public Affairs, 2019. Internet resource.

Mitchell, D. *California Policy Options 2020*. UCLA Luskin School of Public Affairs, 2019. Internet resource.

Gerston, L., and Terry, C. *California Politics and Government: A Practical Approach*. Forth Worth: Harcourt College Publishers, 2001.

Overview of California Legislative Process. California State Association of Counties, www.counties.org/sites/main/files/file-attachments/v2-tab5_-_legislative_advocacy.pdf. Accessed 27 June 2021.

CHAPTER 11

Government in California

11.1. Counties in California

California is divided into 58 counties. According to the California Constitution, a county makes and enforces local ordinances that do not conflict with general laws. A county also has the power to sue and be sued, purchase and hold land, manage or dispose of its properties, and levy and collect taxes authorized by law (for more countywide services, see Table 1).

Many additional powers have been granted to counties by the Legislature. The powers of a county can only be exercised by the Board of Supervisors or through officers acting under the authority of the Board or authority conferred by law.

In California, there is a distinction between a county and a city. In contrast to Californian cities, counties do not have broad powers of self-government. There is also more strict legislative control over counties. The Legislature can delegate or take back to the counties any of the functions which belong to the state itself.

Category	Examples of services
Public Safety	Courts, jails, probation public defense, juvenile detention, sheriff, fire, emergency, animal control
Public Assistance	Housing welfare, nutrition assistance through CalFresh, medical
Elections and Voting	
Tax Collection	
Environment and Recreation	Parks, sport activities
Public Health	Hospitals, mental health clinics
Education	Libraries and schools
Social services	Adoptions and foster care, homeless assistance
Transport	Airports, buses, and railways
Vital records	Birth, death, and marriage certificates

Table 1. Countywide services.

11.2. Types of Counties in California

The California Constitution recognizes two types of counties: general law counties and charter counties. There are currently 44 general law counties and 14 charter counties. General law counties are under the jurisdiction of state law as to the number and duties of county elected officials.

Charter counties have a limited degree of "home rule" authority that may provide for the election, compensation, terms, removal, and salary of the governing Board; for the election or appointment (except the sheriff, district attorney, and assessor who must be elected), compensation, terms and removal of all county officers; for the powers and duties of all officers; and consolidation and segregation of county offices. A charter does not give county officials extra authority over local regulations, revenue-raising abilities, budgetary decisions, or intergovernmental relations.

Charters are defined by California Constitution (Art. XI §3). A county may adopt, amend or repeal a charter with majority vote approval. When counties do not have a charter or, in the case of potential amendment or repeal, such initiative can be proposed by the Board of Supervisors or a charter commission. The amendment or repeal of a charter can also be proposed through an initiative petition.

The initiative petition can be used if citizens of a county want to determine whether to draft or revise a charter and elect a charter commission on the ballot. If this question receives majority support, the 15 candidates for the charter commission who receive the most votes will organize into a commission to prepare a charter (California Government Code § 23700-23714).

11.3. The Board of Supervisors

The Board of Supervisors represents both the legislative and the executive authority of the county. In addition, it has quasi-judicial authority. According to the Government Code (§ 2500), a Board of Supervisors needs to consist of five members. This general law is provided to all law and charter counties, except the charter provides otherwise (e.g., San Francisco and County).

To be a board member, one needs to be a registered voter of, and reside in, the district from which the member is elected. If a county charter does not define a method of filling vacancies, the Governor appoints a successor.

The Board of Supervisors can only perform during their meetings. Individual members of the Board do not have the power to act for the county (Government Code §54950). Meetings are open and public. Moreover, the meetings are recorded and archived.

The Board performs its executive role when it sets priorities for the county. The Board oversees most county departments and programs and annually approves their budgets; supervises county officers and employ-ees; controls all county property; and appropriates and spends money on programs that meet county residents' needs.

The Board of Supervisors can also supervise the sheriff as long as the sheriff performs as a county officer and may investigate the officer's per-formance of county duties. However, in enforcing state law, the sheriff is acting as a peace officer of the state and is under the direct supervision of the attorney general. In addition to being an officer of the county, the sheriff is also an officer of the courts. From this perspective, he or she cannot be under the supervision of the Board.

11.4. Legislative role of the Board of Supervisors

In terms of the county's legislative body, the Board of Supervisors may act by resolution, board order, or ordinance. A resolution is a declaration about future purposes or proceedings of the Board or a policy statement by the Board. Resolutions are often used when the Board makes specific findings of Supervisors. A board order is usually a directive from the Board of Supervisors to its subordinate county officers.

On the other hand, an ordinance refers to a local law adopted with all the legal formality of a statute (California Government Code § 25120). The California Constitution permits a county or city to make and enforce within its limits all local, police, sanitary, and other ordinances and regu-lations that do not conflict with the state's general laws. Most legislative acts, including using police power, are adopted by ordinance. However, there are some exceptions, and specific state laws sometimes indicate whether the action requires an ordinance or resolution. Moreover, there are different forms of ordinances, such as urgency ordinances (required for the immediate preservation of the public peace, health, or safety) and ordinances that are statutorily required to have a noticed public hearing to be adopted (e.g., land use zoning or new fees).

Boards of Supervisors can raise local revenue by imposing or increas-ing a tax, an assessment, or a fee. A county can only impose those taxes, assessments, and fees that the Legislature or the Constitution allow the county to impose and approved by either a simple or two-thirds majority of local voters per Propositions 13 and 62. If a Board of Supervisors decides to impose or increase a specific tax, assessment, or fee, it must follow proper notice in advance and hearing requirements. There are different posting and disclosure requirements for each of these types of local revenue sources.

In this regard, the Board of Supervisors may settle claims that are against the county and may examine and audit the accounts of all county officers as they relate to the management and disbursement of funds. The Board of Supervisors also performs as a quasi-judicial body in appeals of land use decisions and tax issues.

11.5. Municipalities in California

California consists of 482 municipalities (2017)[22]. California law makes no distinction between "city" and "town", and municipalities may use either term in their official names. As in counties, cities derive their power from either the California Government Code (statute) or from adopting a city charter. One can distinguish different forms of cities in California: general law cities, charter cities, and consolidated city and county. The California Government Code governs general law cities; the adoption of charters governs charter cities. The consolidated city and county is a city and a county that have been merged into one jurisdiction and governed by a charter. It is simultaneously a city, a municipal corporation, and a county, which is an administrative division of a state. For now, only San Francisco is a consolidated city and county in California.

---

[22] See, U.S. Census Bureau, "2017 Census of Governments – Organization", https://www.census.gov/data/tables/2017/econ/gus/2017-governments.html (last visited July 28, 2021)

However, cities have a higher level of autonomy than counties because they are voluntarily formed and perform many essential services. Based on Constitution Art. XI and California Government Code § 34871, there is a difference between general law and charter cities. Charter cities have more autonomy in their governance because, through localized laws, their authority expands beyond the general law requirements.

Contract cities: A contract city is a city that contracts for the provision of one or more municipal services with another unit of government or with a private or commercial organization. The first contract city in the United States was founded in 1954 in Lakewood in California.

In contrast, independent cities are cities that provide basic various services to their citizens. In California, most older cities are independent cities. However, many cities today can be considered as a hybrid of both types. For instance, they may directly operate parks programs but contract with the county for police and fire services. Most contract cities do their land-use planning since they were usually incorporated to exert local control over land use.

Unincorporated areas: For those areas that are not within a city (known also as "unincorporated areas" of a county), counties provide law enforcement services through the sheriff's office. For these areas, counties may also provide such services as fire protection, animal control, parks, recreation, public works, planning and land use, water, wastewater, solid waste, and library—services that are similar to those cities provide within their boundaries (known as the incorporated areas).

In some cases, counties and cities provide these services together. These services also may be provided by a private company or by a special district. Counties also have regulatory power within the unincorporated areas (for instance, land use planning authority and building code enforcement).

11.6. Forms of municipal government23

Council-Manager: In this form of government, the council is the governing body of the city, elected by the public. On the other hand, the city manager is not an elected position. Instead, the holder of this office serves at the pleasure of the council, which retains the legal right to dismiss and replace the city manager. The hiring process for a city manager begins with general discussions amongst city council members, often in consultation with voters and professional consultants. After a hiring notice is drafted and distributed to professional organizations, the process then moves to a multistage interview process that includes a review of applications and onsite interviews with qualified candidates. The process ends with a vote taken by the city council.[24]

Usually, the council consists of five to nine members including a mayor (or council president). Mayor is either elected by the council or elected by the citizens of the municipality. The election process of the mayor is described in the city charter. The size of the council is generally smaller than that of a mayor-council municipality. In this case, the council has a nonpartisan character. Among major cities in California, this model is present in San Jose.

The council is responsible for providing legislative direction to the city. The mayor and council, as a collegial body, are responsible for setting policy, approving the budget, and determining the tax rate. The role of the manager is administrative operations of the city based on the council's recommendations. The manager serves as the council's chief advisor. Managers are responsible for preparing the budget, directing day-to-day operations, and hiring and firing personnel.

---

[23] Zimmermann, B. (2017) Does the Structure of Local Government Matter? Fels Institute of Government – University of Pennsylvania. https://www.fels.upenn.edu/recap/posts/1475 (last visited July 28, 2021)

[24] See International City/Council Management Association, "Professional Local Government Management", https://icma.org/en/icma/about/overview/hiring_manager (last visited July 28, 2021)

Typically, the mayor is considered as the political head of the municipality but his/her role is rather legislative and does not have the power to veto legislative actions. According to some experts, the popularity of the manager-council system reflects indicative of a trend toward professionalization in municipal administration (Frederickson et al. 2003).

Mayor-Council: The mayor-council form of government is the form that most closely reflects the American federal government with an elected legislature and a separately elected executive. mayor-council governments are more prominent in older and larger cities, as well as cities located in the Mid-Atlantic and Midwest. Among major cities in California, this model is present in Los Angeles, San Diego, San Francisco.

The mayor or elected executive is the head of the city or county government. The extent of his or her authority can vary from purely representative functions to full responsibility for most operations. The executive body or mayor is usually responsible for: hiring and firing department heads, preparation and administration of the budget, and veto power (which may be overridden) over acts of the legislature. However, in some municipalities, the mayor or executive body may have much larger political importance. In such cases, day-to-day operations can be delegated to administrators that are appointed by and accountable to the chief executive.

Depending on the city's history and the relationship with the surrounding county, the legislative body might go by another name such as an urban-county council, a common council, a board of supervisors, or a metro council. The number of city council members also varies widely. The legislature has such responsibilities as adoption of the budget, passage of resolutions with legislation, auditing the performance of the government, and adoption of general policy positions.

The relationship between the mayor and council government can differ greatly. The differences center around the scope of the mayor's authority and legal power. When the mayor is strong, he/she serves as the city's chief executive and the council is the city's primary legislative body. The variant with the strong mayor has the following characteristics[25]:

- The mayor may appoint and remove departmental heads.
- The mayor drafts and proposes a budget to the city council.
- The mayor possesses veto or line-item veto power.
- The mayor officially represents the city on the state, national and international levels.
- The mayor exercises oversight of the city's day-to-day operations.
- The mayor enforces city laws and ordinances.
- The mayor is not a member of the city council.

When the mayor is weak, the executive role is more shared with the council. The variant with the weak mayor has the following characteristics:

- The City council appoints and approves departmental heads.
- The City council (usually in consultation with the mayor or an appointed administrative officer) drafts a budget.
- The mayor possesses limited or no veto power.
- The mayor officially represents the city on the state, national and international levels.
- The mayor shares oversight of the city's day-to-day operations with the city council, an appointed administrative officer, or both.
- The mayor works together with the city council, an appointed administrative officer, or both to enforce laws and ordinances.
- The mayor may be a member of the city council or the presiding officer of the city council.

---

[25] See National League of Cities, "Mayoral Powers", https://www.nlc.org/resource/cities-101-mayoral-powers/ (last visited July 28, 2021)

The more detailed typology is provided by DeSantis and Renner (2002) depending on the presence of a chief administrative officer:

- Strong mayor-council with an appointed chief administrative officer
- Strong mayor-council without an appointed chief administrative officer
- Weak mayor-council with an appointed chief administrative officer
- Weak mayor-council without an appointed chief administrative officer

11.7. Special Districts in California

Special districts refer to public agencies that provide one or more specific services to a community, such as water service, sewer service, parks, fire protection, and others. California has almost 3300 special districts. We can distinguish dependent and independent special districts.

In the case of dependent special districts, the governing board of either a city or county will also serve as decision-makers for a special district. Almost one-third of special districts are dependent. On the other hand, independent special districts operate under a locally elected, independent board of directors, which oversees district functions. About two-thirds of special districts are independent.

Most special districts perform a single function, such as water service, parks, and recreation, fire protection, pest abatement, or cemetery management. Other districts have multiple functions, such as community service districts. Some special districts provide services for residents in both cities and counties, while others provide services only for residents who live outside city boundaries in unincorporated areas.

While cities must be located in one county, and city boundaries may not cross county lines, special districts may cross city and county boundaries. For example, the Metropolitan Water District of

Southern California serves residents in six different counties and most of the cities within those counties. Special districts generate revenue from several sources including property taxes, special assessments, and fees.

Another type of district is enterprise special districts. These districts run similarly to business enterprises and provide specific benefits to their customers. They are primarily funded by fees paid by service recipients. On the other hand, non-enterprise special districts deliver services that provide general benefits to entire communities. They are primarily funded by property taxes.

11.8. Other types of local agencies in California

Joint Powers Authorities are exercised when officials from various public agencies, such as state departments, counties, cities, and school districts, create a legal entity designed to provide more effective or efficient government services or to solve a service delivery problem. It allows participating agencies to "jointly exercise any power common to the contracting parties," which includes, but is not limited to, "levy[ing] a fee, assessment or tax" (California Government Code § 6502).

The concept of joint power authorities was created in 1921 with Bill 18 passed and allowed any two cities or counties to enter into agreements and provide funds to exercise a power common to each. It was a response to tuberculosis which was a serious public health threat in the Bay Area. During this time, San Francisco has lacked adequate facilities to treat patients with this disease. After the bill passed, Alameda County and the City and County of San Francisco drafted an agreement to share their resources and expand Alameda's tuberculosis facility. In 1923 California Supreme Court upheld this bill.

Typically, joint power authorities are funded through either issuing revenue bonds or an internal revenue stream (Cypher & Grinnell 2007). Each joint powers agreement is unique, as there is no set formula for how governments should use their joint powers. One agency will administer the terms of the agreement, which may be a short-term, long-term, or perpetual-service agreement.

The most common form of joint powers authority is one that serves as a form of an insurance company for local agencies. Through the joint powers agreement, these agencies pool their resources to promote activities to reduce risk and pool their assets to pay claims against member entities (for example, workers compensation claims). Joint powers authorities typically have their board of directors (typically public officials appointed by each participating public entity), their policy development system, and their management structure.

Interestingly, in California, the public agencies entering into the entity do not need to be based in California (California Government Code § 6500). Moreover, Californian public agencies can create joint powers authorities together with federal public agencies based in a different state. Brenstein (2020) argues that it allows "for greater flexibility, expansive power, and generally more applicable knowledge in the execution of specific [area]".

Some experts consider this type of management as beneficial for some sectors, like forestry management, because it allows broad and efficient power without voter approval (Bernstein 2020). Moreover, it is considered to cut costs, reduce overlapping services and use more effectively shared resources.

11.9. Community Facilities Districts in California

Mello-Roos or Community Facilities Districts represent special districts established by local governments in California as measures for obtaining additional public funding. Various levels of local authorities are using this form to pay for public works and some public services. The name is derived from the authors of the law that was enacted by the California State Legislature in 1982.

This law was a response to Proposition 13 that passed in 1978 that allowed local governments to make land-use decisions based on what is expected to generate higher tax revenues. In particular, favoring commercial development, which produces sales tax revenues, over residential development, which generates more limited property tax revenues due to Proposition 13. This dynamic is considered one driving force of the widening housing deficit in California since the 1970s. As a result, the budget for public services has been weakened.

Overall, a Mello-Roos tax is a parcel tax that overcomes the consequences of Proposition 13 because it is not derived based on the assessed value of a real property. In order to form a Mello-Roos Community Facilities District, one needs two-thirds voter approval. The Mello-Roos special tax is based on a formula that is specific to that district, that was approved in proceedings. The formula can be based on a variety of factors but cannot be based on the value of the property. In practice, most Mello-Roos community facilities districts base the special tax on several common formulas, such as the square footage of the improvements, or proximity to a specific improvement, or based on the acreage of the lot.

11.10. School Districts in California

School districts are responsible for educating children from kindergarten through high school. Some school districts provide pre-school services as well. There are multiple types of school districts. The most common are unified districts that include both elementary and high schools. Elementary districts contain only elementary schools and High school districts contain only high schools. Over 5000 school board members govern the more than 1000 school districts and county offices of education in the state[26].

California school districts vary widely, from isolated rural districts with fewer than 20 students to the largest urban district with over 700 000

[26] California School Boards Association (2007) School Board Leadership: The role and function of California's school boards, https://www.csba.org/~/media/51E3FBB839504700825CB 16B7265F3C4.ashx (last visited July 28, 2021)

students. California's public education system also includes community college districts, the California State University system, and the University of California system. The availability of funding for schools is also largely dependent on the state, through the budget process.

Outside the public school system are charter schools that operate independently. While they largely rely on public funds, charter schools are exempt from many of the requirements imposed by state and local authorities. As they only partly receive public funds, charter schools must also rely on private donations and federal grants. The California State Legislature approved the state's charter school law in 1992. According to the National Alliance for Public Charter Schools[27], there were 1234 charter schools in California (2015-2016) with enrolled approximately 58 100 students. This constitutes 9.18% of total public school enrollment in 2015.

In contrast to some other states, in California, public schools and cities/counties have separately elected governing bodies. School board members are usually elected by residents of the school district. Locally elected school boards are a part of this system, as are county offices of education. In addition, some school board members are appointed to county boards of education and to fill vacancies until the next election for the seat is held. The voting methods vary depending on voters and candidates residing area. California does not impose statewide term limits on school board members.

However, terms limits on school board members can still be imposed on the local level. To qualify as a school board candidate in California, a person must be[28]: 18 years of age or older, a citizen of California, a resident of the school district, a registered voter in California, not a current

[27] National Alliance for Public Charter Schools (2016) A Closer Look At The Charter School Movement, http://www.publiccharters.org/wp-content/uploads/2016/02/New-Closed-2016.pdf (last visited July 28, 2021)

[28] California School Boards Association (2007) School Board Leadership: The role and function of California's school boards, https://www.csba.org/~/media/51E3FBB839504700825CB 16B7265F3C4.ashx (last visited July 28, 2021)

employee of the school district, not disqualified by the California state constitution or laws from holding civil office.

11.11. Regional government in California

Another type of local government is regional governments that are established by local governments to combine resources. There are different types of local governments in California. Some of them are involved in the planning and funding of infrastructure in a given area of the state. The others have more general purposes. The California Association of Councils of Governments distinguishes four types of regional governments found in the state:

Councils of Governments are voluntary associations that represent member local governments, mainly cities and counties, that seek to provide cooperative planning, coordination, and technical assistance on issues of mutual concern that cross jurisdictional lines. In this sense, councils of governments serve to develop consensus on many issues that need to be addressed in a subregional or regional context. Their duties should complement and do not duplicate jurisdictional activities, and serve to unify jurisdictions and agencies on matters of mutual concern, but independent of the responsibilities traditionally exercised by the individual members within their communities.

Local authorities usually agree to form councils of governments following discussion and negotiation on common goals and objectives, which are usually consummated by the execution of a joint powers agreement. In most cases, the adoption of a joint powers agreement is specifically authorized by state law (Government Code § 6500).

Most councils of governments in California display similar organizational characteristics. These include voting membership by participating jurisdictions through an Executive Committee or Board of Directors. Representation can be along the lines of *one member-one vote* weighted deferentially based on population or other growth-related parameters, or otherwise determined based on agency/membership representation and/

or affiliation. Other common features of these councils include a variety of policy committees and support task forces or groups which focus on specific issues of concern. They often engage in considerable coordination with member local governments, as well as other special-purpose regional, state, and federal agencies.

Although many councils of governments are formed to mainly focus on transportation planning and programming, some of them have also been tasked by their local governments to address air quality planning; area-wide clearinghouse for review of Federal financial assistance; regional housing needs assessment; hazardous and solid waste management; demographic projections; growth management analysis and development of sub-regional strategies; review of local general plan amendments; area-wide water quality planning; and general planning support and technical assistance as directed by member agencies.

11.12. Regional Transportation and Planning Authorities in California

County or multi-county entities charged by state law in meeting certain transportation planning requirements. Metropolitan Planning Organizations are designations under federal law that encourage large urbanized areas to engage in regional transportation planning. California has 18 metropolitan planning organizations, four of which are multi-county organizations that coordinate planning in three or more counties. Transportation Commissions and Authorities and Congestion Management Agencies are authorities that are located within the multi-county Metropolitan Planning Organizations. They provide a more localized focus to transportation planning within the larger region and often manage county-raised revenue from sales tax measures.

Regional authorities are formed across local jurisdictions in order to address regional plans and priorities. They will establish processes for regional decision-making in an area, identify and develop alternative options for consideration, and prepare regional plans. There are also regional air quality management districts throughout California. There are 35 of these air quality districts in the state and are charged with reducing air pollution in a geographic region.

These regional governmental organizations are utilized by local governments to make regional improvements including in transportation, air quality, and economic development, among areas. Among the larger regional governments are the Southern California Association of Governments and the Association of Bay Area Governments.

11.13. Federalism in California Government

A mandate is a requirement by the state government directing the local government to provide a service or a higher level of an existing service. The state imposes a mandate directly on local agencies; in other words, such mandates are not the result of a new federal law or a voter-approved state initiative but rather new state legislation or state regulations. For local government to be paid by the state for complying with a mandate, it must be found to be a reimbursable mandate.

To determine whether mandates are reimbursable, the Legislature founded the Commission on State Mandates. The Commission on State Mandates is the final arbiter of most mandate claims. Decisions of the commission are subject to review by the courts. The state Department of Finance often brings legal challenges to the courts in cases where the commission has found a mandate to be reimbursable. The courts may uphold the commission's decisions or reverse them. Final decisions of the courts are binding on both the commission and the state.

The Commission on State Mandates has four key functions:

- It hears and decides test claims alleging that the Legislature or a state agency imposed a reimbursable mandate upon local agencies and school districts. Test claims are exactly what the name implies: Claims testing whether a new requirement constitutes a reimbursable mandate that obligates the state to reimburse locals for the expense they incur in complying with that requirement;

- It hears and decides claims alleging that the state controller incorrectly reduced payments to local agencies and school districts;

- It hears and decides requests to adopt new test claim decisions that would supersede previously adopted test claims if there is evidence that the state's liability for that earlier decision under the California Constitution has been modified based on a subsequent change in the law; and

- It determines the existence of significant financial distress for counties seeking to reduce their General Assistance payments.

The nature of this obligation forces local agencies to pay for a new governmental program or procedure, which in turn puts pressure on local tax revenues. In the case of domestic violence offenses, this could be a new law requiring district attorneys to perform database searches of domestic violence defendants to find out if they have committed prior related offenses and requiring those offenses to be admitted into evidence in court.

If the Commission on State Mandates determines that the State Controller's Office has incorrectly reduced mandate reimbursement payments to local governments through an accounting error or other reason, the State Controller's Office is obligated to make good the shortfall in payments. However, there does not appear to be a specific deadline by which this additional payment or payments must be made.

The term unfunded mandates refer to regulations or other requirements imposed by a higher level of government on a lower one, but without accompanying appropriations to cover the cost of compliance. Local school boards frequently complain that laws and regulations imposed by state and federal bodies are unfunded mandates. The actual costs of unfunded mandates are difficult if not impossible to pin down with accuracy, for they often involve nothing more definite than added demands on the time of school administrators.

California voters approved Proposition 1A in November 2004. Among its other provisions, Prop. 1A strengthened protections for local governments against unfunded mandates by requiring the state, for the first time, to suspend any mandate it did not fund during any given budget cycle.

The legal effect of a suspension is that local governments are no longer required to comply with a suspended mandate so, in theory, it provides some fiscal relief. However, in practice, suspended mandates have proved challenging for local governments. In the case of certain mandates, local compliance efforts have to be maintained for reasons related to purely local political pressures or priorities. One example of this is mandatory holding periods for stray animals before they can be euthanized.

In addition, once a mandate is suspended, it not only relieves the state of the responsibility to fund that mandate going forward, it also allows the state to defer payments intended to reimburse locals for expenses incurred as a result of their compliance efforts before the date of the suspension. Depending on the mandate, this can amount to millions of dollars per jurisdiction. The deferment remains in force until the state lifts the suspension. In practice, once a mandate is suspended, the suspension is rarely lifted, and the local agencies often go unpaid in the meantime for prior compliance efforts.

Cities have a range of options as to what they can do in response. As previously mentioned, in some cases — for political or other reasons — cities have little choice but to continue the activities associated with unfunded mandates. But it may be useful to explore the range of options, given the steadily shrinking volume of reimbursement coming from the state.

For example:

- Cities can continue with previously mandated activities, knowing that the costs will just have to be absorbed locally;
- Cities can opt to discontinue compliance efforts for the mandates that have been suspended; and

- Cities can seize the opportunity to examine the degree to which the underlying policy or societal goal driving the suspended mandates matches local priorities and, to the degree that they do, explore ways to create greater efficiencies through cost-saving best practices that may reduce related administrative burdens.

Unfunded liabilities refer to liabilities that are not covered or backed up by assets. If a pension fund or other type of fund has projected debts that exceed its current capital and projected income and investment returns, it has "unfunded liabilities". In other words, a pension liability is a difference between the total amount due to retirees and the amount of money the fund has to make those payments.

High amounts of unfunded liabilities in a city or county pension system are often referred to by pension reform proponents as indicating a pension fund that is in trouble and needs to undergo an overhaul. The unfunded liabilities of a pension plan are often quoted along with what percentage of funding the particular system features, which is a more accurate indication of the health of the fund. For instance, according to the National Association of State Retirement Administrators[29], unfunded liabilities totaled nearly $585 billion throughout the country for post-employment benefits in 2015. California was reported to have about $75.5 billion in unfunded liabilities what represented 1.3% of total state expenditures.

11.14. Funding to respond to the COVID-19 in California

The federal funding is based on legislative acts such as the Coronavirus Preparedness and Response Act; the Families First Coronavirus Response Act; and the Coronavirus Aid, Relief, and Economic Security (CARES)

---

[29] National Association of State Retirement Administrators, Retiree Health Care Benefits for State Employees in Fiscal Year 2015, http://www.nasra.org/files/Spotlight/RHC Brief Final.pdf (last visited July 28, 2021)

Act. In addition, it is based on the federal emergency declarations and funding that reimburse local governments and states for certain costs. Funding is divided into payments to public and private entities. For the purpose of this chapter, only payments to public entities will be discussed.

The state received $9.5 billion[30] from the Coronavirus Relief Fund (CRF) to respond to the costs of the public health emergency (which we discussed in more detail in this post). Second, the state anticipated receiving about $5.3 billion in federal reimbursements for the estimated $7 billion in direct costs of COVID-19 (reflecting a 75 % reimbursement rate). The state received these reimbursements from the Federal Emergency Management Agency (FEMA) under the federal disaster declarations. The precise amount of these funds ultimately depend on the state's actual costs to respond to COVID-19.

In the case of funding dedicated to local governments, most of the funding is provided directly but some funding has to pass through the state. Further, while much of this funding is available broadly to local governments in the state, some funding is dedicated to specific localities. For example, Coronavirus Relief Fund is also available to local governments in California, but only for those with populations of at least 500 000 or above. Similar to the state, local governments in California are eligible to apply for partial reimbursement for local costs to respond to COVID-19, according to the federal disaster declaration.

Local governments will receive nearly $8 billion. The actual amount may differ substantially from this total as local governments request reimbursements from FEMA. Moreover, other public entities such as school districts, community colleges, public universities, joint power authorities, public housing agencies, transit providers, and many others will receive another $8 billion.

---

[30] Legislative Analyst's Office – The California Legislature's Nonpartisan Fiscal and Policy Advisor (2020) Federal COVID-19-Related Funding to California. https://lao.ca.gov/Publications/Report/4226 (last visited July 28, 2021)

11.15. Tribal Governments

California has the highest Native American population in the country. According to the 2010 U.S. Census, California represents 12 percent of the total Native American population (approximately 720,000) identified themselves as Native American. Over one-half of the state's Native American population is composed of individuals (and now their descendants) who were relocated to large urban areas as part of the federal government's termination policy. There are 109 federally recognized Indian tribes in California and several non-federally recognized tribes petitioning for federal recognition through the Bureau of Indian Affairs-Office of Federal Recognition. Tribes in California currently have nearly 100 separate reservations or rancherias. There are also a number of individual Indian trust allotments.

Because each tribe is a separate nation, they each have their own governments, laws, and (in many cases) constitutions. These lands constitute "Indian Country", and a different jurisdictional applies in Indian Country. Many tribal governments provide checks and balances within their government by separating power into branches similar to those in federal or state governments: executive (a governor, president or chief), legislative (a tribal council), and judicial (a tribal court). Tribal governments also have the power to tax their members.

As each tribe is a separate nation, tribal sovereignty comes into power. It means that tribes have the power to govern themselves. Each federally recognized tribe retains the rights of an independent sovereign nation apart from the local, state, or federal government. The U.S. government has an underlying contract with the tribal nations that the tribes possess inalienable powers of sovereignty. As such, the U.S. has signed numerous treaties, statutes, and executive orders protecting the rights of tribal nations. Due to tribal sovereignty, the state- and federal governments typically do not interfere in tribal government. The U.S. Congress does have the power to pass laws governing tribal members; it generally only passes laws to help tribal members by providing necessary services.

The majority of laws governing tribal members and affairs come from tribal governments themselves.

Gaming Regulatory Act (IGRA): In the fall of 1988, President Reagan signed into law the Indian Gaming Regulatory Act (IGRA). This confirmed the rights of tribes to conduct gaming on Indian lands and required states and tribes to enter into a compact (contract) for certain types of gaming. IGRA also created three classes of Indian gaming and provided a different regulatory framework for each class.

Class III (Nevada-style) gaming includes activities such as lotteries, casino games, house-banked card games, horse racing, pari-mutuel wagering, off-track betting, keno, and machine gaming. Tribal-state Class III gaming compacts between each tribe and the state outline: the style of gaming allowed, standards of operation, criminal and civil jurisdiction, state regulation fees, and remedies for breach of a compact.

Class II gaming includes bingo, pull-tabs, punch boards, tip jars, and other games similar to bingo. Card games that are not banked by the house are considered Class II. Regulation of these games is within tribal jurisdiction, subject to oversight by the National Indian Gaming Commission.

Traditional or ceremonial Class I gaming remains within the exclusive jurisdiction of the Indian tribes. These are social games played solely for prizes of minimal value or traditional forms of Indian gaming connected to tribal ceremonies or celebrations.

It is important to mention that in 2000, citizens of California have voted on a constitutional amendment (Proposition 1A) to permit the governor to negotiate (subject to legislative approval) gambling compacts with Indians on tribal lands to authorize slot machines, lottery games, and banking and percentage card games. The proposition passed with more than 64% of voters being in favor of this amendment.

Consequences of Gaming Regulatory Act: The act had significant effects on American Indian nations (Akee et al. 2015). One of them has been sustained revenues for almost all tribes that built facilities. It allowed investing in new programs to address poverty and providing public goods such as education. Moreover, the operation of tribal gaming facilities has also change labor markets on reservations. The consequence of this law has been an increased demand for both high- and low-skill labor workers on the reservation. In addition, tribal gaming affected local and regional migration patterns and improved the overall quality of reservation life as some tribal governments have distributed a share of their gaming revenues to citizens.

On the other hand, Indian gaming facilities have been associated with controversial effects on some communities. It included the disenrollment of tribal citizens, fights over control of the gaming facilities, and factional division in Indian communities.

Statistics (2021)

Number of counties	58
Number of cities	482
Number of federally recognized tribes	109
Number of public school districts	1037
Number of independent elected special districts	2300
Number of special districts	3300

Most and least populous counties in California[31]

Most populous counties	
Los Angeles County	9,969,510
San Diego County	3,347,270
Orange County	3,175,130
Riverside County	2,520,060
San Bernardino County	2,206,750

---

[31] https://worldpopulationreview.com/us-counties/states/ca (last visited July 28, 2021)

Least populous counties

Alpine County	1,209
Sierra County	3,021
Modoc County	8,923
Trinity County	11,721
Mono County	14,526

Five most populous cities in California[32]

Los Angeles	3,983,540
San Diego	1,427,720
San Jose	1,009,340
San Francisco	883,255
Fresno	537,100

[32] https://worldpopulationreview.com/states/cities/california (last visited July 28, 2021)

Works Cited

Akee, R. K. Q., Spilde, K. A., & Taylor, J. B. (2015). The Indian Gaming Regulatory Act and Its Effects on American Indian Economic Development. *The Journal of Economic Perspectives, 29*(3), 185–208.

Bernstein, A. (n.d.). An Introduction to Joint Powers Authorities, Their Funding Mechanisms, and Why California Should Utilize One in Order to Create an Effective Forest Management System to Prevent Wildfires. *Hastings Business Law Journal, 16*, 24.

California Constitution, §§ 3 Article XI (1879).

California Government Code, § 2500 (2021).

California Government Code, § 6500 (2021).

California Government Code, § 6502 (2021).

California Government Code, § 23700-23714 (2021).

California Government Code, § 25120 (2021).

California Government Code, § 34871 (2021).

California Government Code, § 54950 (2021).

Cypher, T., & Grinnell, C. (2007). *Governments Working Together: A Citizen's Guide to Joint Powers Agreements.* California State Legislature: Senate Local Government Committee.

DeSantis, V. S., & Renner, T. (2002). City Government Structures: An Attempt at Clarification. *State & Local Government Review, 34*(2), 95–104.

Frederickson, H. G., Logan, B., & Wood, C. (2003). Municipal Reform in Mayor-Council Cities: A Well-Kept Secret. *State & Local Government Review, 35*(1), 7–14.

Pendall, R. (1999). Opposition to Housing: NIMBY and Beyond. *Urban Affairs Review, 35*(1), 112–136.

About the author

Roger L. Cohen is a university lecturer residing in Redlands, California. His research focus is on political science, ethics, and religious studies. When he is not lecturing, he often can be found at the beach, at a unique coffee bar, or traveling back to his home in New Zealand.

CPSIA information can be obtained
at www.ICGtesting.com
Printed in the USA
LVHW050930260623
750759LV00017B/198

9 781988 557816